GOOD SUCCESS

Advance Praise

"If you are interested in being a better leader by recognizing and learning from the bad ones, this is the book for you. Written from a positive perspective of practical experience, *Good Success* enables leaders to achieve greater personal fulfillment and organizational performance. Dr. Self's insights help you leverage those teachable moments and further develop your emotional intelligence. Dr. Self was my favorite professor at Northwest University. It has been a privilege to apply what he taught. He continues to teach me today to become the leader I have always aspired to be."

—Jeff Masiwchuk, General Manager, PPG Industries, Inc.

"*Good Success* is essentially a comprehensive treatise on what constitutes the character of a good leader gleaned from the failures of bad leaders. Dr. Self adroitly distills a lifetime of wisdom acquired during his remarkable tenure as a teacher and leader in academia and business. Filled with insightful nuggets, *Good Success* has something for every aspiring leader. A well-researched gem!"

—Joshua Brittingham, J.D., Labor and Employment Attorney,
Davis Grimm Payne & Marra

"While earning my MBA I had the privilege of being in the classroom with Dr. Woody Self. I was always impressed with his blend of leadership and entrepreneurial spirit. His ability to combine his passion for teaching and sharing his life lessons were always a joy to listen to as they were entertaining and insightful all at once. Dr. Self understands the delicate balance that it takes to be a good leader and whether you are leading 1 or 1000...it is the personal connection, knowing when to challenge, encourage and build trust that motivates people to be their best. *Good Success* is a fantastic guide on what good and bad looks like in leaders and should be used as a roadmap for how to incorporate all the right characteristics into one's leadership philosophies conveyed through great storytelling. We're all better for the knowledge and stories he shared and his lifelong commitment to shared learning with his students, colleagues and readers of this book as well."

—Mike Coers, District Sales Manager, FedEx Services

"Absent the unique opportunity to work with great leaders one's entire career, it is imperative for emerging leaders to learn from both the good and the bad. In this exceptional book, Dr. Self instills the reader with wisdom to translate train wreck leadership observed, into exceptional leadership that inspires."

—Rick English, Chief Executive Officer, ProCo

"*Good Success: Learning Good Lessons from Bad Leaders* teaches how to navigate, grow, and even benefit from the pain and frustration of working for a bad leader. Dr. Self provides a strategic and practical map for identifying and responding to leadership gaps so one can truly 'learn your best from your boss's worst.' I love this book; I wish I had it years ago."

—Casey Hamar, Client Services Manager, Vocera

GOOD SUCCESS

Learning Good Lessons from Bad Leaders

E. Arthur Self, Ph.D.

NEW YORK

LONDON • NASHVILLE • MELBOURNE • VANCOUVER

Good Success

Learning Good Lessons from Bad Leaders

Published in New York, New York, by Morgan James Publishing. Morgan James is a trademark of Morgan James, LLC. www.MorganJamesPublishing.com

ISBN 9781642797893 paperback
ISBN 9781642797909 eBook
ISBN 9781642797916 Case Laminate
Library of Congress Control Number: 2019950264

Cover & Interior Design by:
Christopher Kirk
www.GFSstudio.com

Morgan James is a proud partner of Habitat for Humanity Peninsula and Greater Williamsburg. Partners in building since 2006.

Get involved today! Visit
MorganJamesPublishing.com/giving-back

To Carol, Adam & Eric
"Fortitudine vincimus."

Acknowledgments

To my many thousands of students, it has been my enormous privilege to have been your Professor, or Dean, or college President, and/or academic and vocational Advisor. You have been and remain a renewing source of personal and professional energy.

My sincere thanks to the several great leaders with whom I have worked and served. You have enriched my life, career, and instincts beyond measure.

My sincerest thanks to all the less-than-great leaders with whom I have labored, for you created marvelous opportunities for learning and ultimately enabled me to write *GOOD SUCCESS*. Without your dysfunction, this book could never have been envisioned or produced.

To Carol V. Self, my developmental editor and chief grammarian, my lasting thanks for your patience and skill. We have walked together through many circumstances that have made this effort possible.

To Dr. Martha Kalnin Diede, Mabeth Clem, and Barbara McNichol, my senior editors who are much more efficient with words than I [will ever be]. I hail your expertise, cleaver, and scalpel.

To my friends and encouragers at Morgan James Publishing, my thanks for the insights and clarity to bring this book to those desiring resolution by achieving *GOOD SUCCESS: Learning Good Lessons from Bad Leaders.*

Table of Contents

Preface

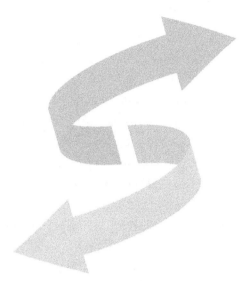

E ach of us bears some resemblance to our ancestors. Hair color, facial features, or soma type can cause us to look like them, while our special, one-of-a-kind features can set us uniquely apart.

So, too, does *GOOD SUCCESS* bear a resemblance to *GOOD LESSONS from Bad Leaders: Discovering Courage Beyond the Chaos,* published on 2014.

GOOD SUCCESS stands upon the foundation of *GOOD LESSONS*. But *GOOD SUCCESS* also stands independently because of the number of new lessons, expansion of prime ideas, and relevant commentaries upon several trends shaping one's career and life, plus new content exclusive to this book.

By GOOD SUCCESS, I mean success that is enduring and will be as relevant in the long run as well as in the short run.

GOOD SUCCESS is not superficial but deep and always good for all who experience it, benefit from it, and share it. GOOD SUCCESS lies in opposition to BAD SUCCESS that is transitory, only good for the few, and has little extensibility or lasting impact upon one's life, career, and contributory value.

GOOD LESSONS enable GOOD SUCCESS. You will see the connection as you read and reflect.

Isaac Newton is attributed to say he stood on the shoulders of giants. This fact remains true in our day as well, and clear-minded and mature thinkers/doers acknowledge it. They move ahead with strength based on this valuable premise.

To a degree, this book, *GOOD SUCCESS,* stands on the shoulders of my previous book, *GOOD LESSONS*. They both provide strength for you to move ahead with resolve in spite of encountering and working with/for bad leaders.

Some of the change experienced in your life and vocation is superficial, some profound, some good, and some not, depending on your point of view and personal reality. It seems no part of life or work remains static. Yet, as the rate of change has accelerated, the view of our ability and even our willingness to keep up has been influenced as well. That's the reality. We must adapt. *GOOD SUCCESS,* like *GOOD LESSONS,* will help you do so.

Survivability has become more of an issue over time, as has relevance. Therefore, you need to ask these additional questions: "Is learning good lessons from bad leaders still possible? Are the lessons written in this book worthy of my time? Are they relevant to my life and circumstances? Will *GOOD SUCCESS* help me survive the bad leader I have, the one I had before, or the one I may yet encounter?"

The answer to these questions is yes. Absolutely yes!

Learning good lessons, especially from bad leaders, is always relevant to your life and career. It can be both a preventive resource to keep you from becoming a bad leader and a palliative resource to assist you in overcoming the difficulties that bad leaders cause.

The message of *GOOD SUCCESS* is enormously relevant. Recent research indicates that a large majority of people who leave their jobs do so because of poor supervisory leadership. People don't leave jobs, companies, and organizations; they leave their supervisors!

Good supervisory leaders make the difference between engaged and disengaged employees who are likely to exit rather than persist. According to author Bridgett Hyacinth:

> A Gallup poll of more than 1 million employed U.S. workers concluded that the No. 1 reason people quit their jobs is a bad boss or immediate supervisor. 75% of workers who voluntarily left their jobs did so because of their bosses and not the position itself. In spite of how good a job may be, people will quit if the reporting relationship is not healthy. "People leave managers not companies... in the end, turnover is mostly a manager issue."[1]

Job satisfaction, career trajectory, and general peace of mind are greatly affected by the quality or lack of quality of one's workplace leadership. Who doesn't want the positive influence of a competent, attentive workplace leader to improve one's life? Who doesn't want to avoid the emotional and career baggage as well as the negative influences of bad leadership?

You can learn a great deal from observing and avoiding the bad behaviors of bad leaders. Your life and career will be altered dramatically when you learn the "best" from a bad leader's "worst."

Observing good and bad leadership behaviors can happen at both the executive level and supervisory level. It's important to address the effects of bad leaders who are higher or highest on the organizational chart and pay scale as well as supervisory leaders who hold positions just above non-management personnel.

GOOD LESSONS received pushback when it demonstrated that some leaders are *infinitely* bad, no matter how bad is defined. Yet, I reaffirm that some leaders are bad, not necessarily because someone believes they are, but because they have proven themselves to be ineffective, inconsiderate, substandard, and disregarding of factors that would otherwise enable them to be good.

The word "mediocre" is a good descriptor for ineffective leaders. Placed together, two Latin words define mediocre as "halfway to the peak." Regarding how well they perform and how well they lead their teams and organizations, bad leaders only make it halfway to the peak.

GOOD SUCCESS again makes a distinction between judging or condemning others. This continues to make sense to those required to conduct employee evaluations and performance appraisals. This section, with its comments and recommendations, remains the same as in *GOOD LESSONS*.

GOOD SUCCESS reflects a greater awareness of the width of the emotional separation between leaders and those led. Despite substantial efforts to promote inclusion and diversity as a means of creating unity and goal attainment, a divide remains in the workplace and in society. This results in intransigence, the exclusion of good people with good ideas, and bad leaders hiding behind their blind spots.

I've noticed a broadening divide in two substantial ways. First, there is an unwillingness to seek to understand another person's point of view on societal and workplace-related issues. Second, although full agreement may never be reached, understanding should be attempted. Good leaders seek to achieve understanding first and then agreement. Bad leaders settle for achieving less-than-optimal levels of both understanding and agreement. They often insist on others agreeing with them and their ideas first.

Moreover, bad leaders continue to be unable to close gaps to create commonality of purpose and outcomes among coworkers. I'm not apocalyptic about this, but unfortunately, there is little unity in the community. Finding agreement on important matters seems an impossibility. It is in this environment that the failures and inadequacies of bad leaders are unexposed or ignored.

When separation and disunity are the norm, how leaders and followers describe one another changes. Leaders pejoratively describe would-be followers as worker bees, laborers, grunts, deplorables, and disposables. Followers describe leaders as being disingenuous, aloof, self-serving, and intractable. This is our current and undesirable reality—not everywhere all the time, but most of the time nearly everywhere.

Learning good lessons will help close the divides. They can be gleaned from even the worst of leaders and workplaces. Short of a profound emotional and spiritual awakening, it falls to good people who have learned good lessons to bridge the gap to community, workplace harmony, and goal attainment.

If good lessons and ultimately good success are not extracted, underestimating how powerful and long-lasting the negative impact of a bad leader can be dangerous. In fact, good lessons can be learned even as bad leadership behaviors are noticed. Game-changing lessons are more likely to be learned with distance and time between the observation of ineffectiveness (with the unsettledness caused by it) and learning good lessons from it.

Additionally, the complexity, demands of the workplace, and pace of life will not slacken. That's the not-so-great, uncomfortable news, but it's an acknowledgment of what we already know. *One is not alone in wondering how to cope.* People in the U.S. and in other developed countries feel the same way.

Both leaders and non-leaders fear that their jobs and workplace responsibilities are becoming unmanageable and thus intolerable. They are not on top of their jobs; their jobs are on top of them.

As we look to the future, we don't see less work, but more. We won't experience fewer complications, but greater complexity. Despite the promise of technology to make our lives less difficult, it doesn't. For example, social media tools designed to make us more connected and intimate many times make us more distant and even more distrusting.

This is our current reality and the societal cards we have been dealt. And it is for many people all too much without planned and purposeful adaptation. Applying the ideas in *Good Success by Learning Good Lessons* is the means to achieving planned and purposeful adaptation. Similarly, have more choices doesn't necessarily make one's life better or one's job less conflicted. However, learning good lessons and achieving good success will provide evidence that you are adapting purposefully.

Regardless of the pace or direction of the world and culture, there are both true and relevant observations about what good leaders do that should be emulated and what bad leaders do that should be avoided. *GOOD SUCCESS* makes this point strongly and repeatedly. It helps create a level of manageability and planned adaptation to one's life and career as the lessons are learned. This book will help you cope, not cop-out.

1. Setting the Cultural, Social, and Business Context

One of the contextual issues I've observed recently is the transition from generations of people who have a *need to know* to a generation of people who have a *need to be known*.

Earlier generations didn't acculturate with social media, so the need was focused on aggregating information and experiences to know about the world. The culture that needs to be known doesn't focus on accumulating information but on accessing it. In this culture, *being known* creates identity; in previous times, *knowing* established one's identity. This difference plays out in the ability and willingness of leaders to lead and followers to follow. The distinction is profound and accounted for by good leaders but not so well by bad ones.

Younger workers/employees have a fear of not being known. That is why they share what seems to be meaningless stuff to older workers. Also, they demonstrate concern for their safety and that of their peers by continually being in touch. Older workers see a much safer world than younger ones do.

Older supervisory workers have the fear of both *not knowing* and *being held accountable for not knowing* what they should have known. Younger workers don't have this fear as much because when they need to know something, they google it. This should enable younger people to make decisions more quickly, but it doesn't. They need more information before a decision can be made. By comparison, an older worker may not know that the data needed can be quickly accessed through the web.

The older worker should be able to make a quick decision based on a low volume of data mixed with their longevity and/or experience. Younger workers need a large data set from which they can construct solutions because they work as temps and at part-time jobs. Thus their information base is broad rather than deep.

In retail, could any leader have predicted the impact the advent and maturity of online purchasing would have on site-based operations? Retail shopping malls are failing right and left. Even automobiles can be purchased online and picked up at a vending machine. Who would have predicted that one doesn't need to go to a restaurant to get a restaurant meal? A "home-cooked" meal can be prepared at a restaurant and delivered to your home by multiple delivery services using autonomous vehicles. How cool is this?

"Consumers Rule" is truer today than ever before. Who would have thought that, by owning a line of scooters and bicycles, Ford Motor Company would see itself as a transportation company rather than only a manufacturer of cars and trucks? Who would have envisioned that Sears, who at one time had the slogan "Sears Has Everything" now has nearly nothing?

Predicting change and *leading* change aren't the same, but some good leaders accomplish both. Bad leaders are more likely to accomplish neither.

Let me mention a commonality, most often ignored, that binds all recent change together. It is data creation and data utilization.

I've taken a deep look at data utilization and positioned it within the context of data monetization and also within the context of automation and robotics. Data utilization, data monetization, automation, and robotics were not discussed in *GOOD LESSONS*.

Having more data doesn't lessen the need for good leadership. After all, no amount of big or good data will compensate for bad leadership. Thinking so is being shortsighted and misinformed. We don't necessarily need more leadership in a digital world; we need *better* leadership in a digital world—leaders who take big and good data and act with it convincingly. Actionable data not acted upon discloses bad leadership while creating a climate for uncertainty and malaise among followers.

Like it or not, we cannot avoid living in this digital world. There is no going back to a non-digital time. Going off grid or even living on the moon or Mars wouldn't be possible without data to get us there and sustain us while there.

The enormous complexity of living in a digital world requires a degree of knowledge, wisdom, restraint, and humility not yet fully developed in most human beings or organizational leaders.

As the sophistication of creating data accelerates via humans and via automation, the way we engage data and optimize it in decision-making will require superior judgment. Thus, the human side of applied data will be judged to be done well or poorly. This, then, legitimizes the premise of the good lessons from bad leader's value proposition.

Data utilization matters immensely. The right data stored properly where it can be accessed, retrieved, interpreted, and applied at the right time and by the right people for the right reason can be enormously beneficial. But if any of these components are engaged wrongly or by the wrong people or for the wrong reason, data can become enormously dangerous.

2. The Power of a False Message

Bad leaders tend to use data badly. It seems this should go without repeating, but that's not true for bad leaders. Most of them do not grasp the magnitude of the power that data possesses, and they fail to use it prudently, responsibility, and confidentially. A recent example makes the case.

On January 19, 2018, a message was sent via official Hawaiian Emergency Management channels that the State of Hawaii was facing a nuclear attack. Of all the U.S. states, Hawaii knows something about sneak attacks. Everyone affected quickly realized that something had gone terribly wrong, either with the potential attack itself or with the person(s) who authorized sending the emergency message.

The first evidence indicated that the person responsible for sending the message had done so accidentally, although he said he sent the message based on what he had been told. The conflicting data was quickly discounted. But what part of the action was based on truth, and what part was based on falsehood? Afterwards, when this event was critically analyzed, it was determined that both human communication and system errors were at fault. The button pusher was thought to be incompetent and above his pay-grade to make such a decision. He was considered an unhinged person unable to rescind the error-filled official message.

Moreover, it was determined that a single person was allowed to send a false message based upon data when the decision should have been made jointly with officials of higher standing and authority. The magnitude of the error was reported by many media sources. It caused alarm, anxiety, and dislocation. Furthermore, the false message direct caused one death as well as parents pushing their children down manholes for shelter.

Perhaps you've heard of "Duck and Cover." It's a phrase used during the Cold War days in the 1950s and 1960s to teach people what to do in case of a nuclear explosion or incoming bomb. Children in schools practiced it like a fire or tornado drill; so did people in offices and factories.

"Duck and Cover" is what followers might need to do when a false message is communicated via a poor decision of a misinformed or over-aggressive leader. Learning good lessons will help you see the false message for what it is, and followers will "duck and cover" when necessary.

The mix of conflicting data, defects in communication systems, and human errors caused the problem in Hawaii. It is too simple to say it was the sole result of an inept employee acting on bad data. It was also the result of maladroit upper management who did not provide proper employee screening and training or anticipate problems with the alarm system.

Yet, within the context of learning Good Lessons from Bad Leaders, this GOOD SUCCESS takes an in-depth look at the Automation and Robotics sector as a case study for examining innovation, data utilization, decision-making, and leadership.

I've already mentioned the retail domain, but there are others such as big data, artificial/ augmented intelligence, entertainment, medical research, Internet of Things (IOT) and Industrial Internet of Things (IIOT), telephony, national and residential security, and 5G connectedness among many others that deserve attention. Each of these sectors requires a degree of human engagement and interaction; each needs good leadership as well. These will be touched on but not fully explored in *GOOD SUCCESS*.

I have focused many of my comments within the context of automation and robotics and which leadership behaviors will quicken or slow down the development of the sector. It is the nature and quality of leadership that will determine how much or how little automation and robotics will be allowed to impact human and machine interactions. Many good lessons can be learned here.

Bad leaders often become bad not because they intend to, but because they work too hard to be liked and not hard enough to be effective. Likeability is nice but not essential to superior leadership. Most people and organizations would rather have a less likeable yet effective leader than a more likeable but less effective leader.

Many bad leaders would rather be liked than effective. Yet, planned and positive results are more likely to occur if leaders/managers like themselves and others while being both effective and highly regarded. It is, in part, the emotional intelligence of leaders that enables their likeability and effectiveness. *GOOD SUCCESS* provides additional insights regarding likeability.

In 2014, the U.S. and most of the world was in an economic malaise. U.S. unemployment rate ranged from a low of 5.6% to a high of 6.6%, according to the U.S. Department of Labor. Five years later, though, economic circumstances have changed for the better. Real wages have increased; more people are working. Full employment sets up a series of economic realities that only marginally affects what bad leaders do and don't do.

Bad leaders tend to be bad regardless of general economic conditions. In really good economic conditions, bad leaders should get better, but they ordinarily don't. With full employment, what happens? Those experiencing a bad leader/supervisor have more flexibility to go elsewhere, and they do.

Furthermore, bad leadership remains more a constant than a variable regardless of economic reality. With a greater demand for talent, people who report to bad leaders are more inclined to seek other employment opportunities rather than continuing to endure intolerably bad leadership. You'd think that bad leaders would get the message and improve, but they don't as this economist's article states:

> Essentially, the idea of full employment is that so few workers are available that companies need to begin raising wages to attract help. Economists technically define full employment as any time a country has a jobless rate equal or below what is known as the "non-accelerating inflation rate of unemployment," Estimates of the measure are based on the historical relationship between the unemployment rate and changes in the pace of inflation. If the unemployment rate is below this number, the economy is at full employment, businesses cannot easily find workers, and inflation and wages typically rise. If not, then there are too many workers in need of a job, and inflation remains low.[2]

The fact that favorable economic conditions have arrived does not invalidate the Good Lessons Affirmation. Learning good lessons remains relevant because bad leaders are still prevalent.

Embedded in the new Automation and Robotics sector are the issues of Data Utilization (DU), Data Monetization (DM), and Emotional Intelligence (EI), each of which will be examined in this book. These three topics reside at the core of current economic success and future economic development.

Furthermore, interesting patterns can be gleaned from the Automation and Robotics sector and extended to other enterprise sectors in which you might be currently employed, might desire to be employed, or into which an entrepreneurial endeavor might be launched.

Automated systems and robots do not completely run themselves; they must be engaged with, by, and for humans. Both automated systems and humans can operate in either superior or suboptimal ways. Just as automated systems require humans, humans require oversight and supervision.

What is it that humans can perform best, and what can automation and robots do best? One way of answering these questions is to examine the enormous energy, human, and financial capital being spent in the creation and optimization of autonomous vehicles, predominately automobiles and trucks. These questions are answered in this book.

Why examine the Automation and Robotics sector for consideration regarding good and bad leadership? The reason is quite simple. It is a mistake to assume that the more automation and robotics are deployed, the less human intervention and leadership are required. As an example, autopilot systems on aircraft require more training of pilots, not less.

> **Automation has made planes safer and more efficient, but the crashes of two Boeing 737 Max jets lead some to wonder if there is a dangerous flip side. Though advanced autopilots and computers are an integral part of any modern jetliner, many pilots worry that the systems detract from developing and maintaining their own abilities. "We've been talking about this in the industry for years. Pilots are losing their basic flying skills, and there's an overreliance on automation," said Les Westbrooks, an associate professor at Embry-Riddle Aeronautical University.[3]**

The A/R sector is not immune to poor leadership and enormous wastes of personnel, equipment, capital, information, and time (PECITs). A/Rs are beginning to dominate as they become the center point of contemporary business and industry, yet good team and individual supervision is still required, regardless of the level of automation.

There are not only moral/ethical questions to address but leadership and management questions as well. For example, "How much automation and robotics are good for humans? How will A/Rs impact human relations? How much should humanity allow automation and robotics to dominate? Who will be dominant; who will be subservient?"

In light of these questions and the new A/R milieu, the issue of good and bad leadership remains pertinent. It is *superior* leadership that will make the A/R sector work to benefit humanity. The substandard leaders in this sector will cause dysfunction and be detrimental to humanity.

When A/Rs are operating optimally, they create abundant value by doing the dull, dirty, dangerous, and dehumanizing operations humans should not or do not want to do.

3. Data Gone Big and Good Data Gone Bad

The use of the term "big data," and the reality of "big data" has expanded dramatically in the last several years. According to the Gartner Group, the term "big data" is defined as "high-**volume**, high-**velocity** and/or high-**variety** information assets that ... that enable enhanced insight, decision making, and **process** automation."[4]

Moreover, Oracle.com states that Big Data is a generic descriptor for . . .

> "Data that contains greater variety arriving in increasing volumes and with ever-higher velocity." And "larger, more complex data sets, especially from new data sources. These data sets are so voluminous that traditional data processing software just can't manage them. But these massive volumes of data can be used to address business problems you wouldn't have been able to tackle before."[5]

Your data can be as big, clean, reliable, current, accessible, and as good as it possibly can be. But when it's badly interpreted, it is not likely to produce the desired ends it could have and should have produced. Good data badly interpreted and applied yields bad outcomes. Certainly, big data can be created and utilized *by* itself *for* itself. But a poor leader's inaccurately interpreting and applying data can negatively affect the utilization of good data, and thus it can go bad.

Consider this example. Your home thermostat can be set or reset locally or remotely, depending on how warm or cold you want it to be. You can program it yourself or let it program and run itself based upon the parameters you give it. If the thermostat is badly made and operates poorly, it will give you a false reading and provide heat when you want cold or cold when you want heat.

Similarly, if a leader continually and badly interprets reliable data, then it is sublimated to the bad leader's idiosyncrasies and decisions. Data in its raw form isn't ordinarily bad or good; it just is. Yet, data may become bad as a result of a leader's nuancing, misinterpretation, and utilization causing it to be bad.

The hit TV show "The Big Bang Theory" proved the point of ignoring the data, interpreting the data badly, and driving people crazy. Often when Penny was giving Sheldon a ride (because he couldn't drive himself), he would refer to the red light that was continually illuminated on the dashboard of Penny's car. She always ignored the warning light, and her willingness to ignore the warning light drove Sheldon crazy. The dialogue was hilarious. They saw the same warning light, but they interpreted its warning differently. The scene was even more exasperating to both Sheldon and Penny because Penny ignored the warning due to her unwillingness to fix it. Sheldon was exasperated because he didn't know what the warning light meant nor had the ability to fix it.

This comedic scene is similar to two coworkers, a leader and a follower, who both see the same red-light data but respond to it differently out of ignorance or unwillingness. In this example, the dash warning light or the data that the dash light provided was not bad; the interpretation of what the light meant was bad. Both the driver and the rider had neither the skillset nor willingness to do anything about it.

This is exactly what happens when leaders cannot see the data. Alternatively, seeing the data doesn't mean seeing the possible danger disclosed. Or the danger is ignored or avoided because the leaders have neither the interest nor the skillset to fix the data warning. This drives followers crazy.

I've concluded that good lessons come from good leaders who are comfortable in uncomfortable circumstances and situations. Good leaders don't slack off from direct confrontation with the opposition when necessary. They know when it is necessary and when it is not. This takes wisdom and humility, both of which will be discussed as examples of good leadership throughout this book.

Introduction

The moment hung in the air and time passed slowly after Denny's name was announced. But when the diploma passed into his trembling hands, thunderous cheers and applause erupted from the audience. Denny gripped the diploma, paused, turned awkwardly to face the audience, smiled, and then triumphantly raised the diploma like it was an Olympic gold medal. The crowd cheered even louder. He didn't rush the moment . . . he couldn't. He then forced his body across the platform while still holding his diploma aloft and the crowd cheered!

I have been a participant or an attendee in a large number of graduation and commencement ceremonies. *Pomp and Circumstance* is permanently on my mental play list. I've heard and seen the families and friends shout and cheer as *their* graduate was announced, but I have not experienced anything that compares to the props Denny received. I've heard cheers for star athletes, those most likely to succeed, for the summa cum lauds, valedictorians, and the disabled as you might expect. But there was nothing like the energy expended acknowledging Denny.

Denny suffered from muscular dystrophy, which made it an enormous struggle to stand and walk, but he did that day. His classmates had seen him face challenges much greater than theirs. He had overcome. With this achievement, he was experiencing great personal joy and public recognition.

The elation I felt for Denny is what I want you, the reader, to feel as you persist, overcome, and learn *Good Lessons from Bad Leaders*. I want you to be able to pump your fists and say that the bad leaders didn't, or are not, getting the best of you.

You may not face physical challenges like Denny's, but you are highly likely to face the private pain and the emotional, financial, vocational challenges of dealing with bad leaders. *Good Lessons from Bad Leaders* will help you seize benefits out of detriments.

You already know that bad leaders are certain to cause uncertainty. They drive organizational dysfunction. They incarnate indecision. They deplete personal energy and team resolve. They exhaust resources and hope. But, through this book you will gain the knowledge and the *good lessons* to overcome the damage, shape your awareness, and build new courage to navigate beyond the chaos.

You may have already written off any chance of benefitting from the chaos bad leaders create. Perhaps you didn't think it was possible. If so, *Good Lesson from Bad Leaders* will help you draw a valuable inheritance from the F.E.A.R. (failures, experiences, anxieties, roadblocks) you've seen bad leaders produce.

The purpose of this book is to help you learn and then integrate the *good lessons* you glean from bad leaders.

You can't always take yourself out of the chaos, but you can take the chaos out of you.

This book will help you do so. This book will also help you learn *good lessons* as a means at looking at employment and life from a glass that is full rather than a glass that is half empty or half full.

Bad leaders can take you off your path, but learning *good lessons* from them can put you back on your path. Bad leaders may take you off your game, but learning *good lessons* through the chaos they create will put you back on your game.

Throughout the course of your life and career, you are not likely to escape the influence of some bad leaders, so you might as well turn the tables and benefit as much as you can from them. You may have experienced this type of leader already. If not, I guarantee that you will.

Good lessons and the courage that springs from them can be learned from leaders who frustrate their coworkers , whose attitudes and actions harm shareholders and stakeholders, and who devalue the standing and influence of the organizations they are paid to advance. They don't produce positive results; rather, they think their actions are exemplary and their leadership laudable.

This book will help you *emulate* the positive in good leadership while being alert, discerning, and able to *avoid* the failures of bad leaders.

Good Lesson from Bad Leaders speaks to the hurt, anger, and discouragement you are likely to feel when beset by a bad leader. It offers alternatives and highly productive responses that put the F.E.A.R. created by bad leaders into your control so you can make them over to become enriching rather than depleting experiences.

Most often, we would rather minimize or attempt to ignore the chaos that bad leaders create and move beyond it ASAP instead of leveraging the hurt and burden they cause for all they're worth. I'm not talking about obsessing over the chaos but making the best of bad situations by understanding and avoiding the leadership behaviors that cause organizations and people to miss the target and fail.

Ignoring bad leaders, or not finding courage beyond the chaos they cause, is not a solution for those seeking to become strong, bold, authentic, and extraordinarily successful leaders. Some jobs and some people can be so odious that it is difficult to derive anything of value from them whatsoever. But because you can learn *good lessons* from even the worst of leaders, you need a method to extract the value.

Good Lessons from Bad Leaders provides you with new perspectives, the hope to persist, and the skills to overcome even the most egregious leaders as well as the most detrimental circumstances they create.

There are no bad lessons, only hard lessons derived from bad events, bad results, and bad leaders. These provide the fertile ground from which you can learn good lessons. Otherwise, bad leaders and the bad situations they create remain only bad.

A *good lesson* is one of high, lasting value. Learning *good lessons* brings your duties, salary, benefits, and workplace social relationships into greater clarity and thus greater meaning. Otherwise, all that may remain from years of dedicated service and hardship at the hands of bad leaders is a sense of loss and profound disappointment. Life is too short to work with those who unmistakably prove themselves to be bad leaders and from which *good lessons* have not been extracted.

But no one else can do it for you. You can extract *good lessons* while still engaged or at any other time regardless of your job discontent or satisfaction. You don't need to be desperate or ready to quit. In fact, learning *Good Lessons from Bad Leaders* may help you to hang tough, because the lesson is worth the effort it takes to learn it.

There are many superb books that detail what makes good leaders good and well-led organizations thrive. These books describe positive leadership traits, behaviors, strategies, and tactics. However, this book takes a different approach. This is *not* about corporate strategy or how to identify great entrepreneurial opportunities. Rather, it is about coping with and thriving through the short- and long-term effects of bad leaders.

Good Lessons from Bad Leaders takes a substantially different, fresh approach to identifying and avoiding fifty-two typical and insidious leadership failures that create chaos, deplete personal resolve, and cause organizations, teams, and individuals to be less effective. To get through the chaos, you must get through it differently, and learning *good lessons* enables you to do so.

Being beyond the chaos is to be at a good and different place in your insights, hopefulness, and capacities. It is *Good Lessons from Bad Leaders* that will place you there.

When you adopt the *good lessons* affirmation, there is no circumstance, negative occurrence, setback, emotional or career injury occasioned by bad leaders from which you can't derive value or from which you cannot learn a *good lesson*.

If you want to increase your influence at work, at home, and in life, then learning these *good lessons* is essential. Indeed, if you don't learn *good lessons* from chaos, all you have is chaos.

The outcomes of having learned *good lessons* are as follows:

- *Good lessons* are the *positive* takeaways from bad leaders.
- Learning *good lessons* enlarges your capacities and stabilizes your emotions.
- *Good lessons* can become safe harbors from the chaos created by bad leaders.

- *Good lessons* provide you with the upper hand, the last laugh, and a lasting return regardless of the toxicity, incompetence, and failures of bad leaders.
- The *good lessons* approach enables you to say "so what" and "nevertheless" rather than "I'm beaten" by the chaos.
- Learning *good lessons* reverses the flow of your energy from bitterness and cynicism to enlightened satisfaction and freedom.
- Learning the *good lessons* accelerates recovery time and moves you more quickly toward personal mastery over the effects of bad leaders.
- Learning *good lessons* builds bridges to professional and personal growth rather than allowing chaos created by bad leaders to detour your aspirations.

As the door hits you in the behind on your way out, the best statement you can make to a bad leader is "I am learning *good lessons* from you. Thanks." And the best statement you can make to a bad leader as the door hits him or her in the behind is, "I am learning *good lessons* from you. Thanks."

Good lessons are primarily gleaned from bad *formal* rather than bad *informal* leaders. Certainly, both formally authorized and informally developed leaders provide environments and behaviors from which you can learn *good lessons*. But is bad leadership from formally appointed persons within the workplace, government, and voluntary organizations that will be examined specifically throughout this book.

In one of my university teaching appointments, I found it necessary to carry a barf bag (like those found below the tray table in an airline seat) to various meetings of the faculty, administration, and staff. I would become physically ill at the drivel I heard, the self-aggrandizement and ineptitude I observed, and the discouragement I perceived among my colleagues occasioned by the statements and behaviors of bad senior leaders. The barf bag became a necessity.

Reconciling the *bad* with the *good* was difficult, because I enormously enjoyed many aspects of my position and relationships with students and colleagues. Although my biggest challenge was to persist while retaining a positive outlook, in the long run, it was worth the effort. I learned *good lessons* that will accrue to the benefit of my readers facing somewhat similar circumstances. I hope you won't ever need to carry a barf bag like I did, because learning *good lessons* will become a better means of coping with the chaos than the barf-bag strategy was for me.

The *good lessons* approach is intended to be salient and beneficial means of overcoming employment and career-related chaos but not necessarily as a generalized remedy for all catastrophes created by bad leaders. My intent is that this book will cause the chaos that you face to be leveraged (made useable) by you as a career and life skills builder. If you can extend the *good lessons* perspective to society and the world in general, all the better.

Chapter 1.

Foundation Blocks

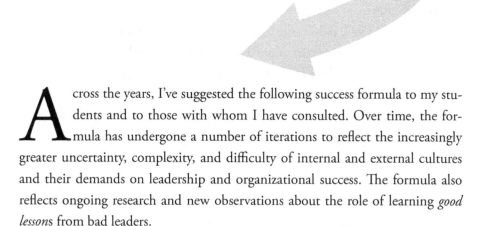

Across the years, I've suggested the following success formula to my students and to those with whom I have consulted. Over time, the formula has undergone a number of iterations to reflect the increasingly greater uncertainty, complexity, and difficulty of internal and external cultures and their demands on leadership and organizational success. The formula also reflects ongoing research and new observations about the role of learning *good lessons* from bad leaders.

1. PD + HW + E + GL = GS

v1.0

Proper Direction + Hard Work = Success

Morphed to:

v2.0

Proper Direction + Hard Work + *Enablers* = Success

By enablers, I mean that additional elements such as new talent, market changes, signed contracts, funding, new discoveries, or helpful PR when they positively coalesce to provide a tailwind and propel an organization toward success. Yet, even with powerful enablers, the extensibility and accuracy of the formula will only have limited success without an ability to learn, integrate, store, and recall *good lessons*.

Most recently, the formula has been revised again to read:

v3.0

Proper Direction + Hard Work + Enablers + *Good Lessons* = Good Success

Although the complexities of personal or organizational success can't be reduced to a simple formula, v3.0 does, however, reflect the critical components through which success is most likely to be achieved. Learning good lessons controls for the inevitable chaos bad leaders create through their miscues and misadventures.

Additionally, v3.0 reflects the following support propositions:

- Proper direction is determined by market need not by wishful thinking.
- Hard work in the wrong direction is just hard work, and it's wrong.
- Combining focus and passion will not compensate for improper direction.
- Enablers have limited shelf lives.
- Organizational culture supersedes the long-term benefit of enablers.
- Without learning and integrating *good lessons,* proper direction, hard work, and enablers will not sustain success.
- Networking alone will not create career momentum and advancement.
- Teamwork alone will not create organizational health.
- Good timing and opportunity do not justify unwise resource expenditures.
- Compelling facts trump exciting presentations.
- Success is driven by learning good lessons, and *good lessons* are best deployed to eliminate personal and organizational chaos.
- Be as aware of the implications of success as you are the implications of failure.

2. Good Lesson Affirmation

I am learning good lessons from every Failure, Experience, Anxiety, Roadblock (FEAR) caused by a bad leader.

By **Failure** I mean…behavior considered as a failing to perform to expectation, lacking success, inability to function to standard.

By **Experience** I mean…an event, discovery, activity, or happening.

By **Anxiety** I mean…uneasiness of mind, apprehensiveness, a sense of impending difficulty or pain.

By **Roadblocks** I mean…barriers and obstructions to progress.

3. Good Lesson Perspectives: Building Upon the Good Lesson Affirmation

GOOD LESSONS:

1. Always provide a floor but never a ceiling.
2. Always open doors but never leave them unguarded.
3. Always create personal energy but never personal aggrandizement.
4. Always provide a next step but never a final step.
5. Always lighten the heart but never dull the mind.
6. Always enable a purpose but never create a license.
7. Always intensify the will but never over-inflate the ego.
8. Always create forward momentum but never backward regret.
9. Always intensify awareness but never oversimplify.
10. Always create steppingstones but never trip wires.
11. Always increase one's contributory value but never decrease the value of others.
12. Always sharpen focus but never minimize risks.
13. Always heighten commitment but never underestimate opposition.
14. Always maximize reward but never minimize challenge.
15. Always smooth the rough spots but never remove an edge.
16. Always create a means of forgiveness but never an abandonment of alertness.

Notice that the affirmation does not contain the words "I will" or "I will attempt" or "I will try." It contains the words "I am," which connotes that you are actively engaged in the process of deriving good lessons from FEAR, and good lessons produce courage, not fear.

Because you are likely to encounter more bad leaders in your career, they, too, will be placed in the active enabling "I am" status, as you continue to move from victim to victor status. This stance also means you do not defer your emotional recovery until a later time, but you step toward recovery now by forgiving the bad leader for the disruptions and pain s/he has caused. By adopting the active "I am" perspective, you do not yield to periods of emotional and vocational turmoil.

Furthermore, as you learn *good lessons*, you prevent hubris from taking root in your life like the kind I have seen embedded in the lives of bad leaders.

Increasing your awareness and understanding of the many negative attitudes and actions of bad leaders will help prevent one from the same missteps. Much of what you will discover in this book will be forward looking to help you identify and avoid the behaviors of bad leaders. Forewarned is forearmed.

4. Become a Good Leader by Recognizing Bad Ones

I once had an insightful conversation with a veteran commercial aircraft pilot during which I asked if he could distinguish between good and bad pilots, other than crashing the plane or ending up in the wrong destination. He first asked me what I meant by "good." I replied, "Competent." He then asked me if I could recognize the difference between a good automobile driver and a bad one. I got the point. Just as one can learn the differences between good or bad pilots and good or bad drivers, one can learn what constitutes good leadership and bad leadership.

Bad leadership, as it is primarily used throughout this book, is about leadership *outcomes* and the influence they have on organizations and the people who comprise them.

Bad leadership can be justifiably linked to some, any, or all of the following definitions depending on the nature and degree of the leader's incompetence, arrogance, or malice.

"Bad," as defined by *Webster's Collegiate Dictionary*, is:

1. Below Standard: Poor, Unfavorable, Decayed, Spoiled
2. Morally Evil, Mischievous, Disobedient
3. Inadequate
4. Disagreeable, Unpleasant
5. Injurious, Harmful, Severe
6. Incorrect, Faulty
7. Ill, Sick
8. Sorry

9. Invalid, Void

Synonyms: EVIL, ILL, WICKED, NAUGHTY. BAD may apply to anything or anyone reprehensible for whatever reason and to whatever degree; EVIL is a stronger term than BAD and usually carries a baleful or sinister connotation; ILL is a less emphatic synonym of EVIL and may imply malevolence or vice; WICKED implies violation of moral law and connotes malice and malevolence; NAUGHTY applies to trivial misbehavior chiefly of children.

Take your pick of any definition for "bad," and you will likely visualize a person or a set of circumstances that a person in a leadership position has created and with which you may be wrestling. You may even find that with each definition, a person or situation quickly comes to mind.

You can easily detect the effects of bad leadership, but learning *good lessons* from these effects is an intentional and worthwhile endeavor. Bad leaders are not necessarily bad because we say they are. They are bad because they prove themselves bad by what they produce or don't produce. Their actions, attitudes, results, and the impact they make on other humans demonstrate that they are so. Bad leaders prove bad because they are judged by truth and reality as untrustworthy leaders, poor stewards of resources, abusers of privilege, or undisciplined, poorly restrained people.

Not all bad leaders are bad all the time, and certainly their successes and failures may be graded in severity. In fact, there are leaders who may be exceptionally good at certain tasks and produce positive results while failing miserably elsewhere. Although not desirable, this is to be expected.

Because most of us have encountered bad leaders at some point, we already have the experiential data from which to form new perspectives and thereby extract *good lessons*.

What you can learn from bad leaders has tremendous value because it helps you obtain release from and give closure to previous personally negative experiences. This perspective also provides an avenue to achieve the emotional strength and upper hand required to move ahead after encountering bad leaders.

Learning *good lessons* from bad leaders is not only a means of creating a set of self-directed leadership and management principles that inform your life and career. It is also a means of overcoming the fear associated with the impact of the bad leaders' bad behaviors and incompetency. The fear of having your life and career sidetracked or dead-ended is real. These fears can be conquered by squeezing out *good lessons* from the very same leadership failures you have witnessed.

The behaviors, actions, attitudes, and outcomes produced by bad leaders substantiate their badness. Let the *good lessons* learned from bad leadership substantiate *your* creativity, resiliency, integrity, and ultimately your own good leadership.

Dismissing bad leaders and their bad behaviors without learning *good lessons* is not profitable for anyone. You learn *good lessons* when you understand that, although past bad leadership behavior cannot be changed, the effects of past leadership need not continue. You can learn *good lessons* if you have the proper tools and perspectives as suggested throughout this book.

Good lessons enable recovery from the effects of bad leadership.

Good lessons truly enrich your life, relationships, and work.

Good lessons create the means to achieving self-mastery.

Good lessons bring closure to previous negative circumstances.

Good lessons are enhancements to your emotional intelligence.

Learning *good lessons* from bad leaders can only occur if you make it happen. Most often, people would rather retreat and ignore (or attempt to ignore) the emotional discomfort and vocational pain that bad leaders produce. Confronting and re-valuing the acts and outcomes of bad leadership is enormously beneficial when done properly. This book will show you how to do it properly.

5. Bad Leader as Thief

Worst among all the "bad" that bad leaders can produce are those outcomes related to theft. Theft ordinarily occurs as a misallocation or misappropriation of resources and is unquestionably related to misuse of personnel, equipment, capital, information, and time (PECITs), which are the primary resources leaders have to manage.

The theft of real property and financial resources certainly has legal and moral ramifications in most cultures where the rule of law creates behavioral expectations adopted by organizations and where leaders are likely to be punished if they steal and are convicted in a court of law. Bad leaders who steal sometimes end up incarcerated.

But that is not necessarily the type of theft I write about here. Theft within the organization may also refer to the theft of a much broader array of resources. Bad leaders can steal your energy, will, peace-of-mind, and aspirations, and they are never held accountable.

The thefts of financial resources are more easily assessed because the loss is quantifiable. The more damaging, difficult thefts are not quantifiable, but they are related to personal and group emotional/psychological state and career well-being, entity reputation, and loss of time.

Thefts that destroy personal confidence, peace of mind, trust, and time are nearly as reprehensible as actually breaking the law and may damage both the individual and the organization in the long term.

If bad leaders haven't looted the organization to a point of insolvency, then recovery may occur over the long-haul and through the aggressive, restorative work of superior leaders who capitalize on opportunities they create in spite of what they were handed when they assumed leadership. If bad leaders have looted to a degree that the company or organization can't recover, that's different altogether. But, in either case, learning *good lessons is* not only possible but is probably the best means to create a fresh perspective, peace of mind, and renewed trust in leadership after financial misdeeds.

Money is recoverable; however, time is not. Bad leaders cause great expenditures of time, distractions, do-overs, and diffusion of energy. Other more trusted, effective leaders are then forced to expend themselves and, as I have heard them say many times, make up for the lost time misspent by bad leaders.

Overcoming a sense of personal violation, which any type of theft creates, requires the expenditure of emotional energy and great financial resources, regardless of the legality, severity, or consequence of the theft.

Bad leaders' thefts may be subtle and covert, bold and overt, planned or spontaneous. The commonality is that most bad leaders deny that their actions result in loss of time, organizational imbalance, or personal well-being. They are seldom remorseful but seek cover from those who may be the very source of greater, more deplorable theft.

If you are prone to steal or otherwise misuse the time, resources, and peace of mind of others, quit it! Such behaviors never end well for anyone, particularly the thief.

> **Bad leaders may steal your time. Bad leaders may also steal your confidence, energy, peace of mind, and trust, but you can recover these resources within the context of the Good Lessons Affirmation.**

You should not deny the facts and realities resulting from leadership failure. Instead, as quickly as possible, you should end the inner rehearsal, turmoil, or malaise that the bad leader has produced.

The closer to the C-suite level the theft occurs, the greater the cascading effect of badness. Bad leadership at lower levels of an organization, although highly undesirable, is likely to have less impact and fewer reputational consequences than bad leadership close to or at the C-suite level. Bad leadership from the C-suite has enormous consequences for the entire organization, but because of distance from the "badness," you may not actually have first-hand knowledge of the failure.

Bad, thieving leadership happening more immediate to your place, status, and emotional commitment to the organization is the more difficult theft to overcome or contextualize within the **Good Lessons Affirmation.**

6. Internal Constraint versus External Restraint

Bad leadership can't be laid at the feet of genetic mis-adaptation or solely upon one circumstance or trait, but rather derives what I call the "Internal Constraint versus External Restraint" continuum.

Consider this example: a young boy is banging on the piano. He is not expressing his inner artist; he is just banging and irritating his mother. Mother has had enough and says, "Johnny, you hit one more key, and you will be severely disciplined." Now, little Johnny has a choice: he can continue banging and suffer the consequences, or he can obey and stop banging. The choice that Johnny makes is a matter of what he views as the most advantageous choice, based upon other choices he has made in similar situations. Is his response based on internal constraint or external restraint?

This internal platform or perspective is sometimes referred to as Locus of Control.[6] Is Johnny more likely to quit banging on the piano because of Mother's external threat or because some little internal bell sounded in his head that says, "Let's play nice with Mommy"? Johnny's internal meter is likely to read, "No way" or "OK, Mommy," but whatever choice he makes will likely be based on the severity of the threat or the value of complying.

To extend this argument to the realm of organizational leadership isn't a big leap. Most leaders have a similar disciplinary clock inside their heads that says, "What will I let control me and my leadership decisions: internal constraint or external restraint?" Do I have an upstream report that says (external control), "This is what we will do, period, no questions asked." Will I defy leadership and drag my feet? Or, will I relent and act as I have been directed, because my internal control says, "A-OK"?

Most good leaders are governed by an internal constraint that says they will comply because it makes sense to say "yes" and choose actions that will result in positive outcomes. In contrast, bad leaders most often ignore internal constraint and may be forced to comply via external restraint.

Sometimes bad leaders will be like little Johnny who, as a challenger to Mother, may take one finger and strike one more piano key and then run for the hills. Similarly, bad leaders are an enormously taxing influence on those attempting to fulfill their commitments and obligations to make the organization work as planned.

> Bad leaders are the vacuous, vapid, consuming persons who don't necessarily kill an organization, although they can. Rather, they're the types of leaders that cause the organization to operate continually with a low-grade fever, never quite right, never fully healthy.

Among the many descriptive words for bad leaders, "vacuous, vapid, and consuming" tend to be the best for the purpose of learning *good lessons* from bad leaders.

Vacuous. . . Empty, marked by a lack of ideas or intelligence, stupid or inane.
Vapid. . . Lacking liveliness, tang, briskness or force, flat-tasting, insipid and
uninteresting.
Consuming… To do away with, destroy, expend, squander, to use wastefully.

These bad leader behaviors can be described as "V2C"… that is, vacuous, vapid, and consuming.

Certainly, if V2C leaders persist in their badness, their modeling and messaging behaviors tend to form new, lower standards for what is acceptable performance. Just as good, high-performing leaders tend to make performance standards higher and results better, bad leaders tend to make standards lower and results poorer.

If you have experienced the reality of V2C leaders, you know exactly what I mean. If you have not experienced V2C leaders yet, you are likely to do so at some point in your career.

You must be alert to the threats to your peace of mind, livelihood, and career at the hands of V2C leaders. You must also be willing to speak out proportionately, affirmatively, and cogently against the threat they bring to the well-being of your colleagues, organization, or business. Cautious, yes; afraid, no.

You can make your feelings and assessments known or just keep quiet and "go along to get along," which is ordinarily a far too conciliatory action to take. King Solomon, reputed to the wisest person to have ever lived, said there is a time for everything under the sun. If you decide to make your feelings known by cautiously identifying and confronting the V2C leader, truth and timing are the most important components. Keeping quiet sometimes makes a lot of sense, for you can live in hopes that bad leaders will overcommit and hang themselves at some point.

7. Evaluating the Leader as Bad: The Good Way to Do It

You may decide to stay quiet because you are unsure if a leader is actually bad. So you must also consider the issue of who has the authority, right, or responsibility to define and determine that a bad leader is, in fact, bad. The topic of judging, evaluating, and assessing others—particularly bad leaders—will be considered briefly here. It will be addressed again after discussing all fifty-two leadership failures and just before the book's conclusion.

Who has the moral authority, responsibility, and ability to discern the attitudes, actions, and competencies of others and then judge them good, bad, and at or below standard? Under what conditions and contexts can such evaluations be made? These are difficult questions, because they are related to issues of fairness, accountability, reward, and punishment. Most people would rather be called anything other than judgmental.

As mentioned earlier, leadership "badness" has gradients and degrees. Let me explain it this way. Recently, I went to the dairy aisle of my local grocery store to purchase a one-half gallon of one-percent organic milk. What I discovered was a large number of other products labeled as milk. There are not only various container sizes from one-half pint to one gallon, but I could buy cow milk, soymilk, goat milk, almond milk, coconut milk, and buttermilk. *And* I could purchase cow milk in fat gradients: whole, half and half, two percent, one percent, low-fat, no-fat, and skimmed. Generally labeled as "milk," these products are all similar but not quite the same.

Like milk, leadership badness has gradients and degrees. You must consider that one person's "milk" requirements and judgments are not exactly the same as another's. What one person considers deplorably bad leadership is only mildly irritating to another. Because it is so subjectively dependent on individual circumstance and interpretation, judging bad leadership actions and attitudes is difficult. Judgments made against objective standards—e.g., timed performance, new businesses developed, or sales quotas—are more easily determined and less affected by emotion and individual interpretation.

Just making judgments in order to aggregate a list of leadership's dysfunctions *is totally not the point.* Making proper judgments, extracting *good lessons* from those judgments, and applying those *good lessons* to produce gravitas is *totally* the point.

This book helps you understand the gradients of badness that might affect the leader's relationship with other people. Not all bad leaders are morally corrupt, nor do they mess up everything all the time. I will return to this topic in the Conclusion, but for now. the focus is on *your* motives as judge rather than on the failures of the bad leader.

One does not need to have the responsibility or the positional authority to make a proper judgment that leads to *good lessons.* Rather, *good lessons* can be learned at any and every level of an organization.

So, under what circumstances are you justified in judging another person as a bad leader? When your responsibility and the facts say so. When you face the necessity of making a determination of a leader's competence, performance, and attitudes, then the authority for an assessment is in place.

You must also honestly consider your motives. Why would you desire to judge another person's performance and character? Sometimes you are forced to do so, even when making such a judgment is the last thing you want to do.

Good leaders learn to judge skillfully by learning *good lessons*. *Good lessons* in aggregation will lead to the proper application of knowledge, which is the definition of wisdom. Wisdom learned through *good lessons* can have an enormous impact on your life and career trajectory. Wisdom can become an enormous personal asset. Wisdom will inform your every judgment. It will also avert leadership blunders and prevent you from being labeled as a "bad leader."

You justifiably have the right to call a leader "bad" because the facts and stats tell the truth. You may also have a responsibility to call leaders bad if you know the leader has engaged in illegal, morally reprehensible actions—ones that hurt and disrupt others and/or damage the reputation of the organization with which that leader is engaged.

Lest you think I'm critical and mean-spirited in judging vacuous, vapid, and consuming leaders, let me remind you of this: These types of people *will* cause you anxiety, grief, and career distress (if they have not already). They feel justified in crushing you and others. Bad leaders cause sleepless nights and bruise careers as they create disasters they blame on others. These leaders will purposefully place you in an emotional prison if you allow them to do so. So, don't think too kindly of them and don't be fearful of calling them what they are: "bad."

Remember, you don't call out leaders as "bad" to make you feel "good." Rather, it is to identify behaviors that prevent you from being called out as "bad" yourself.

Also keep in mind that everyone makes judgments. We make judgments regarding the choice of either driving below, at, or above the speed limit. We judge whether to purchase dill or sweet pickles or both. We make judgments about which entertainment form to enjoy, when to sleep, which cells phone to acquire, and so on.

Our entertainment and media culture places us into the role of judges on a regular basis. If we watch "American Idol" or "Dancing with the Stars" or "America's Funniest Home Videos," we are highly likely to judge participants based on their performances, demeanors, and/or appearances. In these cases, we are judging *comparative* performance and not against an objective standard. Judging can be difficult, but we, nonetheless, make judgments.

When watching basketball, football, and baseball, we see judgment calls being made all the time. Some rule violations are clear cut and can be judged easily—e.g., stepping out of bounds, having one's toe on the three-point line, or catching a foul ball. These are easy. I heard about a baseball catcher who turned and looked at an umpire who had delayed calling a ball or a strike. The catcher said, "What is it a ball or a strike?" The umpire emphatically replied, "It ain't nothing till I call it something." The ump hesitated but did indeed make a judgment.

Some art that you consider great may be considered silly by others because personal taste differs. Some wine is good; some is bad. Some fashion is bad; some is good. Some leaders are good; some leaders are bad. If you determine that some leaders are good, you have already made a judgment. So, don't be afraid to call bad leaders what they truly are.

By judging the failures of bad leaders—their inabilities, non-willingness, and refusals—we are not declaring moral superiority. Rather, we're thoughtfully evaluating the behaviors of bad leaders as they affect our lives and careers. We are not assessing the moral character of bad leaders; rather, we are judging organizational results and the quality of their influence. However, both judgments to criticize and judgments to praise are justified to the degree that a leader's immorality and morality is embedded in their decisions and can have either a substantial negative or positive impact.

Leaders can and should be judged according to how they treat and respond to other people. How leaders treat their responsibilities, use the resources at their disposal, and handle truth are enormously important. They must be part of the evaluative mix. Life is about being discerning, making judgments, and rendering opinions, but when determining performance in the formal workplace and judging bad leaders as bad, often even those who have the responsibility to judge seem to close down and refuse the responsibility. More often than not, people are called upon in the workplace to judge the performance of others against pre-established, objective standards like sales quotas or number of parts made. This task is easier than judging against more comparative, anecdotal, and subjective standards.

The quantitative results of leaders do indeed help create their identity. But what they do and *fail* to do regarding relationships also provides the basis for judging them on a spectrum between good and bad. If you produce bad quantitative and/or bad relational outcomes, then you can be justifiably judged as a bad leader.

In some cases, these types of leaders can appropriately be called toxic. I choose the term "toxic" because it is strongly fatalistic and relevant. Too often, we fail to speak the truth about what is bad, in fear that we may be seen as narrow minded and negative. Yet, the same person (Jesus Christ) who first said, "Judge not lest ye be judged," also said, "By their fruits you will know them."

You should judge accurately and justly without becoming negative, critical, or severe. Developing a *good lessons* mindset will prevent you from focusing on the negative and unproductive; it will stop you from moving beyond judging to condemning.

Garrison Keillor writes about this general "badness" theme in an essay called "The Current Crisis in Remorse." He states:

> Not every wrong in our society is the result of complex factors such as poor early learning environment and resultative dissocialized communication. Some wrong is the result of *badness*. We believe that some people act like jerks, and that when dealing with jerks one doesn't waste too much time on sympathy. They're jerks. They do bad things. They should feel sorry for what they did and stop doing it.[7]

Learning *good lessons* starts with making wise, fair, and instructive judgments. Condemnation has no benefits for either the leader or the person making the judgment.

No one wants to work with cranky, bitter people, and you don't want people to see you as cranky and bitter. As you integrate a *good lessons* perspective into your thinking, you reduce the likelihood of being branded as judgmental and therefore difficult to work with. You will not need to strike back at the bad leader because there is no FEAR caused by a bad leader from which you are not learning a *good lesson*.

8. Eight Questions

This book has been written from my perspective as a practical academician whose research and consulting have enabled organizations and businesses to achieve greater focus and profitability. Additionally, my work has enabled the personal lives of those I have mentored and taught to be more fulfilling and consequential, despite our inevitable encounters with bad leaders.

My work has produced a large body of business plans, market readiness plans, strategic and opportunity opinions, and funding documents that have ultimately created jobs, companies, careers, and lifestyles for others. Yet, I don't describe myself as approaching any savant level of business and organizational management acumen.

However, others have seen me to have the profound ability to extract good from bad, to see a *good lesson* when others can't, and to apply the power of the **Good Lesson Affirmation** to the bad leaders and bad leadership situations that have intersected with my professional path.

For decades, I have recommended to my students and consultees that the blend of formalized learning, focused training, enhanced experiences, exceptional opportunities, *and* learning *good lessons* are the key components to building successful organizations and extraordinary lives.

Additionally, over the last few years, I have intentionally asked everyone with whom I have a serious business or career discussion this question: "What is the best lesson you have ever learned from a bad leader?" The responses have all been insightful, sometimes saddening, often poignant and powerful. One of the best responses was "ninety percent of what I have learned is by watching other people mess up." This individual was successful because he had discovered how to learn *Good Lessons from Bad Leaders*.

Some of the most instructive and meaningful discussions I've had were with nontraditional, adult learners and graduate students who have achieved a degree of professional success, work experience, and leadership responsibility. These occasions may have been in the formal classroom, informally over coffee, or on a study tour. Many times, I have seen the look of learning, as I have watched the facial expressions of students or advisees who have just connected a circumstance or person with a concept or principle. When I perceive this enlightenment, I ask what they have just connected in their minds and if they would like to talk about it. Most times, they do want to talk about it, and terrific learning takes place.

As students have assumed their roles in society and their places of employment, I have often acted as a *de facto* career coach and have repeatedly heard questions concerning the biggest surprises and de-motivators they have encountered in their jobs. I have come to realize that these questions also comprise some of the most daunting questions/realities for the working population in general. Below are eight recurring questions that suggest larger issues in the workplace that negatively affect organizational performance, employee motivation, and personal energy.

The eight questions are:

1. Why is the workplace so political?
2. Why and how did some people actually become leaders?
3. Why and how do bad leaders persist in their positions?
4. Why is so little transparency found among bad leaders?
5. Why aren't there better methods to assess the performance and attitudes of others?
6. Why is the workplace so continuously unsettled?
7. How can good lessons transform me and my work experience?
8. How can I compensate for my lack of (proper) experience?

These questions and the feelings and perceptions behind them are quite normal and to be expected. They reflect real issues, naturally occurring as service time and experience increase. They are ubiquitous and reflect some unfortunate realities of the workplace.

Furthermore, nearly everyone in the organization who is paying attention and is committed to meeting their personal aspirations and organizational objective asks these questions and strongly desires answers to each of them.

These questions must be placed within the greater context of whatever else may or may not be happening in or out of the workplace. Most times, students and clients leave discussions understanding that they must maintain both emotional and financial balance and directional momentum. It is usually not advisable to attempt a wholesale career or personal makeover prematurely in order to reconcile their current job or positional realities.

You cannot always slay all the workplace dragons, but wounding a few and reducing the impact of the dragon's breath will often suffice. "Dragon's breath" is my term to describe the negative influences and organizational culture created by bad leaders. Many early career employees don't have the longevity that builds the emotional strength to withstand the significance of dragon's breath. These employees identify with the eight questions, particularly if they haven't yet earned scars from experience and persistence, or they haven't yet come to grips with the huge difference between working with good leaders and working with bad ones. The chasm is immense.

I confess that I feel protective and even a bit paternalistic when I learn that some of my students and clients have felt the dragon's breath and have been messed with by bad leaders. To some degree, I'd like to prevent it from happening. However, I know that stretching, becoming alert to the realities of the workplace, and developing the *good lessons* perspective is essential to long-term personal and vocational gain.

Patience is also essential to developing the *good lessons* perspective. Employees need a broad perspective in order to create and implement broad-scale solutions to deep, historical problems embedded in an organization and in the behaviors of bad leaders.

Interview and pre-employment processes are not likely to reveal such issues, although they become self-evident after a few turmoil-inducing experiences or several months of experience with the dragon's breath.

Poorly conceived and ill-timed strategies to resolve to the dragon's breath, suggested by those who have not yet earned the privilege to advance such solutions, are likely to cause others to see the newer, younger, or less experienced employees as arrogant. Thus, they're easily discounted and marginalized.

Sometimes, one must patiently deal with only the symptoms of a problem until one's status and the timing is right or the situation is so dire that a more senior person acts. I'm sure that many who read the phrase "or the situation is so dire that a more senior person acts" are telling themselves, "Don't hold your breath."

If you are one of these people, I am confident that you, too, want to ask some or all of the eight questions. Sometimes the best you can do is wait for the questions to resolve themselves or, with time, find a new position where there are fewer of them.

Sometimes experience and dogged persistence are the only way through to answering the eight questions. I intend no fatalism here, only a realistic assessment of what *is*. You do not need complete reconciliation of all eight in order to learn *good lesson* from some of them.

9. Trending to or from G.R.A.C.E.

Grace isn't exclusively a religious word or a short prayer of blessing or thanks. Grace can be justifiably related to the attitudes and actions of all leaders. The best leaders are those who are not only competent, bold, authentic, trustworthy, and effective but those who embody the concept of graciousness in what they say, how they behave, and how they relate to others.

Grace is kindness, courtesy, and tact. It is characterized by charm, good taste, and generosity of spirit. Grace implies cordiality that is warm and ready to respond pleasantly to conversations, requests, or proposals. Good leaders understand the need to demonstrate their grace-fullness. They also understand the powerful connection between treating people gracefully and their desired organizational outcomes.

Grace has the additional qualities of genuineness, truthfulness, and affirmation. There is an implied relationship between grace and being nice. However, being nice doesn't necessarily mean that a leader is genuine, truthful, affirming, or gracious.

Bad leaders trend toward insufficiency regarding grace. They are deficient in kindliness, cordiality, generosity, and warmth. Bad leaders demonstrate their lack of grace-fullness and lack the ability to make the connection between treating people gracefully and the results they want.

Frequently, failures occur due to mismatches between the graces that organizations and nations require and the graces that leaders have the capacity to provide. Good leaders not only achieve the right results, but they achieve the right results in the right ways. The statistical test "goodness of fit" compares an anticipated frequency to an actual frequency. It is also a good descriptor to link the results of leadership with the graces required to achieve that result.

Good leaders must have both the capacity to produce and the capacity to relate. Like shade on a hot day or a cozy fleece jacket on a cold day, they provide a level of comfort. They create stability and vitality. They deliver both bad and good news graciously and without duplicity. They exude warmth and confidence despite the presence of less competent leaders with whom they serve or the general health of the economy. They offer a helping hand, not a grasping hand.

Therefore, all leaders can be plotted somewhere along a continuum running from deficiency to sufficiency. I call this the G.R.A.C.E. GRID, and it is this scale that determines the direction in which a leader is trending. Good leaders trend toward sufficiency; bad leaders trend toward deficiency.

G.R.A.C.E. GRID

Deficiency	Proficiency
Wasteful	Frugal
Scarcity	Abundance
Insensitive: unaware of importance of little things	Sensitive: aware of importance of little things
Foolish	Wise
Unfocused	Focused
Inappropriate or no risk	Appropriate/right risk
Emotionally shallow	Emotionally deep

I define G.R.A.C.E. in the following ways:

- **Goodness** means *quality of character, trustworthiness, honesty, believability, and virtue.*
- **Responsiveness** means *willingness to act promptly, decisively, and appropriately based on the qualities of intuition and awareness.*
- **Aptitude** means *the capacity to learn, ability to grasp (the nature and scope of responsibilities), and the bundle of natural talents, inclinations, and tendencies.*
- **Charter** means *the purpose, direction, and motives of a person's life.*
- **Energy** means *the level of commitment/passion to or for a person's charter.*

Bad leaders frequently have something missing such as responsiveness, a charter, or energy that causes them to trend toward deficiency. They might be the right people in the wrong position, or they demonstrate they can't deliver what the organization needs, or what they can deliver, the organization doesn't need.

Good leaders demonstrate their sufficiency on the G.R.A.C.E. GRID. They prove that they are the *right* people in the *right* job at the *right* time. They demonstrate their goodness, responsiveness, aptitude, charter, and energy to make the connection with their associates, produce desired outcomes at the right time, and expend the right number of resources.

Often it is the leader's lack or abundance of G.R.A.C.E. that creates the degree of buy-in for individuals, the tone for the team or work unit, and the pervasive internal culture of the organization. From the pervasive internal culture springs vitality or lethargy, achievement or failure. Pervasive internal culture and external reputation is either created by design or by default.

The success or failure of a team or work group isn't solely the result of setting the proper tone and then operating within a climate of high expectation or a high-touch environment. Even good leaders find it difficult to establish the proper tone for their teams if informal leaders subvert their efforts or those in higher positional authority fail to set a greater complementary tone for the larger work entity in which their teams fit.

Often organizations suffer imbalances when those with lesser G.R.A.C.E. but bigger egos and higher ranks feel resentful. They are threatened by good leaders with abundant G.R.A.C.E. holding lesser positions. In this case, it is seldom possible to create a dynamic tone among teams or a productive climate within an organization. Most often, the atmosphere is unstable and both parties, the grace-full and the grace-less, are seldom comfortable.

I heard about a college president who was G.R.A.C.E.-less and so threatened by the G.R.A.C.E of professors and other more able administrators that he would not allow anyone within ten feet of his place in any academic processional. He required physical space to self-confirm his status, to protect his inflated ego, and to set himself apart. His inability to share or shine the spotlight on others—showing G.R.A.C.E.—set an organizational tone for incredulity, distrust, and a lack of productivity during his service.

I worked with a warm, G.R.A.C.E-full university administrator who was hired to be an Assistant VP for Student Development. But he was quickly bumped up to become the highest-ranking student development officer (VP for Student Development) within a few weeks of his hiring. He had incredible G.R.A.C.E, and he was not intimidated by faculty and staff of equal or greater talent. He endeared himself to students and the entire campus community. His G.R.A.C.E.-fullness exceeded his lack of senior management experience, and he was enormously well-regarded and successful.

Dr. LeRoy Brown, one of my undergraduate professors, said this about good speakers: "Good speakers are good people speaking well." The same can be said of good leaders. Good leaders are good and G.R.A.C.E.-full people leading well.

Good people may lead well, but sometimes morally bad people may also lead well for a period of time, given proper resources. I separate bad leaders from bad people, although those proving themselves to be bad people don't in the long run make truly great leaders and trend toward deficiency. Bad people and bad leadership are related, just as good people and good leadership are related. Most often, bad leadership behaviors overshadow personal goodness and make the good person less effective. But personal goodness trends toward sufficiency.

In addition, some business concepts/ideas, products, and services are "dead on arrival" (DOA) and can't be well-managed or reach profitability, regardless of the leaders' intents and G.R.A.C.E. In this case, a leader's goodness or badness makes no difference. Occasionally, concepts, initiatives, and organizations only appear to be DOA and can be rescued by good leaders who provide good direction, model commitment, and provide sufficient resources, especially time and hard work.

You may recall the scene in the movie *Princess Bride* in which Billy Crystal, playing Max the Magician, brings "nearly dead" Wesley back to life by giving him a huge pill. He does that because Wesley has a great cause—true love. It is a great comic scene and analogous to a good leader who brings nearly dead organizations or people in them back to life. The skill of leaders like Max bring organizations and people who are nearly dead back to life, but the same leaders who allowed the organization to nearly die in the first place rarely achieve organizational resuscitation.

Although bad leaders have been given the opportunity to lead based on their credentials or degrees, they often lack the G.R.A.C.E. required to lead well. This often disappoints coworkers and those who'd hoped for greater organizational productivity and more personal success because of the credentials, degrees, and assumed competence. As many employers, mentors, and coaches know, "you can't put in what has been left out," and "no amount of experience will compensate for a lack of ability and capacity."

When you have the innate capacity but not the experience, it is your G.R.A.C.E. **G**oodness, **R**esponsiveness, **A**ptitude, **C**harter and **E**nergy that becomes your X factor and sets you apart.

10. Capitalize on Your G.R.A.C.E. to Overcome Your Lack of Experience

It is important to make some comments regarding the issue of G.R.A.C.E. and question #8 from the list of eight questions.

Question #8 is this: *How can I compensate for my lack of (proper) experience?* This is an enormously important one for those who are either unemployed or underemployed. Many people find themselves in the dilemma of not having enough experience or having the wrong type of experience. They have repeatedly heard these statements from potential employers: "You don't have the experience for the job" or "You don't have the right experience/background to get the job" or "If you only had the experience, you'd land the job." It seems that people with jobs to fill only want to concentrate on what you *don't* have and *can't* do rather than what you do have and can do.

How do you counter these arguments and attitudes? If I were interviewing and told I lacked the right experience, I'd say, "Please look at what I *do* have to offer—my goodness, responsiveness, aptitude, charter, and energy. These factors will compensate for my lack of experience."

Ordinarily, the only way to compensate for a lack of experience is time in a related experience. Yet at this point in your life, you can't be older than you are or have more experience than you have. So, to get the job, you must persuade the people doing the hiring that your G.R.A.C.E. compensates for and outweighs your experience deficit.

You should not *deny* your experience deficiency; instead, claim that the characteristics comprising your G.R.A.C.E. will make you sufficient to perform the job with competency. Don't link your lack of experience with deficiency, but your

G.R.A.C.E. with sufficiency. You need to communicate that *whatever* work-related experience you have had, although small, come from learning *good lessons*. *Good lessons* help you close the loop on the lack of experience argument. When placed with your G.R.A.C.E. argument, the odds of landing the job you want increase greatly.

The G.R.A.C.E. strategy will help narrow the gap between what the employer wants and what you offer. Employers don't always know *exactly* what they want, but they always know they seek people who have G.R.A.C.E. first and experience second. And, they are most likely to be confident that they have the processes and systems in place to create the experience. They often hope for more goodness, responsiveness, aptitude, charter, and energy in a hire than they publicly state. Frequently, they would rather *hire to train* than *hire to retrain*. Bad practices and procedures learned elsewhere are expensive and time consuming to purge, and they know it. So, they like to advertise for related experience rather than on the G.R.A.C.E-full characteristics.

The G.R.A.C.E. strategy will strike a positive note, because it is what the hiring people see within themselves as their own best attributes. That is in addition to what they desire to see from their boss, the people they work with, and others they will hire.

The G.R.A.C.E. strategy is most effective during an actual screening or hiring interview, but it can subtlety be embedded in your vita, résumé, and electronically submitted documents. It is a means of helping you think differently about yourself, focus on what you have to offer, and reduce the guilt of not submitting mass numbers of job applications to positions of little interest and might even be unrealistic longshots.

It is said that people get hired based on *what they know, who they know,* and most importantly *who knows them.* The G.R.A.C.E. strategy causes you to be known more quickly and ably by those doing the hiring. It sets you apart from others who don't use it or are G.R.A.C.E.-less

Practice your G.R.A.C.E. arguments well ahead of both the screening interview and hiring interview. Don't use it if you really don't want a particular job. You can use this strategy but don't refer to as such. Rather, think of it as the list of attributes that will enable you to solve a problem or fill a gap the employer has.

Prepare an easily told and quickly understood story or anecdote that illustrates how you have applied your G.R.A.C.E. to solve a problem for another person, group, or employer.

Be realistic and don't expect too much from the G.R.A.C.E. strategy particularly for jobs that require advanced degrees or for a state or industry license. You probably won't be given the keys to the bank vault or the helm of the supertanker. However, the G.R.A.C.E. approach will help get your foot in the right door or on the right boat. That's all you really need to get started. Isn't this exactly what you have said to yourself and to others? "All I really need is a foot in the right door."

Having the precise experience required by an employer may only be developed after securing the job because no two jobs or no two workplaces are exactly the same. Just because you have previous experience is no indication that experience will necessarily signal or guarantee success in a different position. Certainly, there will be some relationship but not one that it so strong, it will completely trump your G.R.A.C.E.

The G.R.A.C.E. strategy also allows *you* to determine helpful data regarding the general character and openness of your prospective employer. If they don't accept your G.R.A.C.E. argument, then it foreshadows the type of environment and the nature of guidance they are likely to provide if you were to be hired. In this way, they indicate the probability of being either a good or a bad employer. From there, you determine if the job might be good or bad for your career, which is something that could not have been determined prior to working for them.

If they accept your argument and you get hired, then that should also indicate the manner in which you are likely to be treated. If you don't get the job, then there should be no regret. It means they truly aren't the people or company you wanted to work for anyway.

Many people won't get the positions they want and be discovered as potential leaders because they don't believe in themselves enough to be mobile, adventuresome, and capitalize on their G.R.A.C.E.

Or, they may have had supervision that was threatened by their G.R.A.C.E. Moreover, no one may have cared enough to correctly highlight their deficiencies and form developmental strategies to improve their G.R.A.C.E.

> Paganini, the great Italian violinist, once stepped on stage only to discover there was something wrong with his violin, just as the audience was ending their applause. He looked at the instrument for a moment and suddenly realized it was not his best and most valuable one. In fact, the violin was not his at all. Momentarily he felt paralyzed, but he quickly returned to his audience, telling them there had been some mistake and he did not have his own violin. He stepped back behind the curtain, thinking he must have left his backstage, but discovered that someone had stolen his and left the inferior one in its place. After remaining behind the curtain for a moment, Paganini stepped onstage again to speak to the audience. He said, "Ladies and Gentlemen, I will now demonstrate to you that the music is not in the instrument but in the soul." Then he played as never before, and beautiful music flowed from that inferior instrument until the audience was so enraptured that their enthusiastic applause nearly lifted the ceiling of the concert hall. He had indeed revealed to them that the music was not in his instrument but in his own soul![8]

It is your G.R.A.C.E., not your experience that is an expression of your soul.

11. Transparency: Distinguishing the Good from the Bad

Because of ultra-high expectations for transparency in and from leaders, question number four, "Why is so little transparency found among bad leaders?" must be considered in depth.

Transparency discloses and enables inherent goodness and strength of character. Also, transparency has a generational component because most early career personnel understand it to mean *openness* and *accessibility*. Older, more experienced personnel add *truthfulness* to this definition. Depending on generation and/

or employment culture, this addition may cause disconnects between *understanding* and *application*.

A lack of access doesn't always mean a lack of transparency on the part of a person, group, company, or even a government. Because of advancements in achieving immediate access to information via Internet technologies, devices, and mobility, a sense of entitlement that results from immediate access appears in many young employees. Generally, they find lack of immediate access to information enormously egregious, especially when they perceive they need it. Many employees interpret a lack of access or restriction of access to people, strategies, policies, and information as an absence of transparency.

Applied to its greatest degree, transparency means "what I want, when I want it, in the form I want it." Nothing else will do.

Transparency defined this way often leads to misunderstandings between worker generations, high emotions, a sense of entitlement, and organizational imbalances. More mature individuals, particularly those who have been in the workplace prior to Internet technologies, view transparency somewhat differently. They seldom have had immediate access to huge amounts of information. These employees acclimated to the demands and requirements of the organization on a different informational basis. Complete transparency—as in complete and immediate access to information—was seldom an issue.

There's a big difference between appropriate and inappropriate transparency. Absolute disclosure and the removal of all policies and hurdles to transparency are sometimes appropriate, sometimes not. For example, using the text TMI, "too much information," is inappropriate transparency. Leaders are not expected or required to disclose everything.

Dr. Kent Keith's Ten Paradoxical Commandments include Number 5: "Honesty and frankness make you vulnerable. Be honest and frank anyway." This has particular merit for considering the issue of transparency. Bad leaders assume the first part of the sentence to be true while good leaders live out the second part of the commandment.

This positive attitude toward transparency includes having a true openness to full review and even intense scrutiny. True transparency ties to what Zenger and Folkman advocate as the center stake of leadership: trust. Bad leaders often rely on a "just trust me" strategy regarding issues of transparency. This approach is particularly prevalent among those who have proven themselves to be serially untrustworthy and not apt to recognize their accountability both to others and to core standards.

Good leaders provide fair, timely, open, appropriate, accurate disclosures. Transparency precedes and follows them like the pleasant, comforting aroma of freshly brewed coffee on chilly day. Great leaders are *fully* trustworthy. Employees trust them because their transparency builds their authority and restrains them from overstepping and exploiting their authority. Moreover, if transparency is defined as genuineness, openness, truthfulness, approachability, accessibility, and full disclosure, then it presents a high management threshold to achieve.

Transparent people and organizations are just that—transparent and open. Those who are least inclined to transparency are those who tend to tout their transparency the most.

One reason for this pattern is that transparency has a hard link to accountability. Bad leaders are likely to disavow this linkage, preferring to ignore it.

Faced with challenge, good leaders see through weak, unclear arguments, get to the heart of the issue, and seldom make the claim of a lack of transparency. On occasion, lack of transparency is strategically necessary, and good leaders know the difference between this type of application and lack of transparency as a means to hide the truth. Yet many times, bad leaders don't have the skills or experience to see through arguments, so they claim their opponents lack transparency.

Sometimes bad leaders hide behind "need to know" arguments as reasons for not being transparent. Stating that someone or something *lacks transparency* can become a strategy to be thrown in the face of any one with whom a bad leader disagrees. So, carefully examine the motives and actions of people claiming transparency while stating that those to whom they may be opposed lack transparency.

There are occasions when a lack of transparency is a strategic necessity. Good leaders know the difference between this type of application and using transparency as a means of hiding the truth. A lack of access to information doesn't always mean a lack of transparency nor does using the lack of transparency argument against an opponent mean the opponent has something to hide.

Good leaders embody transparency. Bad leaders demand transparency of others but seldom see it as a requirement for themselves. For bad leaders, transparency does not easily occur, nor is it a natural first response.

Good managers understand that not all information held by the organization can or should be made available to all constituents. Information that can legally, ethically, strategically, and morally be made available should take place internally and externally. An organization or a leader does not lack transparency when highly sensitive information or legally sealed data is not disclosed.

Truly superior leaders have the ability to orchestrate transparency to a degree that it is productive, rather than unproductive and harmful. Followers grant superior leaders this flexibility, because they have proven themselves to be wise in the use of transparency.

When transparency is defined as genuineness, openness, truthfulness, approachability, and accessibility, then it presents a high threshold and is likely to make a bad leader uncomfortable. Realize that bad leaders aren't necessarily bad because they withhold information. They withhold information as a means of displaying and exercising their power to keep others in the dark when they needn't be.

12. Reactive Protection

Having grown up with a family of three brothers and now having two sons, I've noticed the reality of protective reaction many times. Essentially, reactive protection is expressed in the phrase "I can punch my brother, but you cannot punch my brother."

I have seen this reality played out in the workplace as well, particularly when a third party comes to the assistance and support of those who have been set upon by bad leaders. People who are bad leaders tend to not defend others being beset by other bad leaders. This will be fully discussed in lesson forty-five "Refusal to Provide Covering Fire."

Most of us tend to become protective of those we love and respect when we observe them being beset by bad leaders. Certainly, we don't wish misuse and abuse for others at the hands of V_2C leaders, so we naturally defend others, a desirable trait.

Inexperienced employees tend to seek out counsel as they observe a lack of transparency, ineptitude, disquieting attitudes, and negative influences of bad leaders. Most are not prepared for these issues, particularly Millennials, and their joyfulness of being employed is shaken when these realities set in.

> **Although people at any age, level of seniority, or degree of experience have likely encountered bad leaders, the effect of bad leadership is more likely to cause greater consternation, even pain, among the less experienced.**

Senior personnel are more likely to have encountered bad leaders along the way but seem to be able to accept it as unfortunate yet normal Standard Operating Procedure (SOP).

Fellow workers may occasionally speak up on behalf of those affected by the actions, in-actions, and attitudes of bad leaders. But coming to the defense of others beset by bad leaders carries a high degree of risk. It must only be engaged when those taking the risk are assured of their status and the strength of their arguments.

Whatever the age, experience level, or status of an employee, other employees notice the impact of bad leadership upon an employee's level of commitment, equilibrium, and performance.

13. Bad Bus Driver: Revisiting the *Good to Great* Bus Metaphor

Researcher and author Jim Collins and his associates have created the "bus" example as an easily understood means to describe positive organizational leadership. It's about having the right people in the right seats, on the right bus, on the right road, and going in the right direction. If you are acquainted with this metaphor, you have probably used it. If you are not acquainted with it, I recommended it to you as described in the book *Good to Great* and based upon the prior work of Tom Wolfe in *The Electric Kool-Aid Acid Test* published in 1969.

While the bus metaphor makes great sense, two components of its need further investigation. These are the skills of the bus driver and the conditions of the road. Some organizations have the wrong people behind the wheel, or due to bad road conditions, their driver's skills are insufficient.

Some drivers are bad, regardless of road difficulty or road conditions, just as some leaders are bad regardless of the organization or its stage of development. Treacherous roads require really good drivers, just as difficult situations or crisis circumstances in which organizations find themselves, require leaders who are not prone to the failures discussed later in this book.

Most of us have considered the bus metaphor from a rider's perspective, having seen ourselves or others in this role. The full value of the metaphor is engaged as people see themselves and particularly others from a bus driver's perspective.

I have enjoyed most of my automobile for business and pleasure. In fact, I seldom turn down the opportunity to take a road trip. Thankfully, all my trips have been safe, and on most trips, I made it to the desired location on time. However, the most unsettling trips have not been caused by detours, road or weather conditions, the price of gas, the quality or mechanical condition of the vehicle, or its creature comforts. At the root are the nature, skill, and amiability of the driver.

Some drivers just make me and other people nervous as do certain ineffective leaders. Moreover, people just don't relax with a bad driver. Similarly, people just don't relax with a bad leader. A lack of trust in the driver's skill lies at the core of my inability to relax on. Without trust in the driver, I am never comfortable enough to take a quick nap for fear of going too fast or too slow, going in the wrong direction, ending up in a ditch, or crashing to my death. Perhaps you identify with this feeling—not only while on a road trip, but also in your job? Constantly being diligent, cautious, and worried taxes your mind and body.

When you consider the negative emotions and anxieties created by traveling with incompetent, uncertain drivers, you discover they are enormously similar to feelings created by working with bad leaders. Unfortunately, you may get the same outcomes, as well.

Often followers in an organization also fear going too slow or too fast, going in the wrong direction, not arriving on time, or perhaps ending up in a ditch.

All other components of the bus metaphor can be as they ought, but without the properly trained, motivated driver who performs with skill and purpose, the bus could also crash.

Popular leadership and management books instruct you to emulate the characteristics of effective leaders—certainly this is a good thing to do. *Learning Good Lessons from Bad Leaders* does essentially the opposite. Examine the lives and performance of bad leaders and *don't* repeat their mistakes or emulate them. You learn *good lessons* while traveling the organizational and career road with leaders who are *not* trustworthy, those likely to take you and your organization into mission failure.

14. Defining a Lesson

We learn most lessons in life in this way. We observed and experience. Ape the good, avoid the bad, play in the yard not in the street, don't drink the stagnant water, and by all means don't eat the yellow snow and be cautious of the bad driver!

I had a memorable conversation with an outstanding college football coach, who provided a completely different viewpoint on effective coaching/leading. He contended that the finest football coaching takes place at the high school level rather than the college and professional levels, as I would have supposed. He argued that it takes better leadership to produce winning teams and successful programs where the talent is average, or even below average, than it takes where athletic skills are the greatest.

Since that conversation, I have looked with more awareness into lower levels of organizations for examples of superior leadership and not solely the C-Suite. Good leadership doesn't always surface from where it is expected.

In fact, bad leadership, as well as good leadership, can take place at any level of the organization. You need not look only to a single level to find it. If leaders at lower levels mess up, it is far less likely to be brought to the attention of The Wall Street Journal, Bloomberg, or tweeted, but it will be internally damaging none the less. It is not always the bad leader that gets terminated, but it can be the better leader who is used as a scapegoat and forced to continue their career elsewhere. This type of outcome will be noticed and remembered. It is likely to impact trust.

> Among the greatest employee frustrations are with leaders who *stay* when they should leave and when the organization allows the non-performers to continue as though they were top performers.

When the organization does not definitively deal with a low-performing leader, it causes a pernicious doubt to set in with productive personnel. Frustrations extend to other leaders who fail to act and to the team or organization that enables the quitter to stay.

On many occasions, I have said, "I am not bothered by the employee (or bad bus driver) who quits and leaves, but by the employee who quits and stays." Thus, I am not bothered by the bad leader who fails to perform and leaves; I'm bothered only by the bad leader who fails to perform and stays.

15. Defining a "Good" Lesson

A good lesson is one that you determine to be highly beneficial, desirable, and having transferable and sustained value. You may have learned that sticking your finger in an electrical outlet is not good; obeying the crossing guard is good; and reading the employment manual is also good.

Not learning these *good lessons* leads to bad outcomes. For many people, learning *good lessons* like these happens easily. For others, these lessons are not easily or quickly learned; they require effort to make them become beneficial and sustained.

16. Defining a "Bad" Leader

What is a bad leader? Defining a leader as bad or noting bad leadership behaviors is not a moral judgment. Although many leadership and management problems stem from a breach of a cultural, organizational, religious code or dogma, bad leadership does not fit into that category.

When you think of bad leaders, you most often think of a personality flaw or disorder, perpetual errors in judgment, or a lack of knowledge that affects personal, group, and/or organizational performance. More than intent or will, a lack of performance determines the degree of a leader's "badness."

Bad leaders are those whose may have personal deficiencies that negatively affect the nature, scope, reputation, and performance of an organization. Good trees don't produce bad fruit, and bad trees don't produce good fruit. Jesus Christ provides great distinction between people who produce good and bad fruit, and most bad leaders produce bad fruit. Often a single shortcoming does not create a bad leader, but a series of misjudgments based upon a combination of multiple shortcomings will cause a leader to lead badly.

Not all bad leaders exhibit all fifty-two failures considered in this book. But bad leaders will exhibit many of them. All organizations seek to achieve good results produced by good leaders over the long haul. Often, such is not the case and is the reason so many organizational consultants and personal coaches succeed.

The bad leaders examined here, and the ones you have witnessed, aren't bad at everything. In fact, some bad leaders can be quite good at many things. It's not these good things but the bad things that cause them to be branded. In fact, it is possible that one exceptionally bad aspect of an otherwise good leader will brand that person as bad. Unfortunately, merits/talents are often overshadowed by deficiencies. Great leaders may not do everything to a level of perfection, but they do most things rather well.

We could think of leaderships in terms of baseball. If you were a professional baseball player, you might be good at hitting but lousy defensively. You might be good in the clubhouse but not a great hitter. Coaches, fans, and sports writers judge baseball players on their greatest weaknesses or most critical strengths. I must confess that the baseball example is not a great one because the best hitters fail in their hitting the majority of times. If you could guarantee you could hit .400, then a Major League baseball team would likely hire you. Very few other jobs allow a sixty percent failure rate at the plate, but baseball does. Therefore, other metrics have been created, such as On Base Percentage and Slugging Percentage. They provide additional metrics and spread the hitter's contribution over several interrelated standards.

In contrast, surgeons, dentists, and attorneys must have success rates higher than forty percent, as must leaders of organizations. A sixty percent failure rate just won't cut it. When a big-league hitter fails, everyone knows. When a leader of an organization fails, the failure may not be discovered for years. All the while, the organization may entirely miss the purpose for which it was created. In this case, hitting .400 is tolerable.

Bad leaders make errors both large and small. Indeed, one mission-critical snafu may cause total organizational failure. Both a big hole in the battleship and a pinhole in a rowboat can become a reason for sinking.

17. What Makes a Bad Leader Bad?

Many, many possibilities can make bad leaders bad. For example, an inability to create or communicate a compelling vision that is widely adopted throughout the organization may cause a bad leader to be viewed as bad. Perhaps, inattention to the basics makes a leader bad. Maybe it's a lack of diligence, resilience, innovation, or discipline. It could be a lack of adequate external or internal environmental scanning for threats. Perhaps the leaders just don't learn, or they learn too little too late. A personality culture, rather than a performance culture, that allows the bad leader to persist may be the cause. The reasons are myriad, but I believe at the heart of the matter is the fact that . . .

> Leaders are bad because they are allowed to be so. Boards of directors, superiors, friends, and allies enable a bad leader to remain bad, because they give up helping the bad leader become good by becoming accountable.

Fatigue, inattentiveness, or a lack of proper modeling by supervisors are additional causes for defaulting to bad leadership.

The greatest concern and biggest caution is directed at bad leaders who continually prove to be bad people. *Good lessons* learned from good people performing badly are important, but they are not the anxiety-producing, career-busting ones about which you should worry most.

Certainly, from time to time, an imbalanced person may exercise good leadership behaviors. But good leaders manifest positive personality characteristics such as trustworthiness, diligence, creativity, ability to influence and motivate people who can execute and succeed when measured against organizational goals and mission. Bad leaders are those who perpetually don't do these positive things.

I'm not writing about good leaders who cause an occasional setback or have an infrequent flop. I am writing about those leaders who continually flop and don't meet the standards and expectations of the organizations they were hired to transform.

These same people, for reasons known only to a few, get promoted to higher positions where they manifest even greater incompetency. These are the lucky nincompoops of the workplace.

A no-fault mentality allows these bad leaders to flourish. By no-fault, I mean a lack of accountability for general well-being, success, and/or profitability. No-fault policies may work in marriage dissolutions or in car insurance policy claims, but they do not work in organizations intent on meeting their vision and mission statements—those striving to achieve the benefits for which they were created. Lucky nincompoops who have been, promoted may cause organizational failures because no one measures their success or failure or intends to do anything about it.

This book is about learning how *not* to be a workplace nincompoop by forging *good lessons* while observing the negative behaviors of workplace nincompoops.

Most organizations have personnel who display some degree of nincompoopdom. Some nincompoop behaviors are merely superficial and non-damaging; others can be dangerous and even fatal to the organization—*and* to your career.

There is a difference. Some bad leaders are nice people while some bad leaders are loveable nincompoops.

The positions of good and bad leaders may surprise you. Good leaders may appear at any level in an organization. Let me give you an example. My first full-time job after high school was at Manteno State Hospital as a psychiatric aide on the midnight shift in the admittance and high-security wards. I worked at Manteno when it was the third-largest mental hospital in the world and had thousands of patients. Located just south of Chicago, Illinois, Manteno State was an exciting but dangerous place to work.

Working at Manteno State was a huge blessing to me. It not only provided the income necessary to fund my first two years of undergrad studies but was an exceptionally good place to start making observations about effective and ineffective leadership. The hospital's leadership gave me one of my first ever *good lessons* about complex organizations and inattention to detail. At Manteno State, I first observed that even the deeply imbalanced or disturbed people occasionally exercised some degree of normalcy and solid leadership. Some of the titled and well-positioned people were the source of my first "bad leader" observations.

One of the more effective leaders among those patients who had been given various voluntary ward jobs was a man going through psychiatric evaluation prior to being sent to Menard State Hospital, a facility in Illinois for the criminally insane. He had been convicted of murdering three members of his family. In all respects, he appeared normal and exercised good leadership in his duties.

On one occasion, my older brother, who also worked at the hospital, signed out this patient, and we all proceeded to a local restaurant for Sunday dinner. Signing someone out was entirely within hospital policy and appropriate for that classification of patient and our status. We were not placing ourselves, the patient, or others at risk. So, here we were having a pleasant Sunday dinner with a supposedly insane triple murderer! We thought nothing of it and rather enjoyed the outing. A few hours later, we all safely returned to Manteno State.

Although we took him to dinner and had a good time doing so, I never felt entirely comfortable given his history. But he proved to be a good leader in the specific, controlled task of managing all reading materials and recreational equipment. I felt more comfortable with him than with some of the leaders for whom I would later work. At least, he was honest and transparent.

Since Manteno State—and while spending a lifetime striving to be a good leader and avoiding the inglorious title of a bad leader—I've had the enormous privilege of working with various ineffective leaders, some of whom I describe in this book.

A few were clinically disturbed, but they all had a high degree of competence and incompetence in at least one critical area. Most of them had huge but fragile egos. Many were poor money managers. Some hated their jobs but worked hard to disguise it. Most of them thought they could succeed in another industry. Some of them wanted to be noticed; some wanted to hide. Some worked hard; some believed they worked hard. All thought they were well-liked by their peers.

All thought they were great leaders. Most of them I liked as human beings. To all of them, I owe a great deal of gratitude. They form the core of leaders from whom I've learned *good lessons*.

To what behaviors do bad leaders default? Often, they default to nice behaviors in public and not-nice behaviors in private. Nice is nice, but what most organizations need are *effective* leaders, not necessarily *nice* leaders. I'm not writing about basic civility but about bad leaders who are inclined to default to *not-nice* rather than *nice*.

> *Nice* is too highly rated. *Effective* is not rated highly enough. If you work with nice leaders who are also effective, that's desirable, and you should consider putting down roots and learning from them. But working with *not-nice* leaders who are also *ineffective* should cause you seek employment and fulfillment elsewhere.

18. Current Reality

Without a doubt, historically lean and fat economic cycles have enormously affected the ability of leaders to lead successfully. In lean times, leaders tend to contract for safety and exercise more caution because they have less margin to mess up. In fat times, leaders become less diligent and sometimes even lazy because the sun shines and customers are delighted. Yet, as diligent as great leaders may be while carrying out the full scope of their responsibilities, they seldom have enough of every resource (PECIT) to go around, so they can create both the stability and the innovations required to remain competitive.

Even legendary leaders at the wealthiest companies, NGOs, non-profits, and governments seldom feel they have sufficient resources to achieve all they would like. The problem is substantially compounded for less wealthy or less stable organizations.

To deal with the boom and bust economic realities and establish a perspective from which you can lead despite them, I created the following expectation formula. It condenses work performance, economic reality, and time resource allocation into a single sobering thought.

Leaders are expected to produce...

19. AMAP with ALRAP-ASAP

AMAP (As Much as Possible) with ALRAP (As Little Resource as Possible) ASAP (As Soon as Possible)

Given the pressing, overarching reality of AMAP with ALRAP and ASAP, especially when combined with one or more of the leadership failures discussed here, it foreshadows trouble for individual careers, team productivity, and organizational health.

Leaders of organizations rich in resources can still make good or bad decisions. But when resources are scarce, they have less leeway for bad decisions, and leadership errors become more evident. This scarce environment exposes the failures of bad leaders more easily than in resource-rich times. When things are fat, the concentration goes to enjoying and prolonging the good times rather than determining how to keep the organization from experiencing lean resources and constricting times in the future.

> Leaders need sustained discipline to manage successfully during both lean and fat times, but particularly during fat times when they are prone to become distracted and inattentive due to their success. (See Lesson #29 as cross reference.)

To control for a lack of inattention during abundance and to increase diligence at all times, I created a series of tactics called "prevent offense." Its opposite, "prevent defense," is often used in American football. It's a game strategy to prevent the other team from moving the ball too far too soon and then scoring.

"Prevent offense" describes how organizations can maintain momentum, sustain innovation, avoid complacency, reduce the effect of competition, and keep employees engaged during times of success and abundance. "Prevent offense" tactics should also be used by you to maintain your focus, energy, and momentum during times when others acknowledge your contributions and successes.

20. Learning to See the Good Lesson

In the AMAP, ALRAP, ASAP environment, looking for the *good lesson* may require time and energy. But, as in the *Where's Waldo* book series, spending time looking is a great idea. Adult and child readers alike enjoy trying to find the hidden Waldo and other characters by concentrating, searching, searching again, then rejoicing and luxuriating in diligence and triumph when they finally find Waldo. The reward is worth the search effort, whether in finding Waldo or in extracting *good lessons* from your life, career, and circumstances.

Similar life and organizational processes are not often seen on TV or You-Tube. Among the greatest disinformation and untruths found in contemporary TV are not the highly politicized news programs or the fleshy reality shows but the hunting and fishing reality shows. Most people who watch hunting and fishing shows are those most likely to go into the field and hunt or travel to the lake and fish. The disinformation for the occasional viewer and non-aficionado is how easy the process appears. Given the shows' formats, the chase and capture all take place within a few minutes. But it ain't that way in real life!

Most hunters don't hunt full-time. They don't have all the latest, most effective equipment and products. They may go for years or even decades without seeing, let alone harvesting a trophy. If it were as easy as it appears on TV, then the hunter or fisher wouldn't feel the heart-stopping adrenaline rush when a deer is down or a fish netted. To be a successful hunter, you must leave the TV, bear the heat, cold, pain, and loneliness to be successful.

Learning *good lessons* works the same way. It isn't always as easy as it looks. It takes time and high degrees of commitment and effort. But the exhilarating experience when you capture a *good lesson* is over-the-top worth it.

Good Lessons can be learned from those who have responsibility for your development early in life and from those who have accountability for you in the professional world. However, few people realize that, if they are willing, they can also learn *good lessons* from those who don't care about them. Through their inability, willingness, and refusal, these people can affect you badly if you don't learn *good lessons* from them.

21. Inability, Willingness, and Refusal

As you move into the chapters that follow, you will note that I contextualize leadership failure with three terms: inability, willingness, and refusal.

Inability, willingness, and refusal are default behaviors for bad leaders; they're used here somewhat interchangeably. In most cases, inability refers to a missing innate perception or skill or a lack of ability to avoid bad behaviors and actions. Inability also refers to a lack of inside knowledge or center point for action, what Covey calls "true north." Inability also refers to some internal awareness or savvy that is missing. Inability also refers to knowing the right thing to do, but not having the ability to execute. Refusal refers to a person who has the innate ability, training, and/or knowledge, yet for some reason declines to use them.

Inability is a matter of knowledge while refusal a matter of will. For example, I once owned an Irish setter named Abby. She was absolutely beautiful, but stubborn and willful. She knew she should not leave the yard. She would clearly see me pleading for her to stay home and not run away. She knew what to do and what not to do, but she didn't have the willingness to submit to my commands. She would look over her shoulder at me, catch my eye, and sprint for the next county. Maggie, my beloved black poodle, had the knowledge and awareness of what a relationship with me required and the willingness to submit. I would again have a poodle like Maggie but would never again have an Irish setter like Abby. Both dogs knew what I wanted, but they differed tremendously in their willingness to act accordingly.

Many times, if you see a leader's inability to act, it's likely based on what is missing from their experience, intelligence, and character. The person has not made some inner connection. Yet, when you deal with a leader who manifests unwillingness to act, you deal with someone who may have all the inner intellectual gifts and experience necessary, but not the character or the will.

The willingness of bad leaders to allow, ignore, tolerate, or even enable negative organizational outcomes can be the fertile ground from which you can learn *good lessons*.

Within the workplace, it is easier to deal with inability than refusal because inability is based on an innate deficiency or perhaps a lack of training while refusals are choices. Additionally, if you have an inability in a field like accounting, you can learn that skill with sufficient discipline and without an innate mathematical ability. In contrast, consider someone who has great innate skills with mathematics, has had training and experience in accounting, but refuses to engage in accounting. That person has made a willful choice unrelated to intellect and training.

Sometimes, willful refusal occurs because people have large, personal stakes in particular outcomes, which could lead them to will a particular outcome by refusing good choices. For example, at one of the universities where I served, I came into contact with a young man who I thought had the physical and mental attributes to become a professional football player. He had the perfect size, speed, and competitiveness. However, he thought of himself as a basketball player, although he didn't possess the physical skills to go pro in basketball.

Although I had great affection for this young man, I couldn't persuade him to take a different route to a professional athletic career. I knew him well because his mother had pleaded with the university to readmit him after he had been expelled. His mom persuaded us that his friends at home in Youngstown, Ohio, had either been killed or were in prison, and she didn't want her son to go down either path. Her impassioned plea led us to relent, and he was readmitted.

Several years later while leaving a graduation ceremony, I heard a huge, joyful commotion outside the building. Out of curiosity, I approached the people making the fuss. It was being caused by the student athlete, now a graduate, his mother, and what seemed to be half the population of Youngstown, Ohio. What a time they were having! As I joined in the cheering, the graduate came over to me, wrapped his arms around me, lifted me off the ground, and said to me, "I love you, Prez."

Although he did not heed what I thought was the better path for him (certainly his choice and not mine), I was not dismayed by the choice he made. In this case, I could not fault his choice not to pursue professional football, but I did, and still do to some degree, disagree with him on his unwillingness to at least give professional football a try. He never made it in professional basketball either, but he has been successful pursuing non-athletic-related employment.

22. Asking the Question

Perhaps among the most important questions to ask yourself is this: "What *good lessons* can I learn from the bad leaders I am likely to encounter during my career?"

I arrived at the *Good Lessons from Bad Leaders* idea as a result of many years of teaching management practice in college, scores of consulting jobs, my entrepreneurial and business ownership experiences, assisting and encouraging entrepreneurs, my personal encounters with bad leaders, what my students and colleagues told me about the bad leaders with which they had contended, and lastly by continually asking the question: "What is the best lesson you ever learned from a bad leader?"

This question enables respondents to concentrate on resolution and benefit, rather than on the oppressiveness of prior conflicts. And, whether I ask people at executive, mid-level, or entry-level positions, most often the replies reflect previous turmoil, rumination, and deep introspection.

Respondents are seldom hesitant to reply. In fact, many have thanked me for the opportunity to answer the question. They were eager to disclose their thoughts and feelings as they got a few things off their chests.

Those who had incurred the most pain from bad leaders also seemed to be those who had a profound sense of loss and heaviness of spirit. Their remembrances were often accompanied by a sigh of resolution. Some people had joyfully moved beyond the bad situation caused by a bad leader; many had not. Many bore the emotional scars suffered at the hands of bad leaders; some were still resentful; and some had forgiven and set a new course for themselves, their fellow workers, and organizations.

While listening, I could not help but recall the words of the following poem engraved on the entrance to a college residence hall. It seems enormously relevant in response to the question of learning *Good Lessons from Bad Leaders.*

One ship sails east and another sails west with the self-same winds that blow.

'Tis the set of the sail and not the gale that determines the way they go.

And the winds of the sea are the ways of fate as we voyage along through life.

'Tis the act of the soul that determines the goal, and not the calm or the strife. [9]

23. Incompetency Abounds

As incompetency abounds, why are so many incompetent manager/leaders allowed to keep their jobs? The quick answer is that the *known* incompetent is better than the *unknown* incompetent. Incompetency leads to ineffectiveness and a continuous state of organizational imbalance and ultimately decline. Incompetency will persist as long as it is tolerated.

The personnel policies of professional sports teams clearly establish the value of performance: if you don't perform well, you don't perform at all. You will be benched or traded… period. The best performing athletes play; the under-performing don't… period… end of story. And although the professional sports team's personnel policy seems cold and unfeeling, the sale, trading, or release of players is most often accompanied by the phrase "Well, it's just business." Compare this policy with the difficulty of a RIF or firing of incompetents. They are worlds apart.

Decades ago, Laurence J. Peter and Raymond Hall wrote *The Peter Principle*.[10] At the time, I didn't pay much attention to the central concept of the book: people/employees rise to their own level of incompetence—that is, they are promoted to a level at which they can no longer perform well.

As the pace, complexity, and growth of business and government increases, the Peter Principle makes more sense all the time. The basic trust people have for organizational and political leadership has diminished due to perceptions of increased incompetence.

> **Don't allow yourself to be permanently stuck working with or for incompetent leaders. Their incompetence will rub off on you if you let it.**

24. Summary Statement

What then are positive outcomes of a *good lesson?* Some are insight, patience, perseverance, hope, and quietude, but here are four of special note: ***Awareness,*** which is an initial insight and understanding that something has occurred and exists; ***Deep knowledge,*** which is acute cognizance beyond superficial levels of awareness; ***Wisdom,*** which is the proper application of deep knowledge, and ***Courage*** to face whatever life, your career, and bad leaders throw at you.

A *good lesson* is a virtuous gift that is first received then passed along to benefit others. Without a *good lesson* perspective, problems and bad leaders who cause bad problems have little, if any, positive benefit. But, as you integrate a *good lesson* perspective, *good lessons* become enormously helpful and salutary.

We all like to receive good gifts, and we know the big difference between a good gift and a bad gift. Good gifts aren't necessarily good because they are expensive or inexpensive: they are good because they fit our lifestyles, needs, and interests. Getting a beautiful puppy for Christmas can be a really desirable gift under the right circumstances. That puppy can also be a really bad gift, depending on the circumstances.

When bad circumstances created by bad leaders are turned into *good lessons*, they can be re-gifted as usable gifts for others. In other words, my pain has accrued to my benefit and can work to yours as well.

Unfortunately, the reverse is also true. Bad circumstances created by bad leaders can become bad lessons, infecting the whole organization.

The big problem with bad leaders is that their attitudes, actions, and level of incompetency get normalized into the organization.

People also get absorbed and lulled into the effects of bad leadership. If unchallenged, what bad leaders do and don't do becomes so embedded that those who are brave enough to raise red flags and hold the bad leaders to a higher level of accountability and achievement are likely to be marginalized, if not eliminated altogether.

Bad leaders are not benign. Their influence permeates organizations and the people in them.

Therefore, learning to process and extract *good lessons* is the key to personally overcoming the incompetence and effects of bad leaders and the bad results they create.

25. So, What Are You Going to Do?

Inherent in your response to the personal and organizational chaos caused by bad leaders is the concept of directionality.

By directionality, I mean the trajectory of your response. You can choose not to seek out a *good lesson,* and the trajectory of the chaos caused by the bad leader will become a de facto curse. Or, you can heed the *good lesson* and the direction of your response can result in courage beyond the chaos.

What will you project forward, a curse or courage?

Good lessons are dearly bought, the common lessons,
Such as men give and take from day to day,
Come in the common walk of easy life,
Blown by the careless wind across our way.

Good lessons are greatly won, not found by chance.
Nor wafted on the breath of summer dream;
but grasped in the great struggle of the soul,
Hard buffeting with adverse wind and stream.

Wrung from the troubled spirit, in hard hours
Of weakness, solitude, perchance of pain,
Good Lessons spring like harvest from the well-plowed field,
And the soul feels it has not wept in vain.[11]

26. Recommendations to Extract Value

I recommend you read the following three sections (Inability, Willingness, and Refusal) with the same approach that you found in Summary Statement just above. Read to get awareness, deep knowledge, wisdom, and courage.

Certainly, your degree frustration, urgency of need, and level of experience will form the basis of a "deep dive" and help you learn and remember the lessons in the leadership failure sections that follow. At the end of each of the fifty-two lessons, you will find *good lessons* I want to specifically highlight. I'm sure you will be able to create a number of new lessons of your own as you take time to consider what you read and get the hang of extracting *good lessons*.

I suggest you scan the entire list of fifty-two failures to find one that looks familiar or intriguing. Start there. You might want to take a failure per day or a section per week or go at it straight through front to back or back to front. There is no magic arrangement or sequence to the three types of failures, so read about them using whatever method works best.

The strategy that I use to remember big blocks of information is to adopt what I call R2TM...the Read to Teach Method. When reading, I'm not only reading for myself but for everyone to whom I might pass along what I have read. R2TM then makes me doubly productive and also accountable to those to whom I might communicate what I have learned. This way, I am not just reading randomly and without purpose but for big benefits to me and others. If you use R2TM, you can more successfully log into your mind and heart. I have even gone so far as to read as though I was discussing the failure with the leader who caused it in the first place.

After reading each of the fifty-two leadership failures, ask yourself the following questions:

1. Have I ever seen/heard about this particular leadership failure before?
2. Did it affect me, someone in my family, or someone with whom I work/ed?
3. How did I feel about it at the time it occurred?
4. How do I feel about it now?
5. How will I use the knowledge and lessons learned in this section *to discover* courage beyond the chaos created by the bad leader?
6. How will I use the knowledge and lessons learned in this section *to avoid* committing the failure myself?
7. How will I use the knowledge and the lessons learned in this section *to accelerate* my career?

I suggest that you "lock down" the concept by repeating the **Good Lesson Affirmation** and add the failure that you have just read about.

For example, take Number 11: Inability to Read Between the Lines could be repeated as "There is no FEAR (failure, experience, anxiety, or roadblock) caused by a bad leader from whom I'm not learning a *good lesson*. I have the ability and courage to read between the lines." You might even add the name of a bad leader to the sentence and read it, "I have the ability and courage to read between the lines unlike "Big Nasty" my former boss."

From time to time, I have engaged those who have been so beset and beat down by the bad leaders in their lives and at their places of employment that it is difficult for them to rise above the discouragement. They don't have anyone to provide helpful insights, supportive counsel, or an encouraging nudge. Their lives are just the opposite of the phrase from the old cowboy song "Home, Home on the Range": ". . . never was heard an discouraging word." They find it impossible to rally the internal strength to be *self*-encouraging.

I have occasionally suggested they make use on my last name. My family name, Self, is Norwegian and a contraction of <u>Se</u>a Wo<u>lf</u>. The first two letters were combined with the last two letters and the named morphed into Self. My ancestors made their living from the sea, so the change from Sea Wolf to Self made sense. The short version "Self" has stuck and been in use since the 1100s.

For those who can't summon the courage to be their own self-encouragers, I suggest they think of me as the "self" in "self-encouragement." This approach personifies the role of encourager if they can't play it for themselves.

Perhaps this approach seems silly, maudlin, or pointless for those who have encouragers and mentors, but for those who don't have the emotional strength to be self- encouraging, it can help. Sure, it's only a mental exercise, but a helpful one. Any form of encouragement from anyone, anything, or by any method is better than no encouragement at all.

In many respects, this is similar to the process I used when writing this book. In my minds-eye, I thought of those who would be reading it and how the lessons learned from bad leaders could be encapsulated and communicated. I envisioned how this book might revitalize the lives and careers of readers by viewing the leadership failures they have experienced differently and extract transformative lessons from them. Otherwise, the beneficial process of moving their experiences with bad leaders from a position of *dominance* to a position of *usefulness* is not likely to happen.

Chapter 2.

Good Lessons: Inability

1. Inability to Tell the Whole Truth

"A half-truth is a whole lie."
Yiddish proverb

Telling the whole truth is substantially different from telling part of the truth or lying outright. The whole truth also has significantly different consequences from partial truth or lies. Bad leaders tend to ignore this fact.

I heard about an employee of a railroad company who was only partially truthful when he said he was at his job at the proper time with his lantern in hand at the railroad crossing to prevent the accident. What he failed to disclose was that his signal lantern was not lit at the time of the crash. The fact that his lantern was not functioning made a great deal of difference.

Likewise, a man said he fell off a twelve-foot ladder, but he failed to disclose that he was only standing on the first rung when he fell. It makes a big difference on which rung he was standing when he fell—not only for his well-being but for the accurate perception of the people who heard about it.

Sometimes leaders tell partial truths with little or no real consequence. For example, from year to year, my wife and I board a Washington State Ferry at

Edmonds, Washington, early in the evening on July 4th. We take the ferry to Kingston, Washington, on the Kitsap Peninsula. The ride takes about thirty-five minutes. When the weather and sky conditions are right, we see Mount Rainier in the south and another volcano, Mount Baker, to the north. The panoramic view is about one-hundred forty-five miles.

One particular year, as we were mid-way across the sound on our return to Edmonds, a huge, full, red moon began to appear. Many travelers on the ferry's observation deck were so attracted to the fireworks on the same horizon that they could not process what they were seeing. For a few brief moments, a number of them thought the moon was a new and unusual firework. Their observations were absolutely incorrect, because they expected to see fireworks and were in fact seeing fireworks of a natural kind. Their perceptions were only partially correct.

The captain came on the ship's loudspeaker and explained that the travelers were not seeing fireworks but a "rising moon." This statement was only partially correct. Yes, the moon was appearing, but what the captain said, "We have a rising moon" was not exactly right. The moon wasn't rising; the earth was rotating toward the eastern horizon. Imagine the surprise of the travelers after the captain explained and they recognized the moon—and their misperception. I'm sure the captain's mistake wasn't intentional; no harm was done, but his proclamation was not the whole truth.

Now, according to maritime law, captains of sailing vessels have ultimate authority while aboard ship. Their word is final and must be heeded for the good of the passengers, crew, and vessel. Captains are expected to tell the whole truth all the time because not doing so could have enormous consequences. In this particular circumstance, the captain was completely wrong in his explanation of the moon displaying itself juxtaposed to the fireworks. Right now, you may be thinking, "Big deal. Don't quibble with the captain's explanation or the travelers mistakenly thinking that the moon was some new fireworks display." But here's the point.

Although this is an example of not telling the whole truth, it had little consequence. However, the necessity of telling the whole truth and questioning one's perceptions concerning the whole truth have enormous consequences in your leadership career.

Sometimes, bad leaders do not tell the whole truth, and followers do not test their assumptions about what they have heard and believed to be the whole truth. Bad leaders don't always tell a partial truth. They tell as much truth or falsehood as expedites their purpose.

Furthermore, they seldom take action to clarify—as they should—the assumptions of those they seek to lead. Such leaders are more hopeful that what they say will not be challenged for the whole truth. A challenge may disclose a true intent to deceive or at least to partially misinform their followers and coworkers without being discovered.

Leaders sometimes do horrible things and make duplicitous statements purposefully to mislead. You must determine the wholeness and accuracy of the message received in order to identify a purposefully misleading, duplicitous leader who doesn't have you, your team's or your organization's best interests at heart.

The question then is:

"Why wouldn't a leader tell the whole truth?" They perceive they have more to gain by duplicity than by truthfulness; they perceive they gain an advantage by communicating what's only partially true; or they mistakenly think that telling the whole truth might lessen their power or status.

This belief is quite the opposite of transparency, genuineness, and authenticity.

Two specific behaviors bad leaders tend to manifest regarding accuracy of messaging are sharpening and leveling. Sharpening is adding to or over-emphasizing certain components of messages beyond the truth in order to achieve understanding and buy-in. Leveling is the act of under-emphasizing or down-playing the facts and truth about the facts to achieve understanding and buy-in.

Both sharpening and leveling spin the truth in a certain direction: one up and one down. When or if discovered, both sharpening and leveling cause leaders to be labeled as untrustworthy because they have only communicated a part of the whole truth. I'm not saying that good leaders shouldn't put an optimistic face on the facts, but they should not do so to such a degree that "spin" becomes a lie. Good leaders tend not to sharpen or to level, but to let the message and the truth of the message speak for themselves, all while trusting the hearer with the ability to interpret and understand the facts and truth in the message.

> Good leaders show both concern for the truth and high regard for the listener when they demonstrate their belief that the listener has the intellect and will to handle the truth. Bad leaders, often paternalistically, don't make the same assumption.

Moreover, I'm not suggesting you become entirely suspicious of the leadership's intentions, but that you become as "wise as a serpent, yet as innocent as a dove"[12] and see things as they really are. Great harm has come to lives and careers when reasonable measures of care are not exercised in regard to unreasonable, untimely, irrational commands—the edicts of bad leaders. Most often, these types of demands are not for good superior decision-making, nimble execution, or moving an organization in a new direction. Instead, such edicts serve the purpose of providing notice of a leader's power, the intent to use that power, or, in some cases, the punishment of those who question the misuse of power.

All organizations need someone to whom legitimate authority has been given, or chaos is likely to occur. Few would question this. All organizations have the need to be seen and to view themselves as having leaders who tell the whole, undistorted truth.

Of course, I'm not suggesting that leaders disclose matters that cannot be legally or ethically disclosed, are unwise, untimely, or damaging to people and organizations.

> All leaders spin the facts to promote their ideas, initiatives, attitudes, and actions. Good leaders are more inclined to spin inwardly *toward* the whole truth, whereas bad leaders tend to spin the truth outwardly *away from* the whole truth.

This is not to say that good leaders do not make mistakes. Some margin of error for truthfulness is commonly acceptable in the best of leaders. Still, bad leaders tend to widen the margin of error for complete truthfulness, and it doesn't seem to bother them.

I once worked with a young, first-time entrepreneur. He had a relatively strong working background but no true executive experience. The business proposition he had in mind appeared to have value and was a bit ahead of the market's developmental curve and the competition. I rated the proposed business at 115 out of a total of 150 points on my "likelihood to make it" scale. If he could explain cogently what he wanted to achieve—its features and benefits and why someone would buy the service—then if he created and executed a good plan, the business might have made it.

As we progressed, evidence showed that he had not been entirely truthful regarding his financial background or knowledge. This deficit carried into a proposal regarding a change to the process we had been using to secure second-stage funding. To incentivize a potential second-round investor, he wanted to offer shares from the first round that had closed some months prior and for which no shares were then available. Moreover, he wanted to offer the second-round stock at the first-round price and not disclose this option to current shareholders.

I thought this plan was untruthful and argued that this duplicitous strategy would set us off in the wrong direction. Surely, it would come back to cause a huge breech with other first- or second-round investors who would not have been given the same opportunity. I walked him back from making the decision, but his proposed action to communicate less than the whole truth was troubling. It foreshadowed his lack of ethics and further downstream difficulties.

Another reason to stick with the truth is that after a while, bad leaders begin to believe their own "stuff." With sheer repetition of their untruthful statements, they deceive themselves and think they are truthful when they are not.

Typically, bad leaders who perceive that their statements and messaging have drifted from the whole truth seldom make a correction and get back on the whole truth track. By comparison, once good leaders have realized they have drifted from the whole truth, they will self-correct and realign themselves and their statements, acting in unison with the whole truth.

Another facet of the whole truth is urgency. Perhaps you have seen the statement like "Mistakes on your part don't necessitate urgency on my part" posted on someone's cubicle wall. If a leader makes some uncharacteristic, unreasonable demand for a course of action, a change in it, or a decision accompanied by enormous urgency, exercise caution. At least ask yourself, "What is the source of the pressure and urgency?" Often, the demand for quick action contains less than the whole, complete truth. Additionally, the greater the complexity of the urgent action, the greater is the need to find the whole truth.

GOOD LESSONS:

- Not telling the whole truth has many bad consequences. Good leaders know this. Bad leaders know this but are likely to ignore or minimize the consequences of not telling the whole truth.
- Telling the whole truth *takes* courage and *builds* courage.
- Not telling the whole truth has corrosive effects not only on the untruthful leaders but on all those they seek to lead and influence.
- The motives of good leaders are designed and driven by the whole truth.
- The motives of bad leaders are designed and driven by their version of the whole truth.
- Not telling the whole truth all the time leads to a whole lot of problems all the time.
- Good leaders tell the whole truth all the time, even when it's contrary to their inclinations to spin.
- Good leaders are directed and disciplined by the whole truth. Bad leaders aren't.
- Bad leaders are inclined to tell the whole truth only when it is clearly to their political and ego advantage, or when telling a partial truth is likely to be discovered as a whole lie.
- Good leaders tell the whole truth before they are required to or are forced to admit the truth. Bad leaders only tell the whole truth when they are obligated or forced to do so.
- Good leaders are aware of the implications, reactions, and interpretations of truth embedded in their messages.
- Good leaders engage the whole truth to motivate. Bad leaders use partial truth to manipulate.

Don't take any leader's message hook, line, and sinker without careful consideration of the degree of truthfulness that person has displayed in similar circumstances.

2. Inability to Create and Maintain a Spirit of Fair Exchange

Inherent in western democratic capitalism is the idea of fair exchange. Whether via a bartering system or cash exchange for goods and services, at its core is the notion that both or all parties in the transaction should receive fair exchange in what they desire to receive from the transaction.

Most times, organized markets exist to facilitate such exchanges whether at the local Tuesday Farmers' Market or the New York Stock Exchange. Honest weights and measures and practices are necessary for fair exchange and stable societies. The spirit of fair exchange is essentially a social contract that sets the parameters of fair practice. People often notice the spirit of fair exchange when it is lacking or broken.

Still, without question, people will, at some time, feel as though they have been taken advantage of—ripped off. Whether pitching marbles, playing summer league basketball, receiving a bogus warranty, failing in a relationship, or participating in a complex Ponzi scheme, most of us have felt the emotional sting of being exploited. Its residue is a sense of loss, violation, and anger.

I suspect all of us who have participated in a recreational or vocational competition in which we lost for reasons beyond our poor performance and have felt (as they say in the Dog Pound at FirstEnergy Stadium, the home of the Cleveland Browns) like saying, "We was robbed by 'dem' refs!"

No person, team, or company can expect to win all the time because nature, life, and commerce are just too competitive to let this happen. Nor should any one person or team win all the time, or if it is unfair and leads to the disadvantage of others. For this reason, the United States has anti-trust laws to create a level playing field for all wishing to compete in the marketplace.

I was a child the first time I recall observing a failure of fair exchange and someone getting ripped off. I found out my neighbor kids placed bricks and stones in the middle of bundles of newspapers that were being resold by the pound to what we would now call recycling companies. At first, I thought that their strategy was clever. But after I thought about it, I determined that what appeared to be shrewd was merely dishonest and deceitful. Because I wasn't the buyer of the bundled papers, the lack of fair exchange was no skin off my nose, but I do recall feeling sorry for the guy who bought the papers because of the breech in fair business practice.

Since then, I have often wondered what type of world we would have if everybody disregarded the principle of fair exchange in their personal and business relationships. Utter chaos would result.

Leaders who don't have the ability to recognize the necessity for the creation and maintenance of a spirit of fair exchange can cause enormous disequilibrium within employees and organizations. Take, for example, this story: An employee had been promised a certain time slot for a summer vacation. She had properly applied for the time off and had been pre-approved. Immediately before the start of her vacation, the employee learned that her supervisor had reversed the approval and determined that the employee must forego her vacation until a later date due to an unanticipated addition to the workload. The employee explained that it was 4:45 p.m. on a Friday afternoon and her family was waiting in a rented Winnebago in the employee parking lot. Postponing the vacation would be enormously difficult, discouraging, and even emotionally painful to the employee and family.

Remember, no prior notice had been given for the change. Her supervisor didn't think it would or should be a problem. To the employee's appeal, the supervisor essentially said, "So what?" What type of leader would intentionally or unintentionally create this type of imbalance? A bad one.

You may be thinking how unfair, unjust, and cruel. And, it is! But I'm sure you have seen bad leaders bring about even worse situations because they lack concern about fair exchange. In the mind of the employee, she had earned the vacation. The time off had been approved, and she had done her part. Suddenly, the bad leader had imbalanced the relationship. Not only was the demand to postpone the family vacation vexing, but the cavalier expectation that the postponement should and would not be a problem also exposed a glaring lack of a spirit of fair exchange.

Research supports the importance of a spirit of fair exchange. Fredrick Herzberg's Two-Factor Theory motivational research proved that certain things motivate certain types of employees, such as the ability to advance and grow, recognition, achievement, responsibility, and the job itself.[13] Other factors, which Herzberg called "Hygiene Factors"—reasonable working conditions, supervision, job security, and pay/financial compensation—tend only to maintain employee motivation. Inherent in these findings and several subsequent studies is the notion of fair exchange. Fair exchange makes a great deal of difference to employees.

A lack of spirit of fair exchange is one of the primary reasons organizations fail to achieve buy-in or a full commitment from their personnel. A lack of a spirit of exchange actually has the effect of pushing people away and lessening their productivity. Even worse, getting out of fair exchange with customers can be fatal.

Unfortunately, bad leaders tend not to want to participate in a "tit-for-tat" balancing of relationships and work. In these situations, the scales are weighted toward fairness and not toward the leaders' advantage. The callousness with which they overturn or modify prior planning, decisions, and initiatives can be enormously frustrating. They mistakenly believe they can only win when someone else loses. They do not recognize the value of fair exchange to motivate and inspire their would-be followers. In fact, they appear totally immune to the impact and value of fair exchange.

I suggest avoiding an inability or unwillingness to see the other person's point of view and lack of an innate sense of fairness like the plague. Bad leaders are insensitive to others' contributions. They have a missing gene and are unable to treat people fairly to the same degree that they are unwilling to abide by fair use restrictions in copyright law.

Not all bad leaders manifest an inability to promote an atmosphere of fair exchange, but this glaring inability can become routinized within the behavior of the company, work group, and others, if allowed to do so. Organizations that lack fair exchange perspectives tend to have high employee churn, legal entanglements, and labor unrest. These effects point to leaders who ignore, disrespect, or fail to compensate employees for their ideas, energy, and hard work. These leaders may even see harm in letting another person have a "win." A continued willingness to take advantage of others—coworkers, the supervised, ownership, and even the buying population—reveals a systemic problem characterized by the lack of fair exchange.

Let me illustrate. In one of my university presidencies, my willingness to recognize a spirit of fair exchange was evident in my first meeting with non-teaching staff members. After what I thought was a productive, engaging meeting, the first question I received in the Q&A period was "Are you going to continue the policy of a paid vacation/released time between the Christmas and New Year's holidays?" Little else I said would have had meaning had I not recognized this expectation or the willingness of employees to complete their work to have the additional time off. This was their most important issue.

An imbalance between *what you give* and *what you receive* from the organization tends not to appear on a bad leader's radar screen and fair exchange isn't a big deal.

GOOD LESSONS:

- Being out of fair exchange doesn't bother bad leaders, whereas good leaders work for fair exchange in all relationships at all times.
- You must expect that bad leaders do not acknowledge the necessity and/or value of fair exchange. This assertion can be extended to all relationships within the workplace, whether you deal with employees, vendors, or customers.
- Beware of the bad leader who says, "We'll only be out of balance/fair exchange just this once." Bad leaders will advance this idea, but it indicates a willingness to be out of fair exchange on other things.

Taking advantage of others may provide momentary satisfaction, but in the long run, it corrodes individual spirit as well as undermines good business practice and culture.

- The absence or abundance of fair exchange is a major contributor to organizational culture. Fair exchange is both an attitude (spirit) and an action. Good leaders know this; bad leaders ignore this. Like a rip tide or an ocean undertow, a lack of fair exchange has an insidiously powerful effect on people's emotional well-being and organizational success. Good leaders take ownership of producing and maintaining fair exchange, because they see it as both a means and an end.

---

3. Inability to Take Courage

I have had an ongoing conversation with a young woman in whom I saw great promise. She was smart and had the potential to achieve much with her life, but she lacked the ability to find, derive, and take courage from challenging circumstances. Unfortunately, her challenges became insurmountable hurdles. She was not able to find or extract courage nor apply the courage she should have gained to future challenges. She didn't completely stall out, but neither has she developed her TAGS (talents, abilities, gifts, and skills) to the degree she could and should have. She now works at a major university in a position well short of her potential.

What does it mean to find, draw from, and take courage? Good leaders can find, draw from, and take courage from nearly every challenge. They do this as leaders because they first found, drew, and took courage as individuals not only from bad situations but from good ones as well. This is far more than finding the silver lining, making lemonade out of lemons, or putting a positive spin on PSDs (problems, situations, and difficulties). This kind of courage is an internal resolve that firmly acts to find a way through difficulties. The ability to overcome courage is then extended to subsequent job and career opportunities to which these leaders can "take" their courage reservoir.

Some people completely avoid challenging opportunities and circumstances. Without challenge, there is little need for courage. And, there is a big difference between good challenges and bad challenges, and good leaders can be trusted to know the difference.

Several of my acquaintances have climbed Mount Rainer. At an elevation of 14,410 feet it is one spooky volcano and something to be avoided. But had I climbed and summited lesser mountains, I would be able to draw courage from those assents and apply them to climbing Mount Rainier. As it stands, I have no business on this mountain and attempting to climb it would be a tough challenge.

Bad leaders have difficulty finding those issues or opportunities from which to draw courage. They have not progressively found and taken courage from previous challenges. They may have achieved their job or position as a gift rather than though prior challenge and struggle. Bad leaders lack the willingness to hunt until they find a direction, strategy, appealing product, or a way through the fog. Bad leaders don't have the ability to be resilient until they can find something from which they can discover and pass along courage.

To make the courage sequence work, you must first be confronted by a challenge big enough to require it. Strangely, courage is found in challenge, but many people and bad leaders find discouragement and defeat in challenge. Some people run from or shrink from PSDs. Thus they never find courage.

Others, however, find courage in the face of nearly constant challenge. For example, I've attended many, many graduation commencements and have enjoyed them immensely for their passion, pageantry, and inspiration. Some people find them boring until the person for whom they are attending is mentioned among the list of graduates. That's when the cheering starts. They become alert and engaged, because they are sharing in "their" graduate's courage and achievement.

While I have had many thousands of degree diplomas pass from my hands and am happy for all who graduate, I am the most prone to develop a lump in my throat or even tears in my eyes when those who have found courage in their own physical handicaps make their way across the stage. They may move in wheelchairs, on crutches, or with assistance from others, but they have persisted, overcome, and made it.

Some have overcome even social service agency advisers who attempted to set limits on their success with comments about how they could do no better in life than to take menial jobs or sell apples on the street. One of these graduates specifically sought me out after a commencement ceremony and gave me a picture of herself in her graduation gown with a note of thanks written on the back. She was so happy and thankful for the care and patience of the university and her professors who provided the opportunity to complete a college degree. She was effusive in her praise of me, because I had taken time, when I had seen her on campus, to inquire of her progress and show interest. What she didn't and couldn't know was that, when I would speak with her on campus, I was finding courage through her struggles and resolve. I was the one who was being benefited; she was helping me!

Graduates like her are the ones who are hailed with the most lively, raucous cheering. They are greatly applauded for their courage and achievement. Sound waves of appreciation and affirmation surround them. Some of the words found in the University of Michigan fight song apply to these graduates… "Hail to the victors valiant, Hail to the conquering heroes." These are also the students who have courage for their own challenges and who give courage to others facing challenges.

What does it mean to *take* courage? First, it means to extract courage from challenges you face or to extract courage from the triumphs of others who have or are facing challenges. The Susan B. Komen Foundation's three-day walk is successful because it builds on the courage sequence. Those who have faced or are facing breast cancer can draw courage from the cancer challenge others have encountered and from the challenge that others take on to raise funds for cancer research.

Like breast cancer survivors and those who walk with them, most good leaders are not intimidated by difficult jobs. In fact, some good leaders seek more difficult jobs, but sometimes the difficult jobs just find and/or create the good leader. Bad leaders tend not to seek out the PSD jobs; rather, they avoid them. Good leaders do not go looking for trouble; they just have the willingness to hunt for courage among the problems. Additionally, bad leaders who have not taken their challenges have not extracted courage. Thus they can't pass it along, nor can their followers benefit. They are also unlikely to inspire it in others.

Finding courage *in*, taking courage *from,* and taking courage *to* others is a good way to embrace this idea.

Find and follow a good leader who will place you in PSDs that they expect you to solve. The trust they place in you provides an opportunity to find courage for the task. As much as possible and if you have the choice, avoid the bad leader who will not provide a challenge but only assigns easy tasks. For that leader, the threat of failure and exposure of failure in a challenging task is greater than the reward from a job easily completed.

Courage was a choice General George Washington made and the Continental militia executed when they unexpectedly attacked the Hessian garrison at Trenton, New Jersey, on Christmas night, 1776. The weather conditions were terrible, and the troops ill-equipped to press the attack. They overran the town, and the Hessians surrendered after their head commander had been killed. You may have seen the painting by Emanuel Gottlieb Leutze of Washington boldly standing in a boat while crossing the ice-choked Delaware River from Pennsylvania to New Jersey. It was a courageous, decisive, and well-timed attack—one that got the attention of the British and helped set the course and ultimately the victory for U.S. independence.

Successful, bold, risk-taking leaders, out of the abundance of their courage, are able to take courage or provide it to others. Followers draw courage from good leaders; they don't from bad leaders because bad leaders have no courage from which to draw.

The following poem "Columbus" by Joaquim Miller sums up the process and value of finding, drawing from, and taking courage.

Columbus

Behind him lay the gray Azores,
Behind the gates of Hercules;
Before him not the ghost of shores,
Before him only shore less seas.
The good Mate said: "Now we must pray,
For lo! The very stars are gone.
Brave Admiral, speak, what shall I say?"
"Why, say, 'Sail on! Sail on! And on!'"
"My men grow mutinous day by day;
My men grow ghastly wan and weak!"
The stout Mate thought of home: a spray
Of salt wave washed his swarthy cheek.
"What shall I say, brave Admiral, say,
If we sight naught but seas at dawn?"
"Why, you shall say at break of day,
'Sail on! sail on! sail on! and on!'"
They sailed, They sailed. Then spake the Mate:

"This mad sea shows its teeth tonight.

He curls his lip, he lies in wait,

With lifted teeth, as if to bite!

Brave Admiral, say but one good word;

What shall we do when hope is gone?"

The words leapt like a leaping sword:

"Sail on! sail on! sail on! and on!"

Then, pale and worn, he kept his deck

And peered through darkness, Ah! that night

Of all dark nights! And then a speck-

A light! A light! A light! A light!

It grew, a starlit flag unfurled!

It grew to be Time's burst of dawn.

He gained a world; he gave that world

Its grandest lesson: "On! sail on!"[14]

GOOD LESSONS:

- Having courage doesn't mean you have no fear or have thrown caution to the wind. Good leaders are cautious and respectful of dangerous situations that require the expenditure of resources, particularly human resources and time.
- Good leaders have more than just a sunny disposition and a positive spin on difficulties. They can find good news, capitalize on it, and exploit the smallest ray of light and hope. Bad leaders can't and don't take courage or find a finger or toehold from which to take a next positive step.
- Good leaders will find something, an opportunity, another person, or a circumstance, from which they can take courage and distribute this courage to their followers.
- When good leaders have true, justifiable courage, they infect their followers with it and will lift their emotions toward achievement.
- Bad leaders are less concerned about danger and failure if the resources required to secure a victory do not come from their budgets/allocations.

- Bad leaders are always happy for you to expend your resources to secure their victories. This is true whether during military conflict or in the competitive business marketplace.
- Bad leaders don't ordinarily take courage from difficulty, so those hoping to draw courage from them can't.
- Don't expect bad leaders to hunt for courage until they find it. They will abandon the hunt for something encouraging if the process is too arduous.
- Through courage, good leaders strategically and tactically quicken their pace when faced with challenges. Bad leaders slacken their pace when faced with challenges, and followers take note of it.
- Good leaders know the difference between taking the path of least resistance and the path of greatest value. Bad leaders don't.
- From good challenge springs good hope. From bad challenge springs false hope.
- Taking courage may be just a matter of making the next step not the biggest or most decisive step, but many bad leaders fail to take even the smallest step to draw courage from challenge and provide it to others.

---

4. Inability to Springboard from NOORTS (Noes, Objections, Obfuscations, Rejections, Turndowns, Setbacks)

You are most likely aware of most of the NOORTS, but you may not be acquainted with the subtle differences among them. Some people might say that *differences* exist but not *distinctions*. I suggest otherwise.

Contextualize it this way. If you worked for a company that made mouse traps, and you created what you thought to be a better, less costly device, and took it to your leader, a number of NOORTS might happen. Your new design might be rejected totally, utterly and unreservedly, or it might receive a yes, touted as the next big thing for the company.

1. **Noes** are absolutely nots, no-way whatsoever, period.

2. **Objections** are noes to specific parts of the design, manufacturing, and/ or marketing process. Objections are noes that can be overcome.

3. **Obfuscations** are troublesome noes, because they darken and confuse the path toward the approval and manufacturing of the new mouse trap. They are not strong noes, like rejections, but are a means for the bad leader to put you off the trail and to reduce your passion for a new design. Bad leaders may be skilled at confusing or making the path to approval of the mouse trap more difficult. Obfuscations may be stated as "yes" when they are in fact "no." So, bad leaders might say, "I really like your idea. Let me take a look at it, and I'll get back to you." But they never do. Good leaders may take the mouse trap through a series of noes in order to get ultimately to a "yes," whereas bad leaders will lean toward rejections and obfuscations.

4. **Rejections** are the strongest form of a no. They mean absolutely not, no way at all, and get out of my sight, you idiot! Rejections are repudiations to your idea and to your personhood as well. The new mouse trap is DOA (dead on arrival).

5. **Turndowns,** which means "no" but come back with improvements and production costs estimates, and we'll take another look at it. Turndowns are a weak "no" and may mean a possible "yes." A leader may expect your best effort to bring out the best in the new mouse trap design and roll-out plan before giving approval.

6. **Set-backs** are temporary noes that require more detail, clarification, and specific data to overcome. They may also contain an element of time appropriateness, which means "yes, but not now."

Spring boarding is another essential skill. I've always been intrigued by the physics of the springboard. Perhaps you too have seen diving competitions such as NCAA events or the Olympics. Divers exert downward pressure on a diving board by first jumping up, coming down, and then catapulting upward by the flexing and rebounding of the board. If divers place too much or too little downward pressure on the board, are not balanced as they should be, or don't attain the proper height, then their acrobatic twists, turns, and entry into the water will be incorrect. That makes them unacceptable to their coaches and most importantly to the judges.

Good leaders anticipate bumps in the road. They control for the bumps by turning *unanticipated* NOORTS into *anticipated* NOORTS.

Good leaders and the teams they manage can leverage their problems and rebound from them quickly and ably. Bad leaders hope that all will go as planned but do not anticipate potential NOORTS. They react with surprise when their plans hit speed-bumps or detours.

Good leaders do not place their organizations in harm's way by being dismissive of NOORTS. Bad leaders try to minimize the risks of NOORTS.

Perhaps you've read about the number of elections that Abraham Lincoln lost. You don't hear too much about them or the number of business and personal losses he experienced, but everyone knows about his big win: the U.S. presidency. Lincoln struggled to keep the United States in a union and end the Civil War. His success clearly showed he had survived and learned from his earlier NOORTS to springboard into the White House. He earned his historic place among top-rated presidents in the U.S.

I contend that Lincoln's frequent setbacks in business, stinging losses in politics, and challenges within his family—combined with his persistence and ability to overcome intransigent NOORTS—eventually led to a change of direction for the country and a redefinition of liberty and justice. In a sense, he couldn't deny his personal history, his lack of status or formal education, and numerous NOORTS, but he certainly learned how to leverage them.

Of course, you know it's believed that Thomas Edison was said to have found more than a thousand ways to *not* make a light bulb. He wasn't alone. Other entrepreneurs have faced and overcome NOORTS. For example, I formerly resided in North Canton, Ohio, where the Hoover vacuum was first manufactured. Hoover's innovation, market penetration, and traction were so profound that in Great Britain, the act of vacuuming is often called "Hoovering."

More recently, James Dyson created more than several thousand prototypes of his ball designed vacuum cleaner in order to get it right and ready for market. Now, that's spring boarding!

Liberty, light bulbs, and vacuum sweepers have come into existence only because of the expenditure of resources and the will to overcome, leverage, and launch from NOORTS. This will never change. Progress and discovery will always require it. Don't regret that this is the norm because this state creates opportunity for the diligent, disciplined, and innovative to cull the herd of the lethargic and slothful.

It takes more than a pretty face to get your likeness carved into Mount Rushmore. Examine the lives of Washington, Jefferson, Lincoln, and Teddy Roosevelt and discover how they used springboards to leverage their NOORTS. Each faced NOORTS that were as significant to them in their day as yours are to you. They were able to springboard, and so can you.

In contrast, bad leaders and the teams they manage don't seem to get a lift from NOORTS. They don't leverage the rebound as good leaders do.

Bad leaders are unrealistic in their views that their organizations are not subject to NOORTS like others. They think the NOORTS they encounter will not affect them to the degree that others in the same office, business, industry, or business climate feel.

The more ineffective a leader is, the less that leader has the ability or willingness to learn and teach from NOOTRS. Ineffective leaders are seldom willing to discuss things that go wrong or to extract a good lesson. Why? Doing so would indicate their deficiencies and failures.

One of the false assumptions made by less astute employees is that the higher one climbs in the organization, the easier the decisions become and the less they will need to counter-attack NOORTS. This couldn't be further from the truth. Most of the problems that reach top leaders are ones someone at a lower level couldn't answer. The easily remedied NOORTS seldom get to top levels, but the really tough ones do.

GOOD LESSONS:

NOORTS Happen!

- Everybody has NOORTS. Only the ill-informed think otherwise.

- No personal insulation, isolation, or group denial will prevent NOORTS. The way you minimize the impact and longevity of NOORTS offers a measure of your leadership skills, resourcefulness, and success.
- Good leaders prepare followers for NOORTS by acknowledging they do occur. Good leaders know they can't prevent all NOORTS, but they can indeed leverage them for good.
- Helping others overcome and leverage their NOORTS is a great way to build your reputation and career.
- Good leaders get over their personal NOORTS. Bad leaders don't, won't, and can't.
- Terms like "strategy differences" and "policy disagreements" are often cited as reasons for resignations and/or the "firing" of leaders, when in fact the leader's inability to overcome deeply seated, institutionalized NOORTS caused the separation. Some organizations refuse to be led in new directions or more energetically to pursue greater productivity despite leadership's acumen and commitment.
- No, you didn't get the job. No, you didn't get the sale. No, you didn't get the raise. No, you didn't get the whatever! With a little time and wise counsel, most normal people can place into perspective, reconcile, and leverage the NOORTS of life and business. Good leaders can and will, particularly if they are given the chance and some help in the process.
- Most good leaders can leverage NOORTS; most bad leaders cannot. Be one of those who can.

---

5. Inability to Share in the Meaningful Achievements of Others

An inability to acknowledge or share in the meaningful achievements of others is a clear, certain giveaway of bad leadership, although it may not be as easily detected as other types of leadership failures. It also indicates the type of leader who likely has more of the leadership deficiencies discussed in this book.

The Inability to Acknowledge or Share in the Meaningful Achievements of Others often comes with "Willingness to Bail out and Abandon, Causes, Teams and Responsibilities (and "Refusal to Steadfastly Engage Employee Performance Evaluations". It doesn't often stand by itself in the library of leadership failures.

Bad leaders have difficulty giving others their due "props." These leaders fail to compliment and/or praise others for achievement. Bad leaders are quick to receive the acknowledgments and praise, but slow to give it. They struggle to bring themselves to admit that someone else did a good job. This type of leader experiences emotional pain when giving others the recognition they have earned. Bad leaders mistakenly think that acknowledging others' achievements will somehow detract from their own achievements and reduce their standing or power. Bad leaders also struggle to "apportion" the spotlight with those who have made contributions or successes for which the bad leader desires all the credit.

I'm not recommending that leaders become "bubble-gushers," who are effusive and over-the-top with their praise such as you observe on TV awards shows like the Oscars or Emmys. I suggest their acknowledgments be authentic, timely, and proportional.

The word "meaningful" is an important term in this particular leadership failure. For this purpose, achievements are substantive, ostensible, and earned. "Acknowledgment" is also an important term. Recognition in this sense is associated with extraordinary work-related or career-related success.

While celebrating ordinary occasions such as a birthday, a shared fifty-dollar lottery win, or meeting a standard may be nice, over-celebrating, meaningless recognition, and unwarranted praise degenerates genuine accomplishment. Such praise becomes counterproductive, sappy, and trivializes true achievement.

Bad leaders easily acknowledge and participate in these types of events, but they participate with great difficulty. That's true on occasions in which someone has made a big accomplishment, won a historic victory, or achieved major career success.

Bad leaders behave this way because they mistakenly believe that acknowledging others reduces their personal power and status, and they are humanized to a degree that they don't wish to be humanized. For the bad leader, acknowledging the achievements of others becomes a threat as they fear being upstaged or sharing the spotlight. Bad leaders can't genuinely participate in the progress of others because they mistakenly perceive that the other person's achievement will cause them to garner less attention.

The bad leader's inability to affirm others' achievements indicates an internal aversion to doing so or a willful disregard of the enormous benefits of sharing the progress and achievements of others to create even greater incentives for the celebrant(s).

Celebrating team accomplishments is another important aspect of sharing meaningful accomplishments. Consider, for example, the turtle who found himself atop a fence post and quickly realized he didn't get there solely through his efforts. He praised all the other turtles who made his rise possible. Then he began to pull other turtles up to join him, and together they created a way to balance atop a bigger fence post. They pushed him up in order that he could lift them up. Bad leaders don't do this, whereas truly great leaders give their lives and careers to furthering others' successes.

> **Leaders who don't create or share in celebrations highlighting the achievements of others mistakenly believe that providing praise decreases productivity.**

People who use the "We don't want to give them a big head" argument are likely covering their real motive for not properly acknowledging earned achievement. How lame! You don't spoil an employee by providing acknowledgment for earned achievement but by acknowledging insignificant, phony, unearned achievement.

Leaders destroy their personal credibility and create enormously disruptive environments when they acknowledge and share in the non-achievement of followers with whom they are "tight," while ignoring the real achievements of others who are not their favorites. This behavior is always a huge de-motivator for those deserving praise, while it over-inflates the egos of the undeserving. More insidious yet is the fact that the non-achievers who know they don't deserve praise seldom come to their full potential or make contributions equal to their talents, abilities, gifts, and skills. Through false acknowledgment, bad leaders depreciate the TAGS of followers to the detriment of both the followers and the organizations they serve.

When consulting, I often ask my client, "How well does your organization celebrate achievement?" Responses often foreshadow the organization's climate, *esprit de corps*, financial well-being, and leadership's savvy.

Going further into detail, I ask similar questions regarding supervisory skill: "How well do your supervisory leaders acknowledge and share in the progress of their teams? Please provide an example of a leader who is really good at acknowledging the achievements of others." Responses foreshadow strengths or weaknesses of individual supervisors to share and acknowledge well, poorly, or not at all. Furthermore, responses help to determine the pervasive atmosphere regarding esteem for and care of employees.

I once heard about an organization whose CFO sent out a communiqué to all department heads stating the company would no longer pay for any paper or hospitality products used while celebrating employee work-related achievements. Essentially, if you wanted to celebrate the success of others, you had to pay for your own "stuff." The new policy sent the message that the organization and the CFO were unfeeling "cheapskates" and "killjoys" and that the organization was in financial trouble. It also reinforced the feeling among employees that top managers couldn't bring themselves to share in the accomplishments of others because they couldn't take credit for it. Of course, the new policy didn't apply to those from the C-Suite wanting to celebrate *among themselves* but not when others were honored.

GOOD LESSONS:
- Good leaders always acknowledge the achievements of others on the high side rather than on the cheap. I suggest using the good china, cloth napkins, and real (not plastic) flatware.
- Provide appropriate amounts and types of food and little, if any, alcohol.
- Don't go down the potluck or BYO path.
- Use appropriate, accurate, non-effusive public proclamations and pageantry.
- Don't make recipient(s) or attendees uncomfortable with your jokes or over-familiarity.

- Don't force recipients to speak or respond, but if they do speak, give them a prearranged, specific time limit.
- If you give gifts, explain the protocol for opening them—immediately or later.
- Be punctual, provide sufficient time (not too much or too little), and never before or immediately after a holiday.
- Bad leaders use the opportunity to talk about themselves and new initiatives they want to launch. Don't do as they do.
- Vary the venue and format.
- Don't become event predictable.
- Make every public and private occasion genuine, authentic, and one-of-a-kind.
- Don't overdo it or underdo it.
- Be careful of an open microphone or opportunities for others to vent their feelings and praise of a recipient. These occasions can get out of hand and negatively affect the purpose and spirit of the event.
- If more than one person is providing public acknowledgment, coordinate comments of the speakers and give them a time limit for their comments.
- Never use the occasion for veiled threats or criticizing others who have not achieved or who are not being formally acknowledged. When you do this, you create a high degree of angst, change the spirit of the occasion, cause attendees to exit prematurely, and expose your real agenda.
- Without doubt, you have already seen or will encounter a leader who cannot acknowledge or share in the achievements of others. This must not be said of you.

Bad leaders can't genuinely participate in the progress of others, so be forewarned. Don't look to a bad leader to affirm your achievements.

6. Inability to Use Brakes and Accelerator Properly

Being a passenger in an automobile with a *good* driver can be a pleasant and anxiety-free experience. Riding with a *great* driver can be exhilarating. But riding with a *lousy* driver can evoke anxiety and, in some cases, absolute terror! I'd much rather travel with a driver who evokes confidence and trust than one who doesn't. Similarly, I'd rather work with and for leaders who evoke confidence through their skillful acceleration and braking.

As in most mechanical apparatuses, certain components are required to optimize operations. The braking mechanism is important in addition to propulsion, cooling, and lubrication. Braking systems are essential on bicycles, autos, trains, planes, and roller coasters, etc. Without efficient braking systems, the apparatus loses overall effectiveness.

Not only do mechanical designs need braking and accelerating systems, but they must also be operated properly. Most of us have driven congested freeways on which we have observed braking behavior. We hope to avoid both the driver ahead of us who constantly "rides" the brakes and the driver who only uses the brakes as a last resort to avoid a collision.

Brakes, used properly, make us slow down, avoid obstacles, control skids, set proper speeds, stop ASAP, and in general, increase efficiency and safety.

Proper brake use in vehicles parallels proper use of brakes in organizational leadership. Knowing how properly to apply the brakes in vehicles is as important as knowing how to use the brakes in management and leadership. Many leaders lack this skill. Some bad leaders are on the brakes, then off the brakes; they ride the brakes or don't use them at all. Just like erratic drivers don't evoke confidence, erratic leaders don't either.

These behaviors often cause friction and can be a frequent cause of mechanical breakdown. Friction causes heat, and heat causes brake efficiency to fade. Fading, hot brakes make a palpable, distinctive stink in both vehicles and organizations.

For example, I once drove down from the summit of Pike's Peak in Colorado and rode the brakes too much. A county sheriff had me pull to the side of the road to let the brakes cool, so I would not be a hazard to myself and others farther down the mountain. I have also observed semi-trailer trucks whose brakes have failed while going downhill. The trucks, rather than crashing, took the uphill truck escape exit that paralleled the main road. Nice of the DOT to provide the truck escape!

Few bad leaders get pulled over by higher authorities and forced to let their organizations cool down. Nor do they come upon safe escape routes when things are going downhill and they spin out of control. When bad leaders apply brakes too frequently, too suddenly, and too harshly, individuals, teams, and organizations have a tendency to wear out quickly, causing a loss of control, momentum, and direction.

Some bad leaders, like some bad drivers, can't find the proper relationship between speed and braking. Excessive speed and excessive braking can produce negative results for both automobiles and organizations.

Bad leaders also don't know when and how to take the lead or when and how to let coworkers set the pace. They even sometimes go at great speed in the wrong direction with little care given to the PECITs required to do so or the PECITs required to make a U-turn.

Good leaders set the proper organization pace and rhythm by knowing when to brake and when to shift to neutral or to a higher or lower gear. They also know when to put the hammer down. Bad leaders don't or won't.

Several driving behaviors parallel leadership behaviors, and each behavior has a relationship to organizational health and success.

- Bad leaders ride the brakes and use the accelerator simultaneously.
- Bad leaders don't know their destination or routes to a destination.
- Bad leaders often take short cuts.
- Bad leaders don't allow for detours.
- Bad leaders often disregard warning signs such as STOP, YIELD, EXIT, NO U-TURNS, and RIGHT TURNS ONLY.
- Bad leaders often don't know when to make strategic turns.
- Bad leaders often don't concentrate on the immediate road ahead.
- Bad leaders don't signal their intent or allow time to change direction.
- Bad leaders are easily distracted.

- Bad leaders don't consider the effects of excess accelerating and braking on followers.
- Bad leaders often carry too much baggage and overload their organizations.
- Bad leaders are sometimes asleep at the wheel.

Among the best race car drivers in the world are the Formula One (F1) and NASCAR drivers. Their skills are partly innate but also learned through a great deal of practice and repetition. Not only do they love what they do, they overcome the dangers involved. They must know how to get the most from their cars, pit crews, and race teams.

However, good as they are, not everything always goes right. They occasionally crash. Sometimes the crash is due to mechanical failure; sometimes because a competitor causes an accident and they get caught up in the melee through no fault of their alertness or driving skill. They know when to go fast, when to slow, when to set the pace, when to fall in line and draft, when to conserve fuel, and how to avoid harmful situations and overly aggressive drivers. Yet, like Mario Andretti, the Hall of Fame driver, said, "If everything is in control, you are going too slow."

Unlike skilled race car drivers, bad leaders tend to go too fast sometimes and too slow at other times. Again, they don't know when and how to take the lead or when and how to let co- workers set the pace. They even sometimes go at great speed in the wrong direction with little care given to the PECITs required to do so.

I had a conversation with a New York City cab driver who had been driving for forty years and claimed he had never had an accident. I asked him the secret of his accident-free record. He said, "Never look in the rear-view mirror." Glancing backwards has benefits but focusing on *where you have been* diverts attention from *where you need to go.*

Occasionally, people in a company make an obvious, public mistake in braking or acceleration. Consider, for example, Boeing's 787 Dreamliner. I did some of my writing in a parking lot overlooking Paine Field in Everett, Washington, the location of the Boeing-Everett plant. Boeing's wide-body, commercial aircraft are produced in the main assembly building. The complex is huge, and when combined, the office complex and assembly building are reputed to be the largest building by volume in the world. The building's perimeter is two-and-a-half miles.

As I wrote, I wondered who screwed up the procurement, assembly, and delivery schedules for the 747s, the 777s, and the new 787 Dreamliner. I'm sure it was a confounding challenge, but during 2012 and 2013, I saw unfinished airplanes sitting all over the airfield and the surrounding grounds. The planes were stacked nose-to-tail and wing-to-wing everywhere. I counted as many as fifty-two planes, all unfinished, awaiting parts and personnel for completion. These idle planes reflected billions of dollars worth of value.

Obviously, Boeing had substantial challenges getting the research, testing, certification, and production of the 787 Dreamliner balanced and in-sync. The challenges were immense. A new design, new carbon-fiber construction materials, new production processes, new vendor/supplier chains, and an expectation of manufacturing efficiencies all of which Boeing wanted to extend to their other models and plants. Any one of these design and process changes would have been a major implementation challenge, but by attempting them simultaneously, irregularities, imbalances, delays, and enormous stress occurred.

Still, it was a great day in February 2010 when the first 787 actually took flight. All those who had an interest in the success of the 787, Boeing, and U.S. aerospace breathed a sigh of relief when the plane went airborne.

The 787 was certified by the FAA in August 2011. The first plane entered service on September 25, 2011, and was flown away by ANA (All Nippon Airlines).

Boeing Commercial Airplanes President and CEO Jim Albaugh said, "This airplane embodies the hopes and dreams of everyone fortunate enough to work on it. Their dreams are now coming true." Added Scott Fancher, Boeing's vice president and general manager of the 787 program, "This is truly a great airplane. From the advanced materials and innovative technologies to the improved passenger experience and unbeatable economics, the 787 really is a game-changing airplane."[15]

But wait, there's more!

As you read in Chapter Two, NOORTS have a great deal of impact upon product delivery and organizational success, but what Boeing has experienced with the grounding of its worldwide fleet of 787s in January 2013 is not only an enormous group of NOORTS but also a classic case of improper braking and acceleration The approval and integration of a 787 component part sped along too quickly. Ultimately, a lithium ion battery grounded all fifty delivered planes.

I saw numerous unfinished 787s sitting idle. They were waiting to resolve a battery problem so they could be completed and delivered to customers for entry into passenger service. I am certain the issues of when and how to use brakes to slow or accelerators to speed as well as design, manufacturing, certification, and delivery processes have been an enormously difficult and costly process for Boeing to manage. I don't believe many larger processes exist with the exception of some in the federal government.

But wait! There's even more!

Perhaps nothing has recently and so publicly occurred in the business world that reinforces what I wrote in Lesson Six of *Good Lessons from Bad Leaders*. History has repeated itself. And although Boeing has a new senior management team, record sales, and profitability, it continues in its Inability to Brake and Accelerate Properly issue—sometimes going too fast and not responding quickly enough to slow down when needed. An example of accelerating properly is seeing an opportunity, then organizing and resourcing effectively to capitalize on that opportunity.

On July 1, 2017, Boeing launched Boeing Global Services, its third major business unit. Boeing Global Services is a dedicated services business focused on the needs of global defense, space, and commercial customers.

I love Boeing aircraft. I have flown in them several million miles safely and in relative comfort for the last fifty-five years. Many former students of mine work for the company. My property taxes were kept low while living in the State of Washington because my home was located in the same school tax district as Boeing. Its percentage of the tax pie saved me a lot of money. I have no axe to grind against Boeing.

The problem lies in the fact that Boeing has too great a market share and too little competition. Boeing's own Commercial Market Outlook states, "By any measure, the commercial aviation sector is soaring. More people are taking to the air than ever before, as our industry has now recorded eight straight years of steady and above-trend growth."[16] Boeing projects 42,760 deliveries of new aircraft from 2018 to 2037. This represents a market value of 6.3 trillion dollars. The opportunity is so enormous that it causes the company once again to use the brakes and the accelerator poorly.

Although the 787 was quite late in coming to the market, it has set a new and higher standard for what the air carriers and air travelers expect. What was learned in producing the 787 has been applied to the building of Boeing's second carbon fiber aircraft, a derivation of the 777 called the 777X. This plane is highly anticipated by the marketplace with more than three hundred confirmed orders. The first 777X-9 rolled out of the Everett, Washington, plant on March 14, 2019.

Ordinarily, the rollout of a new plane—especially one whose development is in the multiple billions and whose sales price exceeds 300 million dollars—would be an extravaganza. But this one was subdued and held for Boeing employees only due to the crash of an Ethiopian Airlines flight 302, a 737 MAX. A second 737 MAX crashed on October 29, 2018, in Indonesia. The carrier was Lion Air Flight 610, and the plane was only a few months old. Suspicion over the plane's MCAS (Maneuvering Characteristics Augmentation Systems) software and the two subsequent crashes caused the grounding of the 737 MAX worldwide.

> **The company has suspended deliveries of the 737 MAX and is cutting monthly output to 42 from 52, while maintaining it still has "full confidence" in the plane. Lion Air and several other carriers have said they are reconsidering their orders. Norwegian Air said it will seek compensation for the grounding of about 1 percent of its seats. There's also the prospect of substantial payouts to the families of passengers if Boeing is found responsible for the crashes. In the week after the second crash, Boeing lost more than $22 billion, or 12 percent, of its market value. In April, the company missed its quarterly earnings estimates for just the second time in five years. The entire 737 range accounts for almost one-third of Boeing's operating profit.**[17]

The 737 MAX airplanes are stacking up at the Renton, Washington, plant just like the 787s stacked up at the Everett, Washington, plant in 2014.

Why does Boeing repeat itself? Perhaps the market opportunity is just too great to progress too slowly and lose market share to Airbus and emerging competitors, such as China's Comac (Commercial Aircraft Corporation of China, Ltd.). With 6.3 trillion dollars at stake, who could blame Boeing? Perhaps no

Boeing leader has the courage to slow down and make absolutely sure that its planes were safe prior to delivery.

Braking properly requires enormous discipline when a company or organization has great momentum. Clearly, Boeing doesn't have this degree of discipline and has chosen to manage problems downstream.

Furthermore, for most companies, it is not wise to over-accelerate, then slam on the brakes. But Boeing never slams on the brakes or loses much momentum. This strategy has worked until an entire worldwide line of 394 737 MAX aircraft had to be grounded because 346 people died.

Boeing is good at weathering storms that would sink other companies. Its leaders have chosen to go as fast as they can for as long as they can.

In highly regulated industries like commercial aircraft, if a company doesn't use the accelerator or brakes properly and tragedy happens, then the government will eventually step in and put on the brakes as it did with Boeing. I don't believe Boeing would have self-grounded the MAX.

Boeing is enormously fortunate that it has few competitors and that high demand for its planes continues. The air carriers and the market love Boeing in a way that few companies are loved. They trust that Boeing will eventually get the MAX right, just like the company did with previous performance challenges and delivery delays.

On June 18, 2019, Boeing received orders for two hundred 737 MAX airplanes. Boeing's stock price rose 5.4 percent (despite the deaths, grounding, and inability to use the brakes and accelerator properly.)[18]

However, Boeing's inability to use braking and accelerating properly appears to have finally caught up with them. The organizational culture which allowed Boeing to assume that they would eventually get a new airplane fully "right" *after* it launched, finally unraveled. This cultural expectation will no longer be tolerated by the air carriers, the flying public or the U.S. government.

As a result of the grounding of the MAX and subsequent fallout, major shake-ups occurred within Boeing during the fall of 2019. Moreover, Boeing's customers have lost hundreds of millions of dollars. The President of Boeing Commercial Airplanes was fired and replaced by another long-term Boeing insider. Dennis Muilenburg was stripped of his role as Chairman of Boeing's Board of Directors, while retaining his CEO title, and is now in charge of finding a solution for the MAX disaster. As Boeing's primary spokesperson and apologist, he was called before the U.S. Senate Commerce Committee and the U.S. House of Representatives Transportation Committee. He faced the questioning of legislators and also faced the families of some of those who were killed in 737 MAX crashes. Muilenburg admitted that mistakes had been made and that the MCAS software solution created to correct an airframe design flaw in the MAX did not work as anticipated. The software solution could not be overridden by pilots, nor, were pilots adequately trained to handle the planes performance error when it occurred.

The inability of Boeing to control the urgency and pressure to capture a huge market opportunity by braking and accelerating properly has resulted in the loss of customers, consumer trust, additional loss of billions of dollars of market capitalization, loss of reputation and loss of life. How much better to have braked and accelerated properly.

GOOD LESSONS:

- Good leaders know how to set the correct rhythm and pace for their organizations and people. They know when to press and when to back off. Bad leaders tend to press too hard, too often, and for too long, consuming PECITs in the process. Bad leaders imply that the best pace is a continuous sprint, rather than a steady pace.
- Good leaders know tactically and strategically to apply the brakes and accelerator properly to manage their organizations, so they will neither brake too fast nor too often nor accelerate beyond the capacity of their people.
- When there's an urgency to bring a product to market, particularly when leaders say the product will be a "game changer" and previous delays have occurred, managers may accelerate when they should brake and brake when they should accelerate. When multiple managers engage in uncoordinated accelerating and braking, little good comes from it.
- Most vehicles have a rate of travel at which they are most efficient and happy. And if you pay attention, the vehicle will tell you what that rate

is. Organizations behave in a similar manner. Good leaders pay attention to this reality; bad leaders don't.

- Good leaders have a sense of the resource burn required to set the necessary pace to meet objectives, goals, and mission statements. Bad leaders don't have the same degree of perception.

- Bad leaders fail to achieve either the direction and/or pace required for organizational stability, growth, and productivity. This requires a sense of resource burn, and all leaders should pay attention to it.

7. Inability to Avow or Engage Approachability

Among the many details of studies concerning employee motivation lies the fact that a leader's action or a leader's refusal to act substantially affects motivation. Among the various actions or inactions that cause happy, productive responses from followers is the overt act of avowing. This act is one of the best, most productive ways to motivate. For the bad leader, a lack of avowing is the wellspring of ineffectiveness.

Avowing is, to some degree, synonymous with acknowledging, understanding, noticing, confessing, declaring, and admitting. Avowing is stronger in the sense that it is an action based on acknowledging that certain conditions exist such as personhood and humanity.

Within this context, the act of avowing employees, coworkers, and associates is largely ignored, unintentionally or purposefully, by the bad leader. It's because bad leaders often fail to…

- Avow that I exist.
- Avow that I have relevance and that I matter.
- Avow that I am a human and not a part or a machine.
- Avow that I have motives, feelings, and aspirations.
- Avow that I contribute to the objectives and goals of my work group and employer.
- Avow that I make an effort to exceed expectations that others have for me on and off the job.

- Avow that I am eager to help those with whom I work.
- Avow that I could be working elsewhere.
- Avow that I have more talent than has been engaged.
- Avow that their decisions impact me.

Avowing has approachability as its companion. Approachability is a willingness on the part of a leader to engage in conversation, to participate, to be accessible, to be easy to meet with, and to be courteous. In contrast, a bad leader is distant, aloof, unwilling to engage in conversation, inaccessible, rude, and discourteous. I have even heard the word "stand-offish" refer to a bad leader's lack of approachability.

Often, the bad leader's lack of approachability and lack of avowing become the major source of de-motivation for those they attempt to lead.

The unapproachable leader is closed off to others' ideas, points of view, contributions, and expressions of engagement. Bad leaders might even be unapproachable to the degree that they make little face-to-face contact with those they lead!

The tandem of avowing and approachability creates high esteem for good leaders and is largely missing in bad ones. They generate an internal standard and a mental covenant within good leaders that cause them to engage and treat employees and colleagues with clearly expressed positive regard.

As an example of how avowing colleagues has positive motivational results, I'd like to revisit Manteno State Hospital.

One of my coworkers was a permanent hospital patient. He was unable to care for himself on the outside and was unlikely ever to be released. Although he was not a psychiatrist, nurse, or security officer, he still had an enormously important job. He took great pride in his job and became greatly agitated when anyone tried to impinge upon his responsibility. This job was his, and his alone. Highly valued for the service he rendered, his colleagues avowed him and declared him to be a critically important member of the third-shift team.

What did he do? He made a valuable contribution to the hygiene and order of the ward. He endeared himself to his colleagues because he did an exceptional job of gathering and bundling bed linens. Because not all bed linens needed changing every morning, he created a method to determine which sheets did or didn't need changing and a six-word vocabulary to communicate his findings. Doing a job none of the paid staff cared to do, he would progress down the long line of beds in the ward, slip his hand under the sheets, and yell out in a gravelly voice one of three phrases: "He's all right" or "He's wet" or "He's messed." Then we knew which bed sheets to change.

He was enormously valuable and well-respected. Every employee showed an openness to meet his every concern or need. We all avowed his vital contribution, which built his self-respect and made him even better and more helpful in bed-linen assessment, collection, and bundling. Avowing him and making ourselves approachable for him had tremendously positive results for the entire third-shift team.

GOOD LESSONS:
- Be avowing and approachable; these are the primary tools for building trust.
- Good leaders must engage in public and private avowal of people and teams regarding their value and the contributions they make. This yields approachability and motivates followers.
- Through their acts of avowing and approachability, good leaders enable people to feel that they matter, have workplace significance, and can make productive and meaningful contributions. Through a lack of avowing and unapproachability, bad leaders discourage their followers and make them feel devalued and unappreciated.
- Good leaders know that avowing, acknowledging, understanding, noticing, confessing, declaring, and admitting another's value and contribution as component parts of a team pave the way for organizational success.
- To be a great leader, you must have approachability and avowing as part of your leadership tool kit. Without them, you will always prove yourself less than good.
- When avowing is coupled with approachability, they become springboards to leadership greatness.
- When employees and colleagues feel avowed, high productivity and success follow.
- You can't be unapproachable, inaccessible, emotionally distant, or continually missing from duty and be considered a good leader.

To be a good leader, you must place acts of avowing and the practice of approachability foremost among your actions.

8. Inability to Deploy Ice Cream

Even if they're not personally acquainted with a pressure cooker, most workers have heard or used the expression to describe a job environment—and with good reason. A pressure cooker is a heavy cooking pot that had widespread use before the microwave or Instapot made cooking quick and efficient.

When placed on a gas or electric burner, a pressure cooker had the ability to produce and contain both heat and steam pressure. On top of the lid was a stem with a small hole. Over that hole sat a small rounded metal weight heavy for its size. It too had a small hole and atop of it was a pop-up relief valve. The relief valve vented excess pressure and heat when the cooker became too hot and highly pressurized. I always thought a pressure cooker was dangerous and should be avoided. I knew that if the pressure got too high, it was certain to blow up.

The pressure cooker provided a quickly prepared, better end product than slow cooking. Yet the pressure relief value had even greater value, for it provided safety and well-being for those in the kitchen.

Having a relief valve to take the pressure off of an employee or group of employees is also necessary. I have found ice cream to be that valve. Perhaps for you the valve will be pizza or sushi.

Bad leaders either don't know how or don't care to take pressure off of difficult situations and relationships. Rather, they're inclined to ignore the pressure. While a pressure cooker has a way to release pressure of its own accord, most employees or employee groups don't.

Good leaders find ways to take the pressure off appropriately, whereas bad leaders don't. From time to time as the workload becomes heavy, people become contentious, and their productivity wanes. Good leaders take positive steps to ameliorate the pressure and conflict. Sometimes the tension can be palpable. Before things blow up, a good leader steps in and leads employees out of an impending disaster.

I once stepped into an office during a difficult episode and found the high tension easily discernible. Something needed to be done immediately or the entire office would explode. I told the person in charge to make signs indicating the office would be closed temporarily and that employees would be absent from their posts for one hour. Given the busyness of the office, this moment certainly didn't seem like a good time to take such action. Still, I was willing to take the risk, and we all exited the building and headed for the closest ice cream shop.

Doing this was so shocking, so unexpected, and so much appreciated that it had the desired effect. The pressure was off for a few minutes; everyone enjoyed a one-hour mini vacation. Feeling renewed and relaxed, they all went happily back to work where tensions disappeared and productivity increased. The trip for ice cream proved to be a good and fruitful decision. It wasn't costly or dramatic, but it did produce the outcome I had hoped.

Over the years, I have used spontaneous interruptions to relieve the pressure on over-heated teams. Whether it was stepping away for ice cream or pizza or bringing in Buffalo Wild Wings for lunch, it always worked.

Additionally, I have found mini-vacations to work best with an entire team or work group rather than just one or two team members. If we had to travel a few miles together in the same vehicle, I preferred a smaller vehicle where physical proximity was close and everybody had to accommodate everyone else. This is not a one-on-one but a one-on-many activity. The only time we separated into different cars was when we drove two Mustang convertibles with the tops down. This experience also produced the desired effect. Moreover, ice cream and convertibles just seem to go together.

Why is this simple, yet effective strategy so seldom used by even the best leaders and completely ignored by the bad? It is effective because it is unanticipated. It demonstrates to employees that a supervisor does, in fact, know what is going on and is willing to create strategic interruptions to reduce time pressure.

Time pressure is the first element among those that cause a pressure-cooker work environment. Time pressure is an insidious stress creator. How many times a day are activities controlled or redirected by the clock? From the time people awaken to the "alarm" clock or phone "warning" (good descriptors, but a lousy way to start the day) to the end of the day when the alarms are reset, people are subject to time. If, in fact, a leader can give back time that had already been emotionally spent or allocated to other pressing matters, then that leader has, to some degree, relieved the pressure and created time margins.

Creating time margins is one of the greatest gifts a leader can give.

I've seen this so many times when, as a professor, I extended a paper deadline, or dismissed class fifteen minutes early, or canceled class altogether. You would think that Christmas had come or that someone had won the lottery in spite of the fact that students had paid for the class time. People always appreciate getting time back. You will be considered a heroine or hero when the give-back is strategically timed to relieve pressure.

You don't engage in this practice to endear yourself to others but genuinely to provide release time that will lessen pressure. Even the term "release time" sounds like a reprieve from a jail cell, and it may have ominous overtones. Still, it goes a long way to encourage those under time pressure to breathe easier. I have seen as little as twenty minutes change a person's whole day and dramatically improve workplace attitudes. I never worry about a loss of productivity during a release time. I don't see it as a loss but as an overall gain.

A secondary benefit of this practice is to let people know their leader is paying attention to their issues and workload and is willing to work on their behalf to lighten the load and relieve pressure. As a leader, be prudent; use this approach circumspectly and with an even hand. It will yield great results. Good leaders are not soft or easily taken advantage of, but they are sensitive to time pressure and its impact. By comparison, bad leaders are not likely to see the benefit of extending kindness or compassion when the pressure is on.

With the coming of contemporary, relaxed work schedules, flex time, and telecommuting, you may need to create other release time and pressure-reducing methods. Spontaneously taking employees away from work for tofu and sushi still works, but they seem too serious a food choice compared to naughty dietary indiscretions such as ice cream and pizza.

Bad leaders overlook little things that seem insignificant and unimportant to them, while those in the pressure cooker welcome any gesture that allows them release from time and work pressures. Depressurizing to create time margins yields better mental health and productivity. Bad leaders don't see it this way.

GOOD LESSONS:

- Good leaders know how to relieve workplace pressure. Bad leaders don't and/or won't.
- Good leaders create time margins. Bad leaders either ruin time margins or deny the need for them.
- Good leaders are attuned to what creates the frustrations and tensions of associates in the workplace. They use even the smallest, seemingly most insignificant thing such as ice cream to alleviate a time-pressure-caused conflict.
- When associates make their best efforts, willingly contribute their time and energy above standard, but make no progress, good leaders notice. They step in and deploy additional resources and affirmations.
- Employees appreciate good leaders who notice without being told about conflict and workplace turmoil. Employees expect bad leaders not to notice.
- Bad leaders under-appreciate employee effort, performance, and loyalty during difficult and high-stress periods.
- Don't expect the bad leader to take the pressure off, care, or rise up and call you "blessed" when you give your best effort. It is not in their DNA to do so.

---

9. Inability to Model Loyalty and Ride for the Brand

Loyalty is an enormously valuable attribute, not only for people in general, but for leaders in particular. Good leaders embody, practice, and promote loyalty. Truly great leaders exude loyalty; it's in the fabric of their character, words, and actions. This cannot be said of bad leaders.

Great leaders are never thought disloyal or disdainful by those who have helped that leader achieve greatness. Disloyalty creates negative influences such as distrust, disheartenment, and instability. Loyalty does just the opposite.

Reciprocal loyalty is a highly admired characteristic within leaders. Regardless of position, status level, or task difficulty, followers also expect it. They are loyal to leaders who display loyalty to them. This reciprocal loyalty is normal and good for all concerned. Good leaders know that demonstrated loyalty is a good motivator while disloyalty is a great de-motivator. Loyalty is attractive and winsome in leaders; disloyalty is unattractive and repelling.

For bad leaders, loyalty most often goes only in one direction—toward *them*. They expect others to be loyal to them and their interests but are notably deficient in providing loyalty to others or to the interests of others. This degree of disloyalty trumps achievements and cements reputations.

Some bad leaders are known for their disloyalty and betrayal. General Benedict Arnold, although thought to be an otherwise adequate general, is best remembered as a traitor to the United States during the Revolutionary War. His disloyalty supersedes all other good leadership characteristic he may have had. His disloyalty is particularly odious when compared to the loyalty and honor of General Washington with whom Arnold served.

The historical term "turncoat" refers to someone who, as a military officer, would turn his coat inside out showing one color, or outside in, showing another color. It depended on which side was winning the battle. That's essentially what Arnold did. He first fought with the Continental Army, then defected and fought with the British.

Not all relationships or responsibilities require the same degree of loyalty. If you face a choice between your family and your job, I recommend you choose family. For me, loyalty to God, family, and country trumps all other loyalties. Of course, other things exist to which you should also be loyal, such as friends and an employer. Thoughtful loyalty to your country, family, friends, coworkers, and employer is often viewed positively. Blind, irrational loyalty can indeed be harmful and counterproductive to these same groups. Blind and/or wrongfully directed loyalty is an altogether different matter and a course no one should take.

Alas, bad leaders often confuse steadfast loyalty with blind loyalty. They have a great need for the undivided loyalty of others, while not returning loyalty to others or recognizing appropriate gradients of loyalty. Many times, bad leaders are more loyal to a concept (business or otherwise), cause, or ideology than they are to the people and cultures that the concept, cause, or ideology was created to help. Such leaders may be more loyal to that concept than to those employed to develop and execute the concept, cause, or ideology. They also expect greater loyalty to themselves, their ideas, and their initiatives than to organizational mission and goals. Unfortunately, some leaders are easily disloyal to those they attempt to lead. Bad leaders quickly throw others under the bus, including their closest business associates and even their assigns to signal their disaffection and disloyalty.

Bad leaders also reveal their disloyalty by the speed with which they exhibit egocentric behavior and abandon others' ideas when they perceive there's no personal gain. Without something to augment their status, bad leaders often show disloyalty, as they seldom stand up or stand behind a colleague or company. And, not having loyalty within themselves, they do not model proper loyalty to those they are attempting to lead.

Bad leaders don't have the internal wiring to understand, model, or acknowledge loyalty, even with the smallest, least costly gesture. Moreover, if their personal motives or job performance are brought into question, bad leaders often default to accusations of disloyalty in others. Some bad leaders even go as far as to claim disloyalty in others when asked questions they can't answer or demand solutions they can't deliver.

On the other hand,

Good leaders know that loyalty to a person or organization is built when people see a mutually beneficial, clear path to their self-interests, trust that their leaders see the path, and perceive that leaders have loyalties beyond themselves.

An excellent example of this principle appears in the domesticated canine. Dogs most clearly embody the steadfast loyalty that humans respect. Anyone who has ever owned a labrador or golden retriever, collie, boxer, or beagle knows exactly what I mean. These dogs just cannot be disloyal to a good owner. Good owners make the relationship with their canines mutually beneficial. Similarly, good leaders demonstrate steadfast loyalty to their organizations and to the people who make those organizations run.

> Loyalty is better caught than taught; it is an event with longevity. Loyalty also has appropriate limits: if it doesn't, it will be taken advantage of. Loyalty is not and cannot be only a feeling; it must be a behavior.

Loyalty and disloyalty both have cascading effects. If leadership doesn't model them, then followers are not likely to model them either. And if followers show greater loyalty than the supervisor, they will likely experience negative consequences. Bad leaders can't allow others to appear more loyal than they.

If leaders cannot model or instill company loyalty within the people they lead, then they must instill loyalty to a particular project. If leaders cannot instill loyalty to a project, then they must instill loyalty to people working on the project. Some level of loyalty is better than none at all.

Contrast this limited loyalty with the term "Riding for the Brand," which is a nuanced statement about loyalty. In business, loyalty to a brand, product, or service is precisely what producers want to achieve, and they spend massive amounts of PECIT to secure it. Consumer loyalty is enormously hard to earn and easily lost, especially if the perception of fair exchange doesn't exist, falters, or is lost. The consumer exchange has loyalty that goes both ways: to and from the seller, and to and from the buyer.

This version of loyalty applies even to well-known brands. But like loyalty to a leader, loyalty to a brand must be consistently demonstrated and maintained. Leaders of strong brands will do whatever is necessary to promote and protect them. These brands took generations to build and are worth billions of dollars— Coke, Ford, Apple, and Harley-Davison, as examples. They require leadership and customer loyalty to maintain their value.

Current leaders of entities owning brands and producers of goods and services must not only display brand and customer loyalty, but they should also clearly display loyalty and regard for the leadership and historical achievements of their predecessors. In this way, they demonstrate loyalty to the workers they now lead. I know of a new CEO who was set right by a bold vice-president who stated that the new CEO was wrong in his perception that nothing of value had ever happened before he, the new guy, showed up. The new CEO learned a lesson about humility, the expectations of loyalty, acknowledging earlier leaders, and showing loyalty to the brand. That new CEO was me!

Merely having reciprocal loyalty with customers and loyalty to the workers is not enough. *Riding for the brand* is similar to *esprit de corps* among members of the military. As long as your paycheck comes from the company representing the brand, you give allegiance to the brand and to others riding for the brand. You can't "ride for the brand" and waver in loyalty at the same time. It requires stubborn loyalty, giving your word, fighting, and perhaps metaphorically dying for the brand.

Charles Waite (played by Kevin Costner) typifies this in the western movie *Open Range*. He displays his loyalty to his friend and comrade in arms, Boss "Bluebonnet" Spearman played by Robert Duvall, and to the concept of freely roaming herds of cattle in the grasslands of the west. The movie concludes with a gunfight in which all the bad guys who hate the free grazers are either put to flight or killed. This bloody, gripping scene clearly depicts what lengths cowboys go to show their loyalty to friends, their way of life, and their enormously strong bias to the concept of the brand. Sure it's a Hollywood depiction, but it's an apt one!

Unwillingness to admit your loyalty or positive bias for your company, its products, services, and people creates a false sense of objectivity for some bad leaders. This kind of objectivity trumps other good leadership practices that such leaders might manifest.

GOOD LESSONS:
- Disloyalty gains you nothing. If a relationship with a person or organization has deteriorated to the point that disloyalty looks like a good strategy, then this self-delusion must be exchanged for other non-damaging alternatives. It is better to resign your responsibilities than be proven dis-

loyal and viewed as a traitor. Betrayal has long-lasting, corrosive internal effects and can become a permanent influence in your life. Being typecast as a traitor has lasting career consequences that are difficult to overcome.

- You should avoid like a tornado or a tsunami even the perception that you are disloyal. Just don't place yourself in its path or under its influence.
- Disloyalty is among the worst behaviors of bad leaders. It insidiously eats away at one's self-perception to the degree that one might conclude, "If I am perceived as traitor, I might as well be one." No good will ever result from this self-destructive behavior.
- Be loyal and ride for the brand; people will take note.

10. Inability to Let People Off the Hook Strategically

Over the last few decades, the Fish and Game Departments in many states have adopted catch-and-release programs. Many sport and commercial fisheries applaud the decision to create catch-and-release programs as a reasonable, ecologically sound policy for the management and propagation of the fish population.

Letting fish off the hook makes sense for the fish, fishery stocks, and fisherpersons who get the fun of landing a fish while the fish survives and escapes the frying pan.

"Off the hook" means good things for fish and for humans. Letting people off the hook has tactical value if effectively executed or horrible consequences if badly utilized. You can permanently damage the fish if you do not properly handle and care for it. That's true, too, if humans are not properly let off the hook.

On occasion, you can gain by not emphatically holding people, teams, and organizations accountable to standards, practices, and policies. Occasionally, you achieve more by relenting than by pressing coworkers for one-hundred percent adherence to policy. Most bad leaders don't see the value of the "off-the-hook" strategy—nor do they have the discernment or discipline to engage in it.

However, letting people off the hook cannot become a primary "go-to" or default strategy. Doing so regularly creates lower performance and compliance standards. People see leaders who default in this direction as weak, tentative, and lacking disciplinary grit. That's why letting employees off the hook for their errors or lack of performance can only be used occasionally. If overused, offenders will take advantage of it.

For leaders to try entrapping employees in minor rule infractions seldom makes sense. Serious, big-time, or illegal actions are certainly a different matter. However, bad leaders love to entrap employees—the opposite of letting people off the hook. The off-the-hook strategy cannot be used successfully when company rules and policies are willfully broken or for mission-critical matters. Off-the-hook strategies work when decisions and behaviors that aren't considered damaging simply happen.

I once had a conversation with a supervisor who told me that she had clearly explained to a group of new hires the importance of being punctual and ready to work at a set time. Most of the new employees took on the responsibility to show up on time as required. However, over time, a few employees became careless and began to arrive at work late. Rather than "bust" the employees for their lack of punctuality as the supervisor said she would, she simply stood at their workspaces and looked at her watch without making any comments. They got the message, but they never knew when something might be said about the infractions.

In this way, the supervisor temporarily let them off the hook yet held more influence than if she had unrelentingly held them to the standard. In the long run, she achieved the correct response in addition to exercising greater influence, while not abandoning the standards.

Consider, for example, how such a strategy might work. Alexander the Great once spared the life of a young soldier who had been caught sleeping while on duty. The crime was punishable by death. When the soldier was brought before Alexander for sentencing, Alexander asked the soldier for his name. The soldier replied that his name was also Alexander to which Alexander the Great then said, "Either change your name or change your behavior." He spared the soldier. I'm sure it was a lesson the younger Alexander never forgot, nor did the other soldiers observing the incident.

Like Alexander the Great, a good leader exercises grace strategically and appropriately. Grace is unmerited favor, and using it establishes that the good leader is engaged and aware of both company performance standards and employee behaviors and progress toward achieving standards. The display of grace through strategically letting people off the hook shows discernment and patience on the part of the leader who does what is best for both the organization and the person.

If people are let off the hook for failures or infractions for which they should have been busted, they will speculate on what it means. An off-the-hook strategy must be timely, well thought out, deployed with strategic instead of tactical focus, and only used with those who are likely to receive a better lesson from any other means of discipline. Thus, to deploy this strategy wisely, leaders must know their followers.

Consider, for example, how this strategy might work when an employee would rather be fired than come up to standard. At one time early in my career, I was a high school assistant principal in charge of attendance and discipline. Because I wanted the results of my work to be more helpful and redemptive than solely based on punishment, I occasionally engaged the off-the-hook strategy. It worked well when it worked, and it worked badly when it didn't. The overall results, though, were positive.

I can still recall the shocked relief on the faces of those who were let off the hook or given another means of recovering favorable status when, by all applicable standards, they should have been sent to detention, suspended, or expelled. I recall an instance when school policy called for suspending a student for three schools after breaking a rule. When I informed the student of the three-day rule, he replied, "Screw you; I'll take five." If anything, the student needed to be in the classroom learning, rather than at home or on the street. So the next time this student got busted, I used the off-the-hook approach, believing it was more effective for him than the same three-day rule.

While not a license to ignore the rules, the off-the-hook strategy can have the desired effect and produce more learning and greater continued compliance than dogged insistence on rules and punishments.

GOOD LESSONS:

- Good leaders know when and how to engage an off-the-hook strategy and to intentionally extend their influence for the good of both the organization and the person deserving discipline.
- Good leaders know when to defer the use of the off-the-hook strategy.
- Good leaders who use the off-the-hook strategy do so with precision and to demonstrate they are in-touch with their people and the tasks that their people perform.
- Most bad leaders cannot effectively use the off-the-hook strategy because they are more interested in justice than mercy. They use standards to crush people rather than to stretch and motivate, as good leaders do.
- Many bad leaders feel personally offended when policies and standards are broken as though they and the rules are one. Good leaders don't internalize the rules.
- Bad leaders leverage the breaking of rules to their benefit rather than using discipline as a positive force. Good leaders don't need to do this.

11. Inability to Read Between the Lines Effectively

Good leaders tend to be better listeners than bad leaders. Moreover, good leaders tend to be able to read between the lines better than bad leaders. That is to say good leaders can insightfully read and interpret data, people's actions, attitudes, and circumstances. Good leaders can better determine meaning from what is not being said or written than can bad leaders.

For example, take the following puzzle: R/E/A/D/I/N/G. Some people might analyze the word "reading" and the line between each letter and interpret the puzzle to mean "reading between the lines." They would be correct. Look more intently and see that "lines between reading" would also be correct.

Good leaders demonstrate their effectiveness by their ability to avoid stating the obvious, attempting to make a point that has already been made, or pursuing a point that does not need to be made. The ability to step back mentally and assess what is going on in an email, a public announcement, or a meeting is a skill to be emulated.

> **Leaders who continually state the obvious, make points that have already been made, or state unnecessary points prove they are inattentive, lack new insights, and hurt their credibility. These behaviors are often tolerated but never appreciated.**

Good leaders develop deeper degrees of insight and interpretation regarding opportunities and pitfalls not seen by lesser leaders. Their antennae work well. They connect the dots into new patterns and are able to perceive the moments when more is going on than meets the eye or the ear. Good leaders have a depth of perception that bad leaders don't. Using this knowledge, they can develop trajectories that yield intended results. The ability to read between the lines is a learned skill.

Bad leaders have great difficulty reading between the lines because they and their ideas become the centerpiece of their communications. When their focus is all about being seen as right, informed, intelligent, and authoritative, they miss opportunities to learn what else there is to be seen. When they focus on themselves, they don't develop the necessary sonar to read between the lines effectively, nor do they have the willingness to learn the skill.

Bad leaders see issues and people with a lack of depth and understanding because they haven't developed the skill to see beyond what people say. Many times, what people *do not* say is more meaningful and important than what they *do* say.

Reading between the lines requires enormous concentration. Good leaders frequently demonstrate the ability to focus their minds on what other people communicate and determine what's going on by not dwelling on what they themselves are thinking.

Effectively reading between the lines is a learned skill that sets you apart from those who can't or won't. Reading between the lines enables you to make more informed observations, develop more in-depth arguments, and squeeze more meaning out of what you hear or read. But it doesn't come naturally. This skill requires practice and diligence. But once you've mastered reading between the lines, it can accelerate your career.

One way to learn this skill is to watch movies or TV programs with the audio and text feed off. Interpreting the story without the sound calls for concentration and speculation. After writing down your perceptions, ideas, and thoughts, replay the movie or program to see how accurate you are. With practice, your ability to read between the lines will greatly improve.

Your accuracy in reading between the lines is also based on your degree of knowledge about the topic or issue at hand. This is known as content knowledge and everyone has some form or amount of this. Good leaders with superior content knowledge develop superior insights. They become great leaders and noble people by progressively moving through the "Data to Nobility" process.

Data to Nobility Process

1. **Independent data points**–recognized and properly interpreted
2. **Aggregated data points**–comprised of properly assembled independent data points
3. **Information**–aggregated groupings of aggregated data
4. **Knowledge**–properly aggregated information (and point at which data takes on moral character)
5. **Understanding**–properly interpreted knowledge
6. **Wisdom**–properly applied understanding
7. **Virtue**–moral behavior resulting from wisdom
8. **Humility**–personal behavior resulting from moral virtue
9. **Large-heartedness, generosity, magnanimity**–all a result of morally applied humility
10. **Compassion**–properly focused and engaged generosity
11. **Nobility**–character, state of being, and carriage resulting from moral virtue and properly applied compassion

Because bad leaders lack the ability to read between the lines and because they want to maintain their sense of superiority, bad leaders may actively or passively prevent others from collecting, aggregating, and/or collating information. In this way, bad leaders may also prevent their followers from displaying wisdom.

The follower who can read between the lines must, therefore, exercise great discipline and discretion in using this skill. The better the leader, the better s/he has mastered the data-to-nobility sequence. Bad leaders seldom reach even the humility state because they rarely read between the lines accurately or have the personality to do so.

GOOD LESSONS:

- Reading between the lines is essential to separate chaff from wheat, substance from smoke, and fact from fiction. The mental acuity and emotional courage to challenge the accuracy of spoken or written communiqués allows you to move in the direction of the truth.
- The ability to read between the lines is absolutely essential in any type of discussion, negotiation or meeting. A highly tuned and perceptive ability to read, see and interpret what is *really* being communicated and what is truthful or not truthful is enormously beneficial.

Learning to accurately read between the lines can accelerate your career by creating a competitive advantage that others don't have.

- Good leaders understand the relationship between reading between the lines and personal and organizational success, so they exercise the discipline to learn the skill. Bad leaders are not disciplined enough to develop the art of accurately reading between the lines.
- Good leaders are not gullible and are unlikely to fall prey to the wiles and duplicitous intents of those who are less than truthful and candid in their statements. A good leader often second guesses speakers, presenters, emails, and tweets to determine message veracity and sender transparency.
- Good leaders also read their audiences to determine if people are engaged or wandering away. If they are no longer paying attention, then the presenter or the information is not sufficiently compelling to gain and retain

interest. If audiences are disengaged, good leaders determine the reason and make appropriate changes to re-engage their listeners.

- To improve your contributory value, it is essential to have an extra dimension that your competitors or colleagues don't have. It is often said of highly successful people that they have another gear or zone into which they shift when necessary. I suggest that a fully developed ability to read between the lines can move you into another gear or zone of competency and achievement.

An exceptional example of a leader who was able to read between the lines is described in the book *Endurance: Shackleton's Incredible Voyage*[19] by Alfred Lansing.

Endurance is about Sir Ernest Shackleton and the crew of the Endurance during a failed exploration of Antarctica between 1912 and 1914. Certainly the name of the ship and title of the book are a foreshadowing to the story about the nearly three-year encounter with setback after setback (NOORTS).

The book recounts how Shackleton was able to eventually lead the entire crew to safety and home, although woefully under-resourced. It reveals Shackleton's ability to adapt to ever-changing and life-threatening difficulties by anticipating potential positive and negative outcomes of his decisions. He was a master of not only the clear and obvious consequences of his leadership, but also the highly speculative and risky things. I attribute his leadership to an enormous resolve to overcome unimaginable obstacles, his willingness to think strategies through to their ultimate end, and his ability to fully read between the lines the statements and actions of his men.

The rescue of the entire crew was also the result of his ability to read beyond what the weather, circumstances and even his own rationality was telling him. He was able to successfully read and interpret the differences among speculation, reality and illusion, despair and hope. His reading of what apparent action was necessary for the survival and rescue of his crew was coupled with his incredible discipline to see what could not be foreseen.

12. Inability to Use Talented Personnel Wisely

Good leaders are aware that forcing an employee into a role that didn't fit is clear evidence the employee's talents and interests have been disregarded. It is commonly understood that all people want to use their talents and skills wisely, and they will naturally gravitate to jobs and organizations that recognize, reward, and view them as assets rather than as threats. This is particularly true when economic times are good and employees are in high demand.

Yet, there are bad leaders who purposely re-slot and marginalize their direct reports in positions where the talents, skills, and diligence of others will not be seen as threats. Some unscrupulous leaders even place people in positions where they are likely to fail. And if the misplaced person happens to succeed in the poorly fit job, then fellow workers will notice and hold the survivor in high regard and the leader in disdain. This is likely to cause the bad leader whose inept strategy failed to repeat the marginalization.

Actions of this nature are truly "messed up," but they give clear examples of using talented personnel unwisely. It is risky business, but it does happen.

The motives of bad leaders are often far darker than they will admit.

Misplacement due to supervisory inability or intentional willingness to use personnel unwisely produces negative outcomes. How much better to slot people for success rather than failure and embarrassment? Certainly, appropriately using people's talents and skills wisely seems to be a self-evident policy. But don't be naïve and not realize that people are sometimes purposefully misplaced in order to drive them away, reduce their exposure, or lessen their threat to others.

Willful placement of personnel into situations where they are likely to fail or underperform tells more about those doing the placement than the person being placed. Sometimes, misplacement occurs because the leader is not paying attention; other times, it occurs because of organizational needs.

During my undergraduate days, I had a one night job with a major pharmaceutical company. I had hired on to work the second shift to align with my class schedule and was slotted to work in the handling and shipping department. When I went to work the first afternoon, I was given heavy clothing, boots, and safety gear and told to report to the bovine blood section. About half-way through the shift, I remembered that a couple of guys from my college had contracted hepatitis while working in the same department. I finished the shift but didn't return the second afternoon. I quickly realized I didn't want to get sick nor did I want to work for a company that so quickly and blatantly had broken an agreement about where I would work. In this case, I don't believe it was an inability on the supervisor to place me properly and according to our understanding; rather, it was an intentional placement in a position that was hard to fill due to potential negative health-related side effects.

Many unproductive, goofy reasons exist to misplace others. Perhaps a supervisor wants to deflect from their own weakness, indiscretion, and/or lack of performance. The willful act of misplacing a person draws attention away from the supervisor to the failure of the person misplaced. This sleight-of-hand places the employee in job and career jeopardy while attempting to protect the person or group doing the placement.

Actions such as these do not always achieve the purpose for which they were intended. For example, a radio station held a contest in which female listeners were asked to send in photos of the most worthless kitchen tool or utensil they had ever purchased. Thousands of photos came in, but the winner came from a woman who sent in a photo of her husband. Obviously, his cooking and kitchen skills did not rise to her standards, perhaps because he was better talented in the garage than in the kitchen. Maybe he was forced into kitchen duties only to fail. Unless he had agreed, her act might have pushed him to declare that he would never attempt to please her by participating in kitchen activities again.

Much like the wife who claimed her husband was the most worthless kitchen tool of all, the bad leader gives employees assignments that do not enhance their skills. Instead, bad leaders give them jobs that suppress their talents. Bad leaders frequently do this purposefully as a means of meeting out punishment or in a sorry attempt to get even for a slight, real or imagined. The bad leader might also slot an employee as a sacrificial lamb to lessen the threat that employee poses to a bad leader.

While in a consulting job, I learned of a supervisor who purposefully buried certain personnel in the wrong jobs for as long as possible or until the misplaced employees resigned. This practice was unproductive and unexplainable until it was determined that misplaced employees, more often than not, had substantially more talent and energy than the supervisor. Therefore, they were perceived as potential threats. The situation would not have been amended or other personnel appropriately placed and wisely engaged had the supervisor not been relieved of responsibility in that company.

Bad leaders are not always solely responsible for misplacing an employee. People may willingly accept misplacement due to a number of non-work-related challenges or economic necessities. Times may be difficult. Job mobility may be diminished. Most people have taken positions to fill gaps, to gain income, experience, and/or momentum, but never intended these jobs to be permanent. They were to be episodic and temporary like the few weeks I worked on the kill floor of Armour Packing Company where in one eight-hour shift we took hundreds of cattle from standing on the hoof to hanging in the meat locker. For most of the other guys at Armour, this was a real job; for me it was filler. An employee in a permanent position that does not fit will soon face emotional depletion and could become a detriment to the organization.

Good leaders know that one of the best ways to use talent wisely is, for their own good, to help these employees move on appropriately. An employee once thanked me profusely for dismissing her. I didn't have another meaningful position, and she was only forcing herself to remain in a position to which she was ill-suited (and performing badly), she was relieved to have been let go. In fact, she broke down and cried; she was relieved to be released so she could find something more meaningful and challenging.

Good leaders know that forcing a misfit to achieve failure is inappropriate and unethical. But firing an employee to help him/her find success is a difficult decision that often has positive results and is ethical.

One of the most insidious ways a bad leader can misuse talented personnel is to abuse the other person's time. Bad leaders may abuse their own time, but when they abuse or misuse yours, they fail to deploy your talents and skills effectively. Bad leaders casually and purposefully abuse one of the resources with the greatest value—another person's time. Some bad leaders strategically abuse another person's time as a means of showing their power and/or complicating the person's life as a means of control. Bad leaders fail to realize that once time is lost, that same time can never be recovered. It's gone forever.

While good leaders may accidentally or occasionally abuse another person's time, for them, such behavior is uncharacteristic. Still, even employees may engage in behaviors that demonstrate a lack of understanding for the value of time. Thus, I have often asked in job interviews a question about the candidate's perception of his/her own time and that of others as well as how they have seen both good and bad uses of time. The answers ordinarily provide a sense of how the candidate values such a limited resource and potential reactions when the person sees time being used well and/or used poorly.

GOOD LESSONS:

- If a job is a misfit, get out quickly. Always be cautious and reconfirm job placement prior to making a huge commitment to an employer or opportunity.

Watch out for the bad leader who places people in positions below their talent and experience levels as a means of keeping them in a place and state of mind where they won't be a threat.

- Again, understand that the motives of bad leaders are often far darker than they are willing to admit regarding position placement.
- Don't misplace anybody for any reason on a permanent basis. If you are forced to temporarily misplace someone, tell the person why, for how long and how you will compensate them for the mismatch.
- Keep in mind that "A" class leaders hire and insist on working with other "A" class people. "B" class leaders hire and desire to work with "C" class people. Hiring "A" class people and placing them in "C" class jobs is a misuse of talent and time. Bad leaders don't realize that it is better to

engage the talented employee wisely, despite the ego threats they create, rather than to engage the less talented person.

Good leaders not only place employees in situations in which they will succeed but keep them out of situations in which they are likely to fail.

- Bad leaders don't often take the time required to determine upfront the likely differences between a successful placement and failure placements. They'd prefer to just "get on" with the job.
- Bad leaders often lack the ability or refuse to look for "A" qualities in those of lesser ability. Good leaders continually look for "A" or "B" level qualities in "C" ability people who can be developed with their assistance.

13. Inability to Promote Unity and Diversity

Over the last several decades, diversity-related matters have been justifiably mainstreamed into the workplace, and the benefits of wide demographic input are being realized. Most of the progress regarding diversity has to do with race, ethnicity, gender, and age, but true diversity must be defined much more broadly to encompass diversity of input.

Most definitions of diversity tend to promote a protected class of employees who have previously not been given appropriate access to employment and/ or promotions. However, this model, because it is primarily "front loaded" or "input focused" rather than balanced, tends to fall short in achieving unity of output. Without *diversity of input, unity of output* can't be fully realized, particularly in highly competitive environments. Without unity of output, organizations don't survive.

Diversity has been defined too narrowly and has superseded the necessity of unity of output. Diversity of input, as necessary as it is, cannot solely achieve organizational mission. Good leaders align diversity with unity to produce high-performing groups and organizations. Bad leaders don't see the need for balance and tend to over emphasis either diversity of input or unity of output.

Diversity should also mean every person's ability to help meet organizational goals not only because of a group identity, but also because of each person's independent, one-of-a-kind, specialized personhood. No one can bring to the workplace and the world exactly what *you* can bring. You are one of many, but you are also one of one.

For this reason, over many years of conducting employment interviews, I never have failed to ask this one key question of applicants: "What uniqueness, talent, ability, gifting, or skill do you possess that I can't find in any other applicant?" The interviewees have been enormously diverse, but they tend to fall into two categories: those who do not like the question, and those who do. Most of those who don't like the question don't see themselves as having unique, contributory value. The question becomes difficult to answer. Some people have even seen it as a personal affront.

In my view, if applicants indicate that they have no talents, abilities, gifts, or skills to set them apart from others, then they can carry this perception into their performances. This category of applicant often defaults to overly cautious self-modesty and effacement. In contrast, the question animates some people because they have never been asked it, they like the question, or they have been given the chance to indicate how their contributory value is enhanced by their TAGS (talents, abilities, gifts, and skills), differentiating them from all other applicants. Their answers are ordinarily enjoyable because they are given the opportunity to detach themselves from the societal expectations of a group to showcase their TAGS and display their individual diversity.

Out of that individual diversity comes each person's contributory value. Each person has a unique combination of TAGS, education, life, work experience, and character. When combined, the greatest blend of diversity becomes possible, and it highlights the individual.

Good leaders know that diversity in all of its forms is necessary. They are aware that too many people who think alike will become blind to the realities of the marketplace and lose the competitive advantage that diversity brings.

Good leaders also know that the time for diversity is at the input stage, and the time for unity is at the output stage. They are able to manage both.

Bad leaders often see diversity in all of its forms as a challenge to their authority. They want people who think as they think, believe as they believe, and act as they act. This is *sameness*, not unity. They further believe that sameness of inputs will maintain direction and a competitive edge. It won't.

Unity of output means there is agreement among diverse employees with diverse ideas to produce "best in class" goods and services that meet market demand, enable the entity to be the most creative in their space, and defeat all would-be competitors.

GOOD LESSONS:

- Embrace input diversity to produce output unity.
- Good leaders enhance the contributory value of others; bad leaders don't.
- Good leaders understand that individuals having the greatest diversity of input are also the ones who can make the greatest contribution to unity of output.
- Good leaders understand that diversity for its own sake sells the individual short, as people are lumped together and unable to break free from their group identity and demonstrate their one-in-the-universe TAGS.
- Bad leaders fail to grasp the importance of each individual's importance in producing unity of output.

Bad leaders seldom orchestrate a balance between "diversity of input" with "unity of output." They lean one way or the other, either toward diversity or toward unity, but seldom do they combine both.

14. Inability to Connect Organizational and Personal Benefits

A substantial portion of management science, research, and practice has to do with motivational theory. One aspect of motivational theory has to do with equity theory. In brief, equity theory is thought of as "fairness of rewards for energy expended."

Good leaders fuse personal benefits with positive organization outcomes. Organized labor has played a significant role in U.S. business and economic history because many organizations were unable or unwilling to connect real worker benefits to organizational and managerial prosperity. Workers need and deserve fair compensation and safe working conditions.

Bad leaders fail to take seriously the need to clearly and directly connect the ways in which an organization benefits from the efforts of its employees and the ways in which employees benefit from their relationship with the organization.

Leaders have an initial and continuing responsibility to make this connection. Bad leaders may say they do but demonstrate that they don't.

As an example, some companies encourage their employees to pursue a degree or a certification via employee tuition reimbursement programs. The employee benefits from the additional training, perhaps earning a bachelor's or advanced degree. The manager and company also benefit directly because these employees are then better prepared to do their jobs.

Equity is a fundamental component of job satisfaction for both the employee and others related to the employee. People expect their employers to treat them fairly—in proportion to their perceived contributions. People also expect their employers to treat fellow workers equitably. Thus, any perceived injustice to fellow employees serves as a de-motivator to all. It's one of the primary reasons for job dissatisfaction and a motivator for an organized labor movement.

Recognizing the impact of equity is a nearly innate characteristic for good leaders. This is not true for bad leaders; recognizing the need for equity is not innate or, in their view, essential. At best, the bad leader grudgingly learns to recognize the real need for equity.

Bad leaders exhibit an unwillingness to appropriately confirm the ways through which an organization benefits from worker contributions and the means by which workers are rewarded for their contributions. A one-way street where benefits accrue to the organization doesn't bother bad leaders. They likely won't admit this, but it's the way they behave. As a result, employees feel disposable.

Seldom do bad leaders make the effort purposefully to connect organizational gain to individual gain. The bad leader doesn't recognize the complementary relationship between the employer and the employee. Over time, if equity is not acknowledged, callousness develops in bad leaders, and it frustrates employees and creates churn within the organization. Bad leaders may even entrap workers to perform tasks out of sheer economic necessity. The very worst form of this is human trafficking.

In contrast, good leaders create a workplace ethos in which employees can easily connect their benefits and organizational benefits. The more frequently employees make this connection, the greater the level of engagement and motivation and the better the overall outcomes.

Consider the following scenario. During grad school days, I was general manager of a hotel franchised by a major hotel chain. Although the property was considered a full-service, premium-brand hotel, this particular unit was outside the city limits at the intersection of several interstate highways. The hotel had excellent location and visibility for travelers, but the lack of utility services such as water and sewage disposal caused substantial difficulty. Most of the staff was well-trained and diligent, but I was exceedingly thankful for one particular individual because an enormously egregious job needed to be done every other Friday afternoon. We had to manage our own storm water and sanitary sewage disposal systems, which required regular special maintenance procedures. Although serviceable and up to code, the system required that solids be removed by hand, for example.

The fellow to whom the task fell was named Mike. His job was to put on rubber waders and walk around in the pit to scoop and remove all undigested solids. It was a truly disgusting but necessary task. If ignored, the sewer backed up, which necessitated closing down the entire property until the solid waste was removed.

Mike never wanted to do the job, and I easily understood why. I always had to locate him physically to give him the bad news that "it' now time" to perform this horrible job. So, into the pit he would go to perform the thirty-minute job. Those thirty minutes must have seemed an eternity for Mike.

I did my best to connect this nasty job with the hotels' greater need to serve its customers, and I gave Mike my profound thanks for performing that miserable task. I delivered the same appreciation speech every other Friday afternoon; but when I finally provided Mike with a two extra hours of release time on alternative Friday afternoons, he felt my appreciation. The day he went into the pit was the day he got paid for time off. Once I connected the desperate need of the hotel and Mike's desire to hit the road a couple of hours early on his motorcycle every other Friday, I had confidence the "solid waste" task would get done on schedule. That's all it took.

In such situations, supervisors are often greatly frustrated when they want to configure rewards for extraordinarily difficult or onerous jobs but have neither the freedom nor resources to make that happen. If they assume that their hands are tied, they are even more frustrated. However, the hands of truly good leaders are seldom, if ever, completely tied.

Employees know when a supervisor has gone to the mat for them and when a supervisor hasn't.

Sometimes the situation reaches a dead end, particularly if the person who controls the resources is neither acquainted with the nasty job nor open to creating the means to reconcile the worker's needs with organizational necessity.

Good leaders intentionally create and clearly communicate ways to connect benefits to the individual with those of the organization. While generating these connections may demand creativity, hard work, and trust, good leaders will put in the effort. Failure to make these connections may result in disaster for both the individual and the organization.

GOOD LESSONS:
- If good leaders don't make it pay for workers, then no one will.

For particularly onerous, difficult, dangerous, or boring tasks, good leaders start with by stating the benefits to the individual and then work backward to include the benefits to the organization. Although they discuss both types of benefits, they create the sizzle before the stink.

- Good leaders get serious and creative about securing benefits for performing "dirty" tasks; bad leaders don't.
- Bad leaders are unlikely to extend themselves to improve the circumstances that create "dirty" jobs, but they expect employees to persist without clear benefit or value in doing so. This is at best, a short term solution. Good leaders do not allow this to happen.
- Good leaders don't place people in positions or give assignments prematurely and when workers are only partially trained. It's unethical and unproductive to do so and does not create a positive reciprocal relationship between employees and employer. Workers know when their preparation is inadequate, yet bad leaders often show their impatience and lack of genuine concern and throw employees among the wolves to see if they will survive.
- Don't throw anybody for any reason among the wolves unless you are confident their training and courage will enable them to control the wolves.

---

15. Inability to Leverage Teaching Moments

Just what is a teachable moment? The best leaders I have seen in any, for-profit, non-profit, or NGO environment are those who have the ability and the willingness to take the time to teach in both planned and spontaneous moments. They have the ability, knowledge, and wisdom to bridge from what is evident and known to what is not evident or known. They accurately apply and extend knowledge and willingly seize any moment to teach a principle or concept of real, lasting value. They do so because of their great regard for those they address and their passion for individual, group, and social betterment. They are not parental, and they have consequential things to say. They are not caustic or cutting during teaching moments but leave their colleagues, associates, and listeners with a sense of worth, fullness, and having spent time well. Not only do they know when, what, why, and how to leverage a teachable moment, but they also know when to stay their planned course and avoid an un-teachable moment. The best leaders watch for the perfect set of circumstances, knowing that the opportunity may not ever present itself again. See Lincoln's Gettysburg Address as an example of a profound teaching moment.

> **Good leaders understand that teaching moments have common components: appropriate time; appropriate place; degree of information need; and learner receptivity.**

While a college president, I was asked to accompany a group of students and one professor on a canoe trip to the Algonquin National Forest in Ontario, Canada. It was a well-planned and well-equipped trip. But, while traveling through Toronto at 3 a.m., the college van pulling the canoe trailer with our eight new canoes caught fire and burned to the frame. Thankfully, no one was injured, and no emotional harm befell any of the students. But we were presented with an interesting dilemma: scrub the trip and go home, or persist and create a new game plan.

Over the next few hours, we got another vehicle and lots of new clothing and gear. We pressed on. However, I thought it was highly unusual for the prof to try to turn the shocking fire and near tragedy into a teachable moment. It wasn't the time or place, nor were we in an emotional or physical state to benefit from the teaching, conversation, and debriefing.

As part of this trip, we had planned other teachable moments. We finished the long drive, placed the canoes in the water, and got underway. The next morning, we needed to learn canoeing safety processes. The time, place, and need were present. We were all in our canoes receiving appropriate instruction, including canoe re-entry should a person jump or fall out. The prof asked for a volunteer to help demonstrate proper re-entry techniques, and before he finished the sentence one of the students, a young woman, leapt into the water. It was then that the teachable moment began to go all wrong. Although eager to help, the young woman was a marginal swimmer and enormously shocked and disoriented because of the icy water. The prof failed to leverage this teachable moment that had become much more than he anticipated. Those in my canoe saw that she was in real trouble and rescued her. No one paid much attention to the prof and his ongoing lecture about rescue techniques. He had missed a great teaching moment.

Bad leaders often miss teaching moments or try to force them. When an event or process goes horribly wrong, a bad leader will attempt to force a learning debrief before the learners are calm enough to learn. The fire must be out; the decision made to continue; perhaps the trip even finished before the learners become ready to debrief the situation and learn from it.

When an unplanned learning moment appears, the bad leader fails to notice it or fails to use it to its full potential. Students on that canoeing trip learned far more by actually rescuing their peer than they did by listening to the prof lecture about proper techniques while she became progressively weaker.

Good leaders learn to recognize teaching moments, whether planned or unplanned. They also know that learners cannot learn when they experience undue stress. For this reason, a good leader may wait for a calm moment to give instruction or may deliberately create a low-stakes environment in which to teach. Recognizing a teachable moment is a developed skill and takes a trained eye. You can learn it as you observe and analyze leaders' presentations, actions, and comments. You can learn to leverage teachable moments successfully by learning when to speak and when to be silent.

For example, at one time I was a franchisee of a restaurant chain. I learned that determining the quality of a well-managed restaurant included the attractiveness of entrances, state of repair of its signage, and cleanliness of its employees' shoes—among a long list of other indicators besides the food. Certainly these are not the only tests of operational quality, but they do suggest the seriousness with which we approached our work.

To make my policies stick, I first had to ensure that my own shoes met the standard I wanted my employees to meet. I had one fine employee who wore truly messy shoes to work, and I had to decide what to do. I could ignore the situation, miss a potentially teachable moment, or allow him to slide by, thereby weakening my policy and reducing my credibility. Or, I could take him aside gently, without busting his chops or embarrassing him, and ask what message he sent to patrons and fellow workers by the appearance of his shoes. While he gave an excellent answer, he got my message, and he never failed to meet the standard for footwear again. He learned because he was teachable and because I was able to create a good teaching moment. Most important, he wanted his good character and high-quality work reflected in his appearance.

> **Bad leaders may not be bad people, but they are seldom tuned in enough to take advantage of teachable moments.**

Some bad leaders cannot properly seize teachable moments because they have not come up to standard or adhered to policy as they ought. As a result, they have no credibility to teach others what they do not know or what they do not do themselves. When they try, they lose even more credibility.

Michael Scott (played by Steve Carrel) is the main character on the TV program "The Office." He was particularly inept concerning both planned and spontaneous teaching moments, and his behaviors became the focus of criticism from his fellow workers and much of the story line for the show. He attempted to create teaching moments but never got it right. Don't be like Michael Scott.

GOOD LESSONS:

- Bad leaders often avoid teachable moments because they have not successfully modeled what they want others to learn and do.
- Good leaders teach good lessons because they know how and when to leverage teachable moments to produce good outcomes for all concerned.
- Good leaders capitalize on teachable moments to provide deep insights into human behaviors such as those manifested by customers and competitors.
- Good leaders consider as many factors and desired outcomes as possible before creating a potentially high-stakes teaching moment.

- Good leaders pay attention to receptivity levels and wait for periods of high stress to pass before attempting a teaching moment. They understand the importance of right moments to achieve the desired responses.
- You can learn how to successfully execute teachable moments both by what you do and say when you have the opportunity and by what you don't do and say when you have the opportunity.
- Sometimes silence is the most effective way to teach in a teachable moment. Good leaders know this, but bad leaders feel compelled to fill in the gaps because they aren't intuitive enough to let silence speak for itself.

16. Inability to Endear Themselves

Of the many characteristics associated with superior leaders, one that stands out is the ability of good leaders to endear themselves to those they work with and lead. For leaders to endear themselves to others, they need to display a number of positive characteristics. It is not ordinarily a single behavior or characteristic that endears.

"Endearment" or "endearing" is defined by the Oxford Living Dictionary as "a cause to be loved or liked." I'm not writing about ingratiating oneself to others by use of a false narrative or false motives. Rather, I mean manifesting an attitude or carrying out an action that enables another person to think favorably of you. Not that leaders might want to become endearing to others, but by acting as they did, they organically created endearment. Even great leaders don't set out to endear themselves to others. If the leader is truly great, it just progressively happens.

Bad, uncaring, un-endearing leaders just don't get it. They don't see the connection between cause and effect, between a spontaneous act of kindness and being endearing. For many bad leaders, acts of endearment are just manipulative actions undertaken, not for the benefit of the receiver but for the benefit of the giver.

One of the greatest compliments I have ever been paid came from a professor of English while I was an Academic Dean in the same university. He said in a public setting that he would "follow me anywhere." Although his sentiment was appreciated, its context was not that of a highly critical or dangerous situation, such as running into a burning building to rescue a child or facing the enemy in a military fire fight. So, "following me" was not physically demanding or in a dangerous setting. I believe he meant that I was leading in a direction and manner that was pleasing and beneficial to him, although I had no supervisory responsibility for him.

His viewpoint on how I had endeared myself to him must have been partially the result of being a colleague rather than a fellow worker or direct report. That fact might have changed the game and perhaps his tune. Yet, I had engaged him while he had been going through a difficult health problem that his immediate supervisor seemed to care little about. I had nothing to gain by showing him some basic human kindness. He had assumed that if I had done what I did just *because I thought it a kind thing to do* rather than out of obligation or a direct work-related relationship, I must have characteristics that were admirable. Thus, my act had endeared me to him.

This example is insignificant when compared to the magnanimous acts of generosity and humility that are the source of longer term endearment displayed by highly valued leaders.

A true-life 2016 movie *Hacksaw Ridge*[20] makes this case in a big way. The movie is set in 1945 during World War II as U.S. troops were attempting to take the island of Okinawa. The main character, Desmond Doss, was thought to be chicken-hearted because he was a conscientious objector who refused to touch a gun. In fact, he was physically and emotionally abused for his religious beliefs. But he endeared himself to his fellow soldiers through his selfless and tireless acts of rescuing wounded soldiers from the battlefield. His heroism engendered enormous respect from his battlefield compatriots. Private Doss rescued seventy-five wounded and dying men, and he was the first conscientious objector to receive the Congressional Medal of Honor. His courage endeared him to those who had previously mistreated him. The movie is bloody and tension-filled but resolves into great endearment for Private Doss.

Often a special consideration, kindness, or going out of one's way to encourage and help another creates emotional benefits that spill over into other responsibilities, opportunities, and relationships. Bad leaders often just don't get the point, nor would they take time to show kindness by providing attention to others when they're not required to do so. They don't see the benefit, and thus they don't endear themselves to others.

Bad leaders who fail to show kindness, humility, and genuineness—regardless of the level of success or desired outcomes—will always fail to endear themselves to others. Yet, leaders who show commitment, competence, hard work, and virtue will not.

GOOD LESSONS;

- Good leaders endear themselves; bad leaders can't and don't.
- Endearment is not planned; it is earned.
- Endearment will take good leaders further in tough times than a lack of endearment will take bad leaders in the best of times.
- Endearment cannot be separated from high regard and genuine love.
- Seeking to endear oneself to others by example is better than seeking to impress others though speech.
- Bad leaders distance themselves rather than endear themselves.
- "Flattery" or an "insult" are the opposite of endearment. Avoid them.
- Some acts of kindness leading to endearment naturally fade with time. However, the opposite is true as well. Failing to endear oneself will be remembered by followers for a long time.
- Bad leaders, like bad restaurants, don't endear themselves to people.
- Bad leaders get under your skin but not into your heart.

17. Inability to Use Humor Productively

The phrase "good-humored" refers to being affable, gracious, good-natured and having a positive and helpful state of mind. "Good humored" also expresses being in a cordial mood by making affirming statements and having a pleasant demeanor. Bad leaders are quite frequently viewed as not having these traits.

The opposite of good humored is bad humored. Bad humored is negative, ill-tempered, testy in nature, and used in a supposedly humorous manner to cause pain, embarrassment, and emotional discomfort.

Good leaders who know how, when, how much, and what type of humor to use are frequently thought of as being thoughtful, restrained, and therefore credible. Humor can be used in a number of positive ways: to gain interest, hold attention, entertain, teach, and emphasize important points. Certainly, not all great leaders use humor well, but they know it and avoid using it badly.

Leaders who use humor as a primary means of building their personal brand do so at their peril. The overuse or misuse of humor tends to detract from a leader's authority. Listeners begin to believe that if a leader's message is frivolous, so is the leader. If your humor is viewed as misplaced and negative, you will be viewed in the same light.

Self-effacing humor can be used effectively by leaders to lessen status and perception gaps between leaders and the led. Self-deprecating humor puts skin and humanity on high-ranking leaders. It allows them to not take themselves, their status, or authority too seriously. Really good leaders seldom, if ever, think of themselves too highly. Using humor appropriately enables them to keep themselves and their public comments in check.

Telling jokes, funny stories, or ordinary stories in funny ways is not a required leadership characteristic, but having a quick wit and a ready response is. These are often better examples of a leader's raw intelligence, emotional maturity, or prior training than only being good at telling jokes.

If you are not a naturally gifted comic or don't have rapier-like wit, find and test a few jokes or stories that are appropriate for the setting—ones that will elicit the type of response you want. It's best never to tell a joke that is impertinent to the topic being discussed or the issue at hand. If your audience doesn't easily make the connection between what you are trying to say and your attempts at humor, they will feel manipulated. As a result, your impact as a communicator will be devalued.

With today's politically correct culture, leaders in the workplace must use humor more cautiously than in previous times. Self-restraint in using humor, and thoroughly thinking through the interpretations and shades of meaning of one's humor, are required in diverse and increasing litigious settings.

Leaders who are not good at telling jokes for effect should not attempt to do so. I heard about a prison where the jokes were so stale, each was assigned a number rather than being retold. A new inmate caught on quickly and began to call out numbers for jokes that had previously received raucous laughter. But when the new inmate called out numbers, no one laughed. Wondering why, he asked another inmate why no one laughed at his numbers. The other inmate stated, "Some people just can't tell a joke." Just as some inmates can't tell jokes, there are leaders who can't tell jokes. If you can't, don't.

Jokes that demean are particularly destructive and unnecessary. Good leaders don't weaponize humor. Telling jokes and ordinary stories in a funny way is a different thing. Also, people who are good at telling jokes may not be good at telling ordinary stories in a funny way, so caution is in order. Any joke that relates to a colleague's appearance or body type is never appropriate. Any joke or story meant to minimize a person's workplace status or position is out of order. Celebrity roasts may be the place to do this, but the workplace is not.

GOOD LESSONS:
- Bad leaders are prone to use sarcastic humor. It's difficult to twist a knife and get a laugh with the same joke, so don't try.
- Attempts at off-color humor make listeners uncomfortable and closed to your message. Avoid this type of humor.
- Telling humorous anecdotes about coworkers in a public setting in a positive and enriching way helps build community.
- Humor should be transparent and not layered with dark attempts at retribution.
- If your attempts at humor are frivolous, it won't be long until you are viewed as frivolous, too.
- Don't let bad humor destroy your great logic and good content.
- It is better to avoid using humor to reinforce a good point than to use it badly and destroy your point.
- Good leaders never endear themselves by telling bad jokes.
- Bad leaders never endear themselves by telling good jokes.

18. Inability to Blend Intuition, Emotion, and Reason in Decision Making

Good leaders have the ability and willingness to balance their intuition, emotions, and data-led reasoning to make sound decisions. Lesser leaders not as much, while bad leaders rarely do this. Superior outcomes seldom occur without inputs from intuition, emotion, and reason.

Recall that bad leaders are not necessarily bad people. It may be that their intuitive skills are not fully developed, their emotions are not sufficiently controlled, or their reasoning skills are underutilized.

We hear the term "data driven" on a regular basis. It's a handy descriptor for explaining that a decision or course of action is taken based on objective, actionable data. In other words, it is the preponderance and veracity of the data that enables certain actions to be pushed ahead.

People and the decisions made by them can be driven by data. However, I prefer that people and decisions are *led* by data rather than *driven* by data. Those leaders act as though data is their ally, rather than their master, and data seldom makes decisions. People do.

Often, bad leaders will blame the data for a bad outcome. Yet data doesn't make its own decisions most of the time. There are certainly AI, IOT, and algorithmic exceptions through which machines and systems, led by data, will make their own decision without human interpretation or intervention. But data-driven decisions often make humans secondary elements in a decision where the comfort of having no accountability can be claimed. For example, someone who is stopped by a police officer states, "Sorry, officer, the car just drove itself through the red light." Bad leaders tend to hide behind this type of argument.

I think of it differently, based on what I experienced while leading complex organizations and observed in my consulting. When intuition, emotion, and data are in balance, the union creates compelling arguments upon which sound decisions can be made.

According to *Merriam-Webster's Collegiate Dictionary*, intuition means "a quick and ready insight and the power or faculty of knowing things without conscious reasoning." Reasoning, on the other hand, is defined as "the use of reason, the power to think and exercising the faculty of logical thought."

Decision making based solely on data might be argued as a superior strategy. Decision making based solely on intuition or gut feelings is not always bad or deficient. Decision making based on prior positive outcomes gives rise to greater accuracy, whether based on intuition, data, or a balanced combination of both.

Some years ago, my personal physician, an otherwise skilled MD, misdiagnosed his own illness. He relied on his own feelings and intuition to treat what he thought was his illness rather than seeking treatment from another MD. His choice led to greater physical problems and eventually to his death.

We tend to trust those whose decisions are accurate, regardless of the input basis on which they were made. When trust is not achieved, it could be because the decision makers were not balanced in using intuition and data analysis. Perhaps they were making decisions outside of their swim lane or beyond their interpretative range.

Intuition-based decisions are not data-based but experienced-based. As such, they can be affected more by luck than superior data or rationality.

Good leaders frequently make decisions that disregard their intuition because the mass and accuracy of the data suggest that to do otherwise would be foolhardy. But they are cognizant of the fact that they are doing so.

Some leaders are viewed as good based upon the fact that they are lucky. Lucky and good are far better than unlucky and bad. But even an outstanding leader's balance of data-led, intuition-informed, emotion-apprised decisions can go bad based on a number of uncontrollable and unanticipated circumstances.

I had a graduate student who had a great idea for importing a special vintage of wine not available in the U.S. He found distributors and retailers willing to shelve his product. He found that customers were willing to pay the price he needed to make profitable margins. He based his decision to execute his plan on solid market data and intuition that his import wine business would be economically feasible. However, to get the product into the U.S., he needed to transport the wine via a container ship through a Canadian port. His container of wine sat on a freighter during an extreme cold snap, and it did not have high enough alcohol content to keep it from freezing. The entire shipment was lost and uninsured based on the nature of the loss. His emotion-apprised choice to hurry and ship during the cold season proved devastating to an otherwise solid business endeavor.

Frequently, decisions based on intuition are those that can be made quickly and have little resource consequence. It's one thing to decide what kind of cookie to buy: Oreos or Vanilla Wafers. It's quite another to decide to move your manufacturing operations back from China to the U.S. because the resource expenditures (PECITs) are so great and the risks consequential.

GOOD LESSONS:

- Followers trust the "gut instincts" of good leaders, and they don't trust the "gut instincts" of bad ones.
- One gains intuition primarily through past positive experiences and by observing what good leaders do well that bad leaders don't.
- Bad leaders are less inclined than good leaders to monitor their emotions in unfamiliar circumstances and with difficult people.
- Good leaders know when their associates are being overly influenced by emotions. Bad leaders don't.
- Good leaders admit to being overly influenced by their emotions and instincts, while bad leaders don't.

---

19. Inability to Be Comfortable in Uncomfortable Circumstances

I'm sure we would rather see lions free on a range than in cages. However, there are some similarities between being a skilled leader and being a skilled lion-tamer that are worthy of our consideration.

Like people, lions have the capacity to act passively or aggressively, depending on their nature and mood. Also, like people, some lions are more easily taught than others; they accept the authority of the trainer or have a calm demeanor. A hungry lion is more than likely to act differently after eating.

It is the courage and skill of the trainer that brings out the desired behavior of the lion. Professional tamers never become overly relaxed or indifferent to the harm a lion might cause. They survive in the space between carelessness and carefulness and become as comfortable as one can in uncomfortable, threatening situations. Good lion tamers can do this; bad lion tamers—well, you get the picture.

> Many times, bad leaders are uncomfortable in their own skins. They are not comfortable with themselves as human beings or as managers; they have not reconciled their self-image to the role and status expectations others have conferred on them.

Bad leaders are also prone to be uncomfortable with their own skills, which is evident in their self-doubt and shaky relationships with others. A lack of comfortability within their skins and with their skills is often the source of discomfort in difficult circumstances.

Perhaps you've heard the phrase, "Never let them see you sweat." It is a reference to one's sense of comfortability in trying situations. Bad leaders, finding themselves in sweat-producing circumstances, often "zone-out" and/or "shut down." This behavior is noticed and despised by their followers.

I recently heard of a college president who announced a change in university policy to a group of students. This policy change upset the direction of the students' lives so much that the majority would have to leave the institution and pursue their interests and diplomas elsewhere. But it was not only the change in policy that was devastating for students; it was also the abrupt, uncaring manner in which the message was delivered. Add to that was the fact that, after the announcement, the president was nowhere to be found. He dropped the bomb and left, leaving other college personnel to dispel the students' anger and help plan their exit strategies.

The college president was clearly uncomfortable in this tough situation, and it was noticed by all, included the local press. He should have stayed engaged to shoulder the consequences of the change in policy and face the people to whom the change in policy was most injurious.

Bad leaders often demonstrate that, when the going gets tough, they do, too. This is the wrong message and could also foreshadow further leadership gaffs.

Observers both inside and outside the college saw the bad behavior. They are likely to remember it the next time circumstances become uncomfortable.

Good lessons can be learned from good leaders who are comfortable in uncomfortable circumstances. Why? Because they don't slack off from direct confrontation and pressure when necessary. They know when it's necessary to hold ground and/or confront others—and when not to. This takes wisdom and humility. Confrontation with humility is found in strong, competent leaders.

Good leaders don't necessarily create safe places on every issue for every person within the organization, nor should they. But providing some level of safety is necessary to create stability when uncomfortable challenges arise.

GOOD LESSONS:

- While experiencing an uncomfortable situation, bad leaders often ignore or deny the source of the discomfort.
- Good leaders rely on themselves to lead their people and organization out of difficulty rather than giving up or assigning the responsibility of creating a solution to others.
- Bad leaders can become needy, see themselves as victims, and seek emotional support from others due to difficult circumstances. These leaders are difficult to follow.
- Becoming too comfortable in a difficult situation is a form of self-deception for the bad leader.
- Good leaders do not abandon their posts or their people when the pressure is on, but exercise emotional strength, courage and resolve.
- Good leaders don't panic when faced with difficult circumstances; they keep their emotions in check and immediately determine the source of the difficulty. They also don't prematurely engage a strategy to get out of the uncomfortable circumstance.

20. Inability to Release Prior Success

Clinginess is a type of adherence that prevents one from releasing something out of one's hand or off one's fingertips, like a light piece of paper or a cellophane wrapper that stays attached. One might shake one's hand, but static electricity or an adhesive allows it to persistently hang on. If one attempts to remove it with other hand, it clings there, too.

Clinginess is a good thing when applied as a part of a wrapping or package. But it becomes a nuisance when it's not performing according to its original purpose.

Often, failure and success behave in the same way. For example, letting go of failure is something we have been told to do. Releasing and forgetting it so it no longer impedes us is good advice, and we get it. We have all failed at something, and letting failure drag us down is self-defeating. But *not* letting go of success can also become self-defeating. Moving on isn't easy, particularly when a success has contributed to the formation of our self-image and how we view the present and future.

Motivational speakers have made a great deal of money helping people let go and move on from career and family setbacks, divorce, job loss, and even someone's death. But I've yet to hear a motivational speaker insist that one move on from success.

In fact, this book is about developing the insights and forward-looking strategies needed to drive ahead in spite of the difficulties encountered due to the failures, inabilities, and refusals of bad leaders. Past successes become illusionary and more difficult to turn loose than a failure.

Supervisory-level leaders are apt to cling to success as much, if not more, than those in the C-Suite or board room. But there is no level of an organization at which clinging to success for too long remains an effective strategy. When clinging to success becomes a behavior for lower-level leaders, operational stagnancy could result. Who hasn't heard the phrase, "But we've always done it this way"?

Depending on a past success has a tendency to percolate both upwards and downwards within the organization or institution. Clinging to the right things for too long makes them wrong.

Dr. Robert J. Herbold wrote a book titled *Seduced By Success: How the Best Companies Survive the 9 Trips of Winning*. As a senior leader at Proctor & Gamble, then as COO of Microsoft, Dr. Herbold has the background and deep insights to make observations about how and why big and successful corporations stall out after success.[21]

He cites three reasons big companies get stuck on their successes: (1) neglect: sticking with yesterday's business model; (2) pride: allowing your products to become outdated, and (3) lethargy: getting lulled into a culture of comfort.

What he observes at a high level of corporate life is what can be observed as an inability of leaders well down the ladder. In either context, hanging on too long to a past success wears thin as a model for future success.

You may remember the old TV sitcom *Married with Children*. It starred actor Ed O'Neill as Al Bundy, a father and not-so-great leader of a dysfunctional Chicago family. His wife, Peggy, and children, Kelly and Bud, each had their own issues. Al's life was stuck in the past. As an ineffective father, shoe salesman, and human being, he often would look back and state that he had once scored five touchdowns in a single high school football game. Scoring five touchdowns was the highlight of his past life, current life, and most likely the highlight that would follow his life forever. He couldn't get past it; he couldn't let it go. It colored his thoughts and actions, particularly when things got crazy, which they often did.

Al seldom had solutions to the myriad of dilemmas the Bundy's faced. His past success of scoring five touchdowns served to create his identity, gave him some comfort, but it prevented him from achieving new family and career successes.

Not a cognitive knowledge-based, but an emotion-based overreliance on a past successful event (or series of past successful events) can shape a single response pattern. That pattern causes leaders to be less effective by not thinking forward. An attitude that our past success will carry us forward is delusional. That's why Dr. Herbold titled his book *Seduced by Success*.

Bad leaders are high-centered on past successes and the aura that success casts on those who enabled it to occur. These leaders are not pleased when those who were not a part of previous successes are not impressed with using the past template as the future template. Nor are they charitable when the previous aura that shone on their leadership brilliance is not acknowledged.

Leaders who follow this pattern achieve a level of personal comfort for themselves, but not for followers. Followers frequently decide that progress is stagnant because leadership is stagnant, and their personal energy and commitment is moribund because their leadership is inept.

We live in the type of business and organizational world where this happens with surprising frequency. As comfortable as an old pair of athletic shoes are, at some point in time, they must be tossed. The inability of a supervisor to let go of a previously successful process, product, or person causes the interests of a younger or newer employee to fade. It causes the leader's credibility to fade, as well.

Certainly not everything old is bad, and not everything new is good. Yet, with some bad leaders, everything that is new is bad, and all that is old is good. Newness, goodness, and/or oldness are not the issues. Leadership effectiveness happens when it's judged by a willingness to *not* cling to former success.

Leaders are considered bad when they cling unswervingly to processes and procedures that were once successful. These are often more difficult to release because they have been routinized within individuals and organizations. With products or services, release is far easier because the market determines the need to let go.

Moreover, clinginess is particularly irritating when it manifests itself in regard to human capital. Positively recalling the exploits of athletes, actors, politicians, business luminaries, and employees of the past goes nowhere these days. What counts is what's *now*. Hearing about the exploits and contributions of successful workers from the past is not a motivator. It's like drinking a soda that has lost its fizz.

So to create a sustainable company future, it is not just the inability of older, higher-placed leaders to let go of previous success. It is also an over-dependency on technology and human-free connections that cause younger workers to resist releasing success to achieve greater success. Each work generation has its own form of clinginess.

GOOD LESSONS:

- Past success, whether created through individuals, teams, or entire organizations, has a limited shelf life.
- Success should be remembered but not consciously idolized or unconsciously allowed to impede future success.

- Past success as a deterrent to future success seems to be incongruent. It isn't.

- Bad leaders tend to believe that successes of the past are more influential and powerful to our future than they really are. They expect that we should learn more from the past than we really can.

21. Inability to Anticipate Conditions and Intentions

The capacity and sophistication of tools now available to the weather forecaster is enormous and powerful. The National Oceanic and Atmospheric Administration (NOAA), an entity of the U.S. Department of Commerce, states that there are six weather monitoring systems they use:

1. Doppler Radar
2. Satellite Data
3. Radiosondes (weather balloons)
4. Automated surface-observing systems (weather stations) include over 10,000 National Weather Service Cooperative Observers
5. Supercomputers
6. AWIPS–a computer system that syncs data from the other systems and presents it graphically on a computer screen.[22]

These powerful systems monitor weather conditions so forecasting can be done more accurately. Yet, even with these tools, the data is not always read and interpreted with absolute accuracy. Weather forecasters say, "Don't blame me. I don't make the weather; I just forecast it." Weather monitoring can only *anticipate* what will happen; it cannot guarantee what will happen.

Certainly, other occupations do the same. Predicting the weather is similar to how a handicapper picks horses to win races or how a broker predicts the surge or plunge of a company's share price. Some people even read tea leaves or chicken bones to make predictions. This, of course, is not scientific, but nonetheless, it's used to increase the likelihood that a certain set of input causes (data) will create the desired effect. Each of these requires skill in reading the data and anticipating results.

As good weather forecasters become competent at anticipating and predicting the weather conditions, so, too, must good leaders anticipate the conditions and intentions of their followers.

Weather forecasters anticipate that a certain type of weather pattern will develop. With the pattern will be wind direction and velocity, temperature, humidity, and barometric factors in the mix. Good weather forecasters anticipate whether threatening or pleasant weather conditions will occur. They are also good at helping create appropriate responses to what they anticipate might happen.

Like good weather forecasters, good leaders must have the ability to read the data at hand, interpret that data correctly, and anticipate what the mix of data will mean at some time and location in the future. They anticipate and act according to the conditions.

Although anticipating, predicting, and forecasting are pretty much synonymous, anticipating seems to have a greater intensity, because it implies there is an awareness and perhaps an effort to get ahead of what is predicted or forecast.

Good leaders seem to have a depth of insight they use to get ahead of conditions. Bad leaders seldom get ahead of challenges, but challenges seem to get ahead of them, thus placing them in a reactive or "make-up" response.

For both weathercasters and leaders, it's always better to be ahead of the storm rather than in it.

Bad leaders are not good at anticipating conditions or intentions while good leaders are good predictors of conditions. They must be also good predictors of intentions.

I haven't always been good at anticipating the intentions of others, and it has cost me greatly. The biggest disappointments I've had in business occurred when I didn't correctly anticipate the intentions of my partners. This was true both when things got really tough or when they were really good.

Perhaps you've heard that comics, politicians, and public speakers "read the room"—that is, they anticipate the attitudes, reactions, and responsiveness of listeners and mold their comments in that light.

The ability to anticipate is more of a learned behavior than an inherited trait. Observing or understanding the likely behaviors of teammates is learned. It's like a football quarterback who knows a receiver so well that he can predict what the receiver will do given a certain set of circumstances. Sometimes no verbal signal or even a nod of the head is needed to make a play. It just happens because the two have practiced together so much, they know what the most productive response will be. The magic of a long gain or a touchdown follows. Truthfully, though, the magic did not *just* happen. It was the result of anticipating the defense and both players knowing exactly how the other would react.

Motorcycling has become my primary mode of escape—but not my primary mode of relaxation. The vast majority of time motorcycling on public roadways is not relaxing, although it is enjoyable. Motorcycle riders flex between brief moments of enormous joy (even euphoria) and moments of sheer panic. That's because good motorcyclists must be competent at anticipating the intentions of others.

Properly anticipating road conditions, movements of stray animals, and the intentions of others on the road is essential for one's safety and survival. Anticipating what others may do and what you must do to stay upright is required. Anticipating road conditions is easier than anticipating the actions of people driving vehicles because road conditions are more static and predictable. One can't always read the intentions of other drivers.

Yet anticipating the intentions of others is something good leaders do with far greater accuracy than bad leaders. If a bad leader cannot predict the intention of others— customers, clients, competitors, employees, superiors, or others—either positively or negatively, then the team, workflow, and organization will suffer, perhaps critically. When cyclists improperly interpret the intentions of others, it can be fatal. It is the same with bad leaders.

Working with a good anticipator makes one's life far more relaxed and tolerable than working with someone who does not have this trait or skill. Being good at anticipation makes good leaders better.

You may have heard or read the idiom "Red sky at night; sailor's delight. Red sky in the morning; sailor's warning." This means that an informed and wise sailor will anticipate taking an action by reading the sky. The good sailor might stay in port, change direction, slow down, or speed up while battening down the hatches.

When bad leaders are inattentive to the storm, its fierceness, its direction, and its duration, it always unsettles coworkers. The wise leader, like the wise sailor, never sets sail directly into the path of a potentially disastrous storm.

GOOD LESSONS:

- Good leaders anticipate. Bad leaders aggravate their people by not getting ahead of challenges.
- Good leaders properly anticipate external societal environments and internal social climates. They accurately predict the reactionary intentions of their followers.
- Followers become frustrated with bad leaders when they feel as though they never get ahead of challenges. Rather, they are always battling from behind rather than from the lead.
- Bad leaders are not good at anticipating the results of their decisions or non-decisions.
- Good leaders have a high degree of confidence that the outcomes of their decisions will be as accurate as they predicted them to be.

22. Inability to Distinguish Truths

Throughout these pages, I've written about a number of inabilities, willingness, and refusals in which bad leaders engage as they conduct their supervisory responsibilities. The commonality among these lessons is *avoidance*, a continuing theme. So do what good leaders do and intentionally avoid the bad behaviors and choices bad leaders make.

Bad leaders have the tendency to make everything all about them. It's uncanny how bad leaders do this with such consistency and alacrity. This action becomes saddening, even maddening, because issues that should be topic-specific, activity-specific, or data-specific will be redirected to focus attention on the bad leader.

I've seen this happen in initial or hiring interviews when the focus is not on the job seeker but on the person conducting the interview. Rather than being other-centric and results-centric, the focus turns to the bad leader. This happens because either the leader is needy or is intent on proving positional power. When this occurs, others in the conversation ordinarily disengage and let the "all about me" leader continue until the meeting time runs out.

As donors to a non-profit organization, my wife and I were invited with other donors to attend a dinner cruise on Puget Sound. We anticipated a beautiful summer evening on the water with those who had a mutual interest in the mission and progress of the charity. Much to our dismay, we didn't hear anything about the nonprofit whatsoever. Everyone there was held captive to a one-and-one-quarter-hour speech by the CEO—and he talked about himself the entire time. As CEO, his role in the success of the non-profit was understood, but we didn't need to hear exclusively about his unparalleled leadership and influence in the community. Nothing was spoken that accrued to the benefit of the non-profit and the clients it served. Moreover, no one cared to hear about an editorial the CEO had recently published in a local newspaper, which he profusely claimed had received wonderful reviews. Again, there was no mention of value gained by the non-profit.

As the ship approached the dock, I leaned over and whispered to our tablemates, "If he's going to say anything about the charity and nothing more about himself, he had better hurry." Just as I finished my comment, the ship's horn sounded, and we arrived at the dock. The CEO didn't miss the opportunity to promote himself, but he sure missed an opportunity to promote the non-profit or provide an opening to contribute to it.

> **When bad leaders act as if everything important is all about them and they are the cause of all that is good, they make others feel minimized and of little or no consequence.**

The second theme to be assiduously avoided is the belief that "my truth" is the only truth. This is a behavior observed in bad leaders, but it is increasingly being seen in followers and in the culture in general.

When everyone's "truth" is the only one that matters, thought patterns become routinized in an organization, and that organization becomes nearly impossible to manage.

Good leaders are not me-centric or "my truth"-centric. They do not channel conversations or exchanges back to themselves. Good leaders can also distinguish among my truth, current truth, and real truth. Bad leaders can't.

"My truth" is the most subjective of the three. It is idiosyncratic and only relative to the person making the statement. When one person's truth is the *only* truth, there are no other truths upon which we can agree or build community.

Current truth lies between relative/subjective truth and absolute/objective truth and is subject to a time window. Current truth is good for a season but maybe not forever. Current truth is mostly transitory. What is current truth today may not be current truth tomorrow or even later today. This is due to the rate at which data, information, and knowledge is expanding, as previously discussed.

Current truth is based on the data or knowledge at hand. It may change when there is new, different, or even conflicting data. Real truth is irrefutable, unchangeable, timeless, and stable. It is the type of truth upon which individuals, groups, companies, and countries can agree and build community.

Confusion in the workplace and culture occurs when real truth is dissected and willfully disbelieved. How is it that coworkers and citizens can examine the same data, information, and knowledge, yet arrive at far different implications and applications of that truth when there are none? Truth has clearly spoken for itself! Perhaps they concentrate too much on *their* truth and the *current* truth rather than on *real* truth.

Good leaders take divergent aspirations, diversities, and personalities and meld them into a single whole for the good of the whole. Not every leader has the ability to get everyone on board, aligned, and striving for the good of the whole. Therefore, leadership must produce good for the whole through the efforts, views, aspirations, diversities, and personalities of those willing. Those unwilling to contribute are likely so because the only truth they acknowledge is their own.

Every policy, activity, or effort that works to the benefit of the whole is only beneficial when it is first beneficial to them. This is subjective self-delusion. If bad leaders think this way, it will have a destabilizing effect on their people and the mission of the organization.

GOOD LESSONS:
- Real truth enables. Current truth confuses. My truth deludes.

- Many bad leaders behave unwisely by not believing the real, irrefutable, and objective truth disclosed through trusted data.
- By not believing or acting on real truth, bad leaders lessen the frequency of making good decisions and increase the frequency of making bad ones.
- Good leaders are alert to politicized data and don't accept it as real truth.
- What person who has more and better objective data would care to follow a person who doesn't?
- Good leaders don't believe everything they hear. More often than not, bad leaders believe everything they think.
- "My truth is the only truth that matters." Tell that to your boss and see how long you have a job.
- Those who believe themselves to be able, enable others. Those who believe themselves unable, disable others. This is real truth for both good and bad leaders.

Good Lesson Affirmation
There is no FEAR (Failure, Experience, Anxiety, or Roadblock) caused by a bad leader, from which I am not learning a good lesson.

Chapter 3.

Good Lessons:
Willingness

1. Willingness to Tolerate Inconsistency

T he first time I heard of Six Sigma, I was immediately attracted to the idea of achieving error-free production processes. Having a philosophy and methodology to strip out errors and inconsistencies to 3.4 defects per million opportunities (DPMO), thus reducing costs and redoes, made sense to me. I soon made the jump to applying Six-Sigma principles to the problem of inconsistent leadership behaviors, specifically to bad leaders' behaviors.

Certainly, Six Sigma principles are more applicable in some environments than others, for they cannot completely reduce human error or control human variability. Still, reducing the errors of bad leaders would be terrific.

> Leaders lead badly when they consistently show a high tolerance for inconsistency and error.

Bad leaders allow inconsistencies in personal behaviors, in product design and manufacturing, in service delivery and support, in policies and procedures, and in behavioral expectations and employee performance. They themselves don't demand or model consistency. They are unable or unwilling to articulate the host of benefits derived from consistency, dependability, and predictable standards.

And they don't value consistently keeping commitments to employees, suppliers, and customers.

Bad leaders are prone to make on-the-fly decisions that conflict with previously established policies and procedures. They are not on the same page as others, but it doesn't bother them. If bad leaders were baseball pitchers, they would give the nod to throw a strike and then would throw a curve ball.

Inconsistency can destroy an organization's success. Consider the tale of Bill Knapp's family restaurant chain. Just the name makes me think of bean soup, great cheeseburgers, and au gratin potatoes. Bill Knapp's existed from 1948 until 2002 as a model of consistency for mid-market, casual dining in the Midwest. The food was not only well priced and tasty, but it was also incredibly consistent from restaurant to restaurant. If I liked a menu item at one Bill Knapp's, I could get exactly the same-tasting item in a different location. There was an appealingly consistent flavor, texture, color, aroma, and serving temperature to all of its food products but especially to the bean soup. Either because the soup was cooked in a central commissary or the chefs at the various units strictly adhered to recipes and standards, the consistency and value of the bean soup was assured.

Today, the consistency of bean soup at Bill Knapp's and the inconsistency observed in bad leaders seem far apart, but in fact they are not. The consistency and predictability of Bill Knapp's were its distinct competitive advantages. When the chain lost these, it lost its place in the market.

Inconsistency tends to lead to more inconsistency and toward lower standards and less success. By comparison, consistency tends to lead to greater consistency and toward higher standards and greater success.

Consistency and inconsistency engage directionality and longevity. Some products and services tend to persist in success, and others don't. Like good products, good professional sports teams tend to be consistently good, and bad teams tend to be historically and consistently bad. The bad teams just can't seem to make the jump to be among the better teams. On occasion, they might surprise their fans and have a championship season, but their predominate performance, season after season, trends toward poor. Good teams are, by-and-large, good because they do not tolerate inconsistency in their core principles, players, coaches, and office operations.

One reason such patterns occur is that consistency and inconsistency both play into your beliefs about yourself. When you establish self-belief regarding standards of success, both inconsistent and consistent directionality can occur. For this reason, some organizations never seem to get out of their own way. Inconsistency leads to less adherence to standards, and bad leaders tolerate it. Consistency produces greater adherence to standard, and good leaders expect it. In fact, they do not tolerate inconsistency.

Consistency bespeaks the value found in uniformity and the value inherent in predictability. The bean soup could only be consistent and up to standard if it were properly prepared, served, and judged to be so by the consumer. It's not just one component of the process that creates consistency, like texture or taste. All processes, standards, and outcomes must work together to create whole-systems consistency. It's like having a beautiful new car. It could have a great interior and exterior design as well as excellent audio and electronic toys, but if it has a faulty engine that refuses to start, the overall quality of the car will be judged on the inconsistency or "badness" of its engine.

When bad leaders are pretty good at most leadership functions yet highly dysfunctional in one, then that one inconsistent behavior gets the most attention. More than that, it creates vulnerability for the leader and frustration and lack of trust among followers.

Either bad leaders don't recognize inconsistency or see inconsistent outcomes or behaviors but do nothing about them. The leaders who intentionally ignore inconsistency most vex their followers. By their inaction, these leaders communicate that inconsistency will be tolerated and that consistency doesn't matter, but they will never admit it aloud.

This inconsistency is sometimes quite obvious in sports. For example, the "Jordan Rules" appeared when Michael Jordan played basketball. This euphemism stemmed from an inconsistent application of basketball rules by referees that allowed Michael Jordan to get away with rule infractions that others were not allowed. Due to his talent and cultural status, Jordan was afforded a special set of rules that applied only to him. Jordan's special treatment became a huge frustration to opposing teams and their fans. Although decried, the special rules undersold his talent and reduced the integrity of the game. The inconsistency was obvious and became a disservice to both him and to opposing teams.

Regardless of who creates or allows inconsistency to continue, planned inconsistency lessens credibility. The special status of some employees who are allowed to break rules or not meet standards creates an unhealthy organization and a minefield for those attempting set things right.

GOOD LESSONS:

- Good leaders do not create policies that are impossible to implement consistently. Bad leaders create policies, practices, and procedures that are difficult to apply consistently.
- Good leaders are extremely attentive to the consistent application of access to information and themselves.
- Bad leaders are not cognizant of the need for consistency regarding rewards, discipline, and punishment.
- Good leaders either abide by a policy or change it for the better. They will not discredit themselves by intentionally disregarding a policy or by allowing employees to disregard it.
- If a rule or operational standard is continuously ignored or inconsistently applied, it will morph negatively into another lower standard, ordinarily not for the betterment of an organization.

Bad leaders are mistaken in their belief that inconsistency is a good way to keep employees off balance and therefore productive. It isn't.

- When leaders tolerate inconsistency in their personal behaviors and management practices, employees notice, and the leader's status and influence diminish.

- Inconsistency leads to unpredictability; unpredictability leads to chaos; and chaos creates a habitat for the non-productive leader.
- The inconsistent application of rules and standards by bad leaders can become enormously frustrating because it creates uncertainty for those attempting to meet standards and smugness for those who are exempt.

2. Willingness to Enable Covetousness

Although I was raised a son of a Christian minister and should have known sooner, it took a while to discover that the Ten Commandments make a great deal of sense from a human relations, business, and leadership point of view. I must confess that the commandment I least understood was Number Ten: "Thou Shalt Not Covet." It really didn't seem to fit among the others about loving God, not murdering, and not being a false witness against your neighbor. It now makes a lot of sense and is in some ways similar to commandment number Eight: "Thou Shalt Not Steal."

Covetousness is defined as a condition of the heart that causes one to desire and to take action to possess that which is rightfully owned by another.

I began to recognize and understand covetousness after gaining experience in complex business and educational organizations. Coveting soon became evident because it was so corrosive to smooth operations and productive relationships.

Covetousness is a tactic frequently used by bad leaders to compensate for their miscalculations and lack of attentiveness to internal trends.

Covetousness can become a standard procedure and a destructive organizational way of life. It is not a practice upon which one should build a career and reputation.

Covetousness is a sure sign of an undisciplined leader who will search within the organization for resources allocated to others and attempt to make them their own. Bad leaders hope that capturing the resources of other persons or groups will make their staff better, their budget bigger, their workload lighter, and their status more secure. Watch out for the covetous folks! They'll steal you blind and show no remorse in doing so. No resource is off limits to them.

These types of unscrupulous leaders have designs on and plans for PECITs that have been allocated elsewhere. They don't care about the extra work or the organizational dislocation they cause to others if they are allowed to desire, then take, and finally control.

I have encountered many bad leaders who, although they would not admit it when challenged, provided strong evidence of coveting my budgets, my personnel, and the ideas/initiatives of my teams. These leaders don't plan or spend their resources wisely. They always make an argument for more. They don't go through all the hassles of finding their own personnel. Rather, they are likely to poach the ones that others have recruited, hired, trained, and acclimated.

Bad leaders are unwilling to pay the price and go through the difficult processes that good leaders go through to manage well. Instead, they expect that resources allocated elsewhere will rescue them.

You may have experienced the frustration of finally getting your ideal team in place, only to have it raided by someone within your organization who should have known better. Then you're left to start the process again. I'm not writing about a competitor who has made a better, more attractive offer or a prudent, justified reassignment, but an inside person who becomes an internal raider.

Most organizations have policies to prevent this or at least a means of compensating for the heists. But those that covet will go unchecked until someone above them on the organizational chart brings it to a halt.

Most exasperating are senior leaders who not only allow covetousness but encourage it through their own actions. Be alert! This may be those leaders' most obvious, negative enabling behavior.

Coveting not only occurs in personnel matters; it also occurs in regard to superior processes and ideas that can be picked off and claimed by those who did not envision or create them. I have even seen acclaim heaped on those who have stolen the ideas of others and claimed them as their own, yet they did not feel a bit of regret or shame in the process.

The covetous are always alert for ideas with clout that they can grab and claim as their own.

The act of covetousness is most blatant when bad leaders attempt to secure additional financial resources from allocations other than their own. Someone else argued for and received these dollars to operate, but they become the target of redistribution. Occasional, temporary re-distribution of budget dollars for the good and re-balancing of the organization are not at issue. It's those dollars that some people seek for narrow purposes and their own benefit.

What do you possess that has been coveted? It may be a corner office, a more suitable cubicle, a territory, a membership, a parking place, a relationship with a client, customers, or preferred vendor. It could be your time, your opportunities, your job, or your status. Nothing is off limits to the covetous leader or co-worker, even your office furniture.

I once came into my university office to find that the guest chairs assigned to my office were missing. I wondered who had the nerve to remove them from a senior VP's office. After a search, I found them in the office of another VP down the hall. His administrative assistant thought they looked better in that guy's office and removed them from mine without authorization. I soon learned that if people would covet my office chairs, they would attempt to do the same in more consequential matters. Through experience, I became alert to the ways covetousness can disrupt relationships and organizational tranquility.

Just look at what coveting the ring did to Gollum in *Lord of the Rings*. Don't be like Gollum!

GOOD LESSONS:

- Build your reputation as a good leader who refuses to covet the PECITs of others and who won't manipulate the facts to deprive others of the resources they require to carry out their responsibilities.
- Good leaders strongly discourage their direct reports from coveting the resources of others. In doing so, they encourage more discernment in cre-

ating budgets and caution in resource expenditures. If not, their people are likely to go on the hunt for the resources of others as a first response to resource shortfalls.

- Good leaders don't need to possess what belongs to colleagues. Instead, they lead well, are productive, and manage effectively with the resources provided.

- If you need additional resources, don't go through back channels to acquire them. Create your plan, state your case to the right people, and move ahead whether additional funds are made available or not. Don't pout if you don't succeed in your requests. Good leaders don't.

- Be alert to the leader who trolls for resources to snatch away. Their behavior is likely to occur during periods of high stress, at predictable times within the budget cycle, or when they have recently lost personnel.

- Make convincing initial arguments regarding your budget needs so your teams can live within its allocation and won't need to covet the resources of others.

---

3. Willingness to Impoverish

Willful impoverishment is so pervasive that nearly every world culture has a political, social, or literary example of it. Remember the story of Cinderella? Cinderella was financially, emotionally, and physically impoverished at the hands of her stepmother who intended that one of her own daughters escape work, marry the prince, secure the privileges of court, and experience the long tail of being the royal mother-in-law.

We are happy when Cinderella goes to the ball, meets the prince, fits the shoe, and marries him. The wicked stepmother and stepsisters' actions are discovered and punished for their impoverishment strategies.

While Cinderella is a folk tale, her experience of impoverishment is a real strategy used by bad leaders to deny access to resources. Most individuals have or will encounter it to a greater degree sometime during their careers.

You might think that a willingness to impoverish as a display of power is a rare thing and the stuff of folk tales. However, I have come to realize that for many bad leaders, it is a standard practice.

Bad leaders within organizations, cultures, and governments will block, change, and purposefully distort reality to serve their own ends, including the planned impoverishment of others.

Perhaps you recall or have seen videos of the enormous May Day parades in Moscow during the heyday of the Soviet Union. They were impressive. It was sobering to see tanks and missiles on display as a show of military power, realizing that western nations, particularly the United States, were the primary targets of all that military might.

What was not realized was the enormous toll it took on the Soviet economy and its citizens to produce and maintain all those armaments. To a lesser degree, the same thing could be said about western nations and certainly the U.S. However, the stunning reality was the willingness of the Soviet leaders to callously impoverish their people to maintain their military and personal power. The USSR eventually imploded, not because the guns and bombs were too few, but because the ideology to support the impoverishment of its people would no longer be tolerated.

On a smaller scale, the bad leaders' "impoverishment" catalog includes practices like keeping someone waiting. It marks a display of power highlighting the importance of the leaders' time and their ability to waste another person's time.

A last-minute rescheduling, cancellation, or relocation of a meeting without notice, a planned lack of punctuality, or a failure to provide a timely email or Twitter response are examples of a willingness to rob subordinates of resources needed to carry out their responsibilities. It's a form of impoverishment. These are common yet deplorable practices for bad leaders and exactly the opposite of what they should do. Withholding praise, encouragement, or information is also a form of intentional impoverishment.

Impoverishment is used as a means to humiliate, punish, control emotions or resources, or send a message. It is a choice to deny assets—including ideas, information, solutions, and/or approvals—when they are available and within a leader's power to allocate. Bad leaders use impoverishment as a means to achieve status separation and intimidate others. This tactic causes followers to perform less ably and may deter those who desire to move up in the organization. Intentional stalling, thwarting actions, and blocking conduits are also examples of willful impoverishment.

Acts of impoverishment can also be intentional personal "put downs" that diminish the emotional or vocational well-being of fellow workers. Impoverishment emanates from the heart of leaders who don't value or serve associates properly. They don't have a grasp of what is required to keep the best interests of others in mind.

Most large-scale impoverishment strategies can't be successfully executed without the agreement of co-conspirators, as in a Ponzi scheme. Most bad leaders need others to share in the execution of the impoverishment, but the larger the number of participants, the greater the likelihood of discovery.

If an impoverishment mentality is allowed to succeed or go unchallenged, it is likely to spread within the organization, and it will corrode trust, relationships, and productivity.

The act of impoverishment has another side.

Bad leaders impoverish in order to enrich themselves and those people and programs they believe have merit when often they factually don't.

Bad leaders may not actually steal resources, but they deprive others of the enrichment and flexibility that resources enable.

Willing impoverishment expresses qualities of a leader's character but it's not a proper expression of the leader's legitimate power. Insidious and unproductive, impoverishment can be seen at all levels of an organization but tends to skew to lower levels.

The willingness to impoverish reveals the character of its devotees who tend to get eliminated earlier rather than later in their careers and while at low levels of the organization. Such leaders seek to secure power to determine where resources are expended, to fund their agenda, and to keep resources out of the hands of those they consider threats. These leaders believe that, if they can keep people impoverished and ignorant, then they will be in control.

Occasionally in my college classes, I demonstrate the distortion and destructive outcomes of having too many links in a communication system and the willingness of those in a chain to impoverish others through creating message inaccuracies. I start a secret message at one end of a long chain of students and see what occurs by the time the message gets to the other end. For example, I once whispered, "Its fleece was white as snow." When the message got to the other end, it came out as "Her slip began to show." This was among many other interpretations!

I knew that some mischievous student would likely distort the message on purpose to get a laugh and hope I would point a finger of accusation at a classmate, allowing this act of sabotage to go unnoticed. The results of this exercise could be hilarious. Yet, I always let students know that people within organizations will block, change, deny, and purposefully distort the truth to serve their own ends—to the planned impoverishment and embarrassment of others.

Bad leaders often use a progression of four steps to gain control. When asking for *more information*, they really desire to *determine what is communicated*. When they ask for better communication, they really *seek greater power*, but they won't admit it. When they secure greater power, they are really *after more control*.

The first two in the progression—information and communication—are more innocuous than power and control, what bad leaders really desire. By aggregating power and control, bad leaders gain opportunities to allocate resources. When they choose unfairly, preferentially, and capriciously to control and punish by denying resources, they show their willingness to impoverish.

Early in my academic teaching career, I agreed to serve as the Sports Information Director at a small college. The biggest sport on campus was men's basketball. It was my job to report the scores of games to the wire services, so the results could be distributed to media outlets. To successfully do this job, it was necessary to get access to a telephone immediately after a game and inform the wire services before their 10 p.m. deadlines. This happened before cell phones and the Internet, which would have made the task enormously less difficult. But because the basketball games often went long, I had to sprint across campus to my academic office to get access to a phone. Although it wasn't a large and sprawling campus, it was a pain to reach my office in time to meet the deadline.

To solve this problem I asked the head of public relations to contact the athletic director (AD) and request access to a telephone in the gymnasium where the games were played. The head of PR said I should make the request for access directly to the AD. So, I asked him for access to a suite of offices with a phone

I could use immediately after the games. He agreed but stipulated that I would have to find him to open the locked office after each game.

This system worked well for a couple of games, although it was difficult to find him among the exiting fans. Also, he seemed irritated that I would break into his post-game activities to have him unlock the door. So to speed up accessing the newswires, I came up with what I thought was an easy way to solve the problem. I requested I be assigned my own key to the office containing the phone; then I wouldn't need to bug him after each game. Well, by asking for a key, you would have thought I was attempting to break into Fort Knox or to steal his first child. The AD hit the roof! In no uncertain terms, he indicated that key control was totally within his discretion, that I didn't need access to *his* phone in order to do *my* job. Geez, Louise, this simple request set off a firestorm.

As I look back on this, I have come to understand that asking for a key to access an office phone was not the issue at all. My proposal and the AD's subsequent response were all about his willingness to withhold a resource and be helpful. It was a show of power and intentional impoverishment more than anything else. I guess he didn't like the teaching staff or (as I surmised) the top PR guy either, so he'd take any opportunity to put us in our places by denying requests related to athletic facilities.

This was the first time I had ever encountered an impoverishment attitude, and I still remember its sting. Had I not perceived what was actually going on, it would have negatively affected my self-esteem and perhaps my performance downstream. I realize that purposeful impoverishment is a normal but negative behavior for bad leaders.

Because of its detrimental effects, I am amazed at how long bad leaders are allowed to get away with malevolent behavior.

Without experiencing a sense of fair play and justice at work, employees easily lose their commitment to their jobs.

When I perceive purposeful impoverishment used among those supervised, I quickly deal with it to the long- and short-term benefit of all concerned. If you see corruptive power, you must do the same.

Unfortunately, we are all acquainted with corruptive power. But it is the *sting* of corrupted power that's difficult to teach and learn without actually going through it.

I have often spoken with beleaguered leaders and employees about how this behavior can be detrimental to everyone's confidence and energy. Once they realize that Cinderella is not entirely a folk tale, they can understand this deplorable fact of organizational and political life. And they must deal with the problem to increase motivational energy, degree of engagement, and confidence while resolving to *not* behave in a similar fashion.

GOOD LESSONS:

- Good leaders don't purposefully impoverish. They justify their actions when they are forced to withdraw resources for reallocation elsewhere.
- Good leaders are alert to the attempts of bad leaders to impoverish others and will actively thwart them because they understand such actions are wholly unproductive and divisive.
- Good leaders deploy assets to achieve positive benefits for all concerned and not only for the few who have a most-favored status.
- Good leaders build their influence through their right actions, attitudes, and willingness to share.
- Good leaders know that the allocation of resources indicates priorities. They are thoughtful and attentive regarding what budget priorities communicate to internal and external constituents. Resource allocations send strong messages about what is most important and what is less important by what gets funded and what doesn't.

Bad leaders impoverish others by withholding resources and support when resources and support are within their power to allocate.

- Bad leaders aggregate and consume resources while followers remain resource-starved. Good leaders don't allow this to happen.

- Bad leaders attempt to build their power through impoverishment; good leaders don't.

- Bad leaders care little about what resource allocations communicate unless the allocations impinge on their ability to control rewards or to enact impoverishment.

- Bad leaders are indifferent to the effects that resource impoverishment and reallocation have on the motivation and job satisfaction of those from whom resources have been withheld or unjustifiably taken.

- Bad leaders deny assets to demonstrate their willingness to impoverish. Don't emulate them.

- As a good leader, you must act decisively when you learn that purposeful impoverishment has occurred among those you supervise. Deal with it quickly. Letting the impoverishment continue sends a deleterious message about the strength of your leadership and your sense of fair play.

4. Willingness to Bail Out and Abandon

Not one of the images associated with the idea of a bailout has a positive connotation.

Among them are bailing out of a crashing plane, a failing relationship, a dead-end job, a boring evening, or a release from jail.

A "bailout" relates to financial or business failures when the government steps in to rescue a poorly managed organization or a business that has been impacted by economic decline.

The noun "bailout" has some positive overtones if doing so enables you to escape undesirable circumstances. Depending on your political and economic position, bailouts could be seen in a positive light. Nonetheless, both the verb "bail out" and the noun "bailout" have underlying threads that indicate something went wrong and is not as optimal as it should be.

"Bail out" refers to an action taken in response to not finding a way through a difficult situation, not hanging tough, or not gutting it out. It occurs when one gives up, gives in, or runs out of energy or will power to persist.

Bail out is what bad leaders do; abandonment is what followers feel.

Bad leaders tend to bail out or give up on challenges and people. They lack the skills or interest to exercise patience until the tide turns, situations improve, or people learn. The next step for bad leaders after bailing out is abandonment. There is no more negative emotional abyss than to realize you have been abandoned.

Yet, bad leaders rarely give abandonment a second thought. They are not likely to provide assistance and a bailout for you and your team. They will just bail out themselves and abandon you, your team, and your ideas or work in progress.

The ability to recover from a stressor such as abandonment is called resilience. Some people seem to naturally have more of this quality than others. In truth, however, resilience is a learned skill. Those who have not been abandoned may have difficulty understanding it and overcoming the emotional toll from it.

In the face of abandonment or other setbacks not of your own making, learning to seek help from others and develop long-term stable relationships is essential for your emotional, physical, psychological, and spiritual well-being. These relationships also help you resist the urge to bail out, thereby abandoning your post, people, and responsibilities.

Bad leaders show their willingness to bail out and abandon their duties, teams, and the initiatives they have led by their emotional choices. Emotional abandonment can be as destructive as physical abandonment. Again, I've often said, "I don't mind when an employee or leader quits and leaves, but I do mind it when an employee or leader quits and stays."

Such leaders often make self-centered choices, indicating their inability to place themselves on the other side of challenges and obstacles. These choices show such leaders act on emotional and psychological stimuli rather than on intellectual reason and/or factual evidence.

Callousness and indifference to the potential harm that abandonment causes aren't a problem for bad leaders.

Bad leaders place themselves and their interests above the needs of others, and they discount the effect of their abandonment. They tend to see it as no big deal, when, in fact, it is an extremely big deal in the eyes of the persons being abandoned.

Bruce Springsteen wrote a song about a guy who bails out. He abandons his family and seems justified in doing so because he has a "hungry, hungry heart."

Got a wife and kids in Baltimore, Jack

I went out for a ride and I never went back[23]

What a sad commentary on being a bad husband and irresponsible father.

Bad leaders tend to abandon those people, plans, and responsibilities for which they previously might have appeared to show strong commitment. So, the weaker the original commitment, the greater the ease with which abandonment occurs. Bad leaders tend to hide their weak commitment, hoping no one will perceive they are inclined toward the path of least resistance, not the pursuit of highest value. This is not the same as a justifiable, evidence-based change of mind. Rather, it's a profound change of support for previously agreed-upon plans and people.

This behavior is what I call "rabbiting," named for the western jack rabbit. Western jack rabbits are extremely fast, unpredictable runners. When threatened, they sprint quickly away, only to stop abruptly, look around, park themselves, or sprint away again in another direction. Their behaviors vary among sprinting, stopping, changing direction, then repeating the process—just like a lot of bad leaders. Leaders who, in spite of prior understandings, agreements, and even public announcements, tend to make quick turns and race in another direction. They abandon their prior commitments to the surprise and dismay of their colleagues and fellow workers.

I was employed at a university whose president "rabbited" on a regular basis. The university advancement staff and volunteers had worked for months on the creation of a capital campaign, leadership gifts, and pre-launch event. We followed the pre-approved and agreed-upon plan and had begun executing the plan. We had printed all support documentation and PR collateral, prepared press releases, and got ready to launch the public phase of the campaign.

Yet when we were introducing the plan to our alumni leaders and campaign volunteers at the launch event, the president rabbited. Certainly he had the right to change his mind and redirect the campaign, but we sure wished he had told us about it prior to this event. As it turned out, he changed the entire approach to the campaign on the fly while speaking at the campaign launch.

For the staff and volunteers, the air went out of the room. Shock appeared on our faces, as we were caught off guard, feeling abandoned and embarrassed.

We had experienced excitement and anticipation until the bailout, abandonment, and betrayal came. In a few brief moments, all of our work was spontaneously discarded. We wiped the egg off our faces and started again. After the incredible surprise, we were left with an inferior capital campaign plan created by a leader who had rabbited. The staff never regained momentum; the president lost support; and the campaign failed to raise the funds we had anticipated.

> When leaders abandon commitments and mutually agreed-upon plans, they violate deep cultural codes by placing their interests ahead of the interest of others and failing to provide "fair warning." They engender resentment and are less believable. They might as well wear a *Caution!* sign around their necks.

When bad leaders abandon their people and their duties even with threatening circumstances and uncertain outcomes, they create an environment in which the re-establishment of trust is nearly impossible.

Betrayal is hard to overcome. It takes a high degree of commitment and maturity to return to normalcy and productivity. Once the followers perceive an act of abandonment as betrayal, their attitudes change, and restoration of confidence becomes unlikely. One of two events usually occur. Either the leader who has bailed out moves to a job where the abandonment is unknown or will have less impact, or those who experienced the abandonment/betrayal will determine that the bad leader they know is better than the bad leaders they don't know. They reconcile to the status quo.

At times, it is necessary to make changes in strategy, policy, and personnel—totally justifiable. But leaders who prematurely and continually abandon products, policies, and people as a standard operational practice are not likely to be revered or trusted in the future.

In the workplace, I have seen bad leaders who having abandoned their people and then find that those abandoned cover for them and justify the behavior. It's like the Stockholm syndrome in which captives become sympathetic to their captors.

It would take a good amount of deep therapy to unpack this type of unmerited support, but it seems to be a form of mistaken loyalty as the abandoned persons discount the betrayal. The bad leader exercises a form of control in which their support is exchanged for job and financial security. When analyzing the situation, innocent employees sometimes blame themselves, the work group, or the job rather than the bad leader who has abandoned and betrayed them.

Abandonment is most clearly evident when, for no justifiable reason, bad leaders choose to dismiss or devalue and reassign people as a means of hiding errors and problems they have created. Bad leaders also use this technique to deflect criticism.

An organization can easily abandon a single person when that person's project or initiative no longer suits the goals of the organization. It is one thing for a person to be abandoned; it is quite another to have a product, service, or project into which you have poured your intellect, energy, and future be abandoned. The feeling of betrayal is very much the same.

This is one of the reasons I have advised would-be leaders to exercise caution and never become too closely identified with a single, speculative initiative that narrowly defines their abilities and value to the organization. If the project is abandoned, they too will be abandoned. Many times, teams of employees are viewed as having been so closely integrated into a failed project or identified with failed leaders that when the project goes out the door, they do, too.

Bad leaders' willingness to bail out and abandon their followers has yet another dark side. They might treat their followers as beasts or boxes to be used until they fall apart. For example, consider the horses used during the Alaskan Gold Rush. Just a few miles north of Skagway, Alaska, lie the infamous Chilkoot and White Horse Passes—two of the primary routes to the Yukon gold fields where the gold rush started in 1896.

Chilkoot Pass proved to be an enormously difficult, dangerous climb. As the route went through Canada, Canadian officials required that 1500 pounds of varied provisions be in hand before the would-be miners were released to continue their quests to the gold fields. A portion of White Pass came to be known as Dead Horse Trail. In their obsession to reach the gold fields, would-be miners would pack their horses and cruelly work them to death. The hopeful miners rolled the bodies of their horses off the path to accumulate in the valley below. An estimated three thousand horses died while carrying supplies up and over the steep mountain.[24]

Some of the worst leaders are those who treat people as though they were horses to be abused, worked to exhaustion, and abandoned to die.

The willingness of bad leaders to abandon those who have labored on their behalf to the detriment of their own careers is a difficult reality that could take years to overcome. I have had a few employees and students who have expressed their inability to trust due to previous painful abandonment events. It is my sense that the leaders most willing to abandon their teams are those who have, at some point, felt the most abandoned themselves. Thus, they justify their actions. Conversely, those leaders who have been most supported and cared for are the ones least likely to abandon others.

You may recall a "Seinfeld" TV episode in which George Costanza pushes his way through a group of children during what he thought was an escape from a fire. George proves himself to be a despicable and unfeeling person, only concerned about his safety to the detriment of others attempting to escape.

Like George, bad leaders are likely to look to their own well-being first and foremost, ignoring the needs of others in the process. The selflessness that allows others to be considered before oneself is admired in good leaders. Its opposite is not admired, nor should it be emulated.

I wonder how the passengers and crew felt when the captain of the cruise ship Costa Concordia[25] bailed out on them and abandoned ship after running aground in Italy in 2012. It seems they were justified in calling him Captain Coward. He, like many other bad leaders, did not give abandonment a second thought.

GOOD LESSONS:

- If you change your mind on a plan, person, or initiative, don't "rabbit." Provide proper time for others to process the implications of the change.

- Don't make public announcements without prepping those who will be most affected by abandoning previously agreed-upon initiatives.
- Announce a change in direction to your immediate associates directly; otherwise, the change is likely to be seen as abandonment. Don't rely on someone else to do this for you.
- If you are forced to resign, make sure (as much as possible) your team is fully aware of the circumstances and your near-term status. Don't leave them feeling abandoned, even if you have been terminated.
- Bad leaders are those unwilling to commit themselves deeply to the improvement of others. They continually look for new career and personal opportunities and the fastest way out of their obligations. They are most likely to abruptly abandon their duties and their teams while feeling justified in doing so.
- Bad leaders mentally justify and minimize the emotional impact of bailing out and abandoning their associates.
- Bad leaders do not see bailing out and abandonment through the eyes of employees or coworkers but through their own dispassionate eyes. Don't be like them.
- Bad leaders create churn, doubt, and organizational anxiety through the sequence of bailing out, abandonment, and betrayal.

Bad leaders behave as though humans are disposable and unaffected by overuse. Good leaders never do.

- Bad leaders create workloads so excessive that they endanger the well-being of their followers. This act abandons sound leadership principles and betrays followers. Bad leaders think that burnout is an example of an employee well used.
- There is nothing wrong with self-interest but a whole lot wrong with selfishness, which lies at the heart of unwarranted abandonment.
- Strategic plans *du jour* are evidence of an over-eagerness to bail out.

5. Willingness to Provoke Purposefully

As a child, I had a friend with whom I enjoyed riding bikes, ice skating, and playing baseball. But I always felt more comfortable when we played baseball at my house, a city park, or at our school. When we went to his place, I was terrified by "Sarge," his next door neighbor's huge German shepherd guard dog. This was not a warm, fuzzy, friendly type of animal. He was a big, noisy, teeth-baring dog intent on attacking whomever was unfortunate enough to foul the ball over the fence. Bothering Sarge was the last thing we wanted to do. I still get chills thinking about that mean old dog, but I have come to realize his behavior was the result of his owner training and provoking him to be vicious.

In the movie *Taken*,[26] Liam Neeson plays the role of the father of a young woman abducted and sold into sex slavery by human traffickers while in Paris. You may recall the scene where the father confronts the abductor on the phone. Their conversation is an excellent example of how the father is justifiably provoked and what actions he will take if his daughter is not immediately released.

The word "provoke" applies to what many bad leaders cause to happen among those they should serve and motivate. "To provoke" means to arouse and stir up, but this definition seems like the definition for "to motivate." A definition more pertinent to bad leadership is "to induce to anger, frustrate, irritate, and incite in order to arouse a negative course of action."

The insidious part of provoking someone to negative action is that such behaviors can indeed degenerate into harm and failure. On occasion, even good leaders can frustrate those with whom they work based on an opposing point of view or time pressure, not intentional provocation. Provocation is an unproductive motivational strategy in which leaders motivate followers by making them angry.

Bad leaders can be labeled as provocateurs when they attempt to frustrate and purposefully arouse employees to take a certain course of action or inaction. The techniques include deliberate angering, poking, prodding, and intimidation. Many of the bad leaders' actions seem like using an electric prod to move cattle. Unsurprisingly, people don't react well, and this technique leads to personal frustrations and team turmoil.

Provocation is not a means to properly motivate people.

Provocation is a form of intimidation. It is also a distraction from more important issues, because followers concentrate on the provocation rather than on their goals. At worst, provocation can be wholly unproductive by minimizing the regard followers have for leaders and leaders have for followers.

On occasion, provocation may have some brief, short-term benefits, but in the long run, it just doesn't work. Continued use of provocation is not only hurtful but difficult to correct once it has taken root. Why? Because it is a condition of the heart of the user. Provocation always causes some degree of harm.

Good leaders do not motivate others to action by intentional provocation. At their core, they have the best interests of all those people they lead. Such leaders balance rationality and emotion to motivate their followers toward achieving great results. Great mentors and coaches don't use this strategy and nor should good leaders.

Leadership by provocation is not uncommon, but it's a more subtle form of ineffectiveness than other behaviors reviewed in this book. When uncovered, it is clearly seen as an ineffective and disruptive type of leadership.

Such techniques are likely to appear in coaching. For example, at a junior high school basketball game I attended, at half time, I witnessed a coach verbally assault, humiliate, and attempt to provoke his players. Everyone else heard it too! Although I sat at half-court and a long way from the locker room, I heard his intense barrage on the players.

Previously, I had seen that same coach grab a player and throw him into a courtside seat in a moment of anger. That told me what he was capable of. As the verbal assault raged on, I could bear it no longer and hurried to the locker room to intervene. I asked the coach to calm down, back off, and use other means of motivation than his negative, mean-spirited provocations. He demanded I exit the locker room, which I did. The remarkable thing was not the coach's lack of judgment and indiscretion or even my boldness. It's amazing that the players cheered loudly when I came to their defense and called out the coach for his abusive language and provocations.

Provocation reflects a person's character. Like that coach, bad leaders who use provocation see little downside to its application because they are hardened to its usage. This is the kind of leader you don't want to work for or in whose hands you wouldn't care to place in your future.

I worked at a university whose chairman of the board saw his primary role as getting under the skin of the faculty and staff as a means of keeping them in line. He was willing to frustrate, badger, and provoke faculty members to develop attitudes and take actions that would hurt their status when it came to promotions and tenure. Additionally, because of his vindictiveness, he would use any means or person, including senior administrators and other trustees, to do his bidding. This caused a great deal of animosity and unrest as it would in any organization. He was particularly pained whenever faculty members were legitimately acknowledged for their academic achievements and contributions to the institution.

Unfortunately, this type of provocation is not an isolated case but a more widespread occurrence than what is expected of humane, non-profit organizations. Provocations of this nature are wholly unnecessary, unproductive, and insidious to an organization's mission and desired results.

GOOD LESSONS:

Good leaders inspire; bad leaders provoke.

- Good leaders enable followers to concentrate on achieving goals, not on the frustration and irritation they feel as a result of provocations.
- If you provoke and frustrate friends, you probably won't have any.
- If you provoke and frustrate customers, you probably won't have any.
- If you provoke and frustrate those you lead, you probably won't have followers to lead.
- If you provoke others to action, you will always be remembered as a person who excites, irritates, and negatively induces, rather than one who positively influences others toward good actions.
- Leaders who provoke others to action will always be remembered for their provocations and not for their achievements.
- Bad leaders who provoke others to action may obtain results they desire, but they won't have the trust and esteem of those they attempt to lead.

- Provocation can become the only trump card for bad leaders. They will use it when they have exhausted other means to persuade and motivate. Followers will eventually notice. Then it will take ever greater provocations to elicit the behaviors and results the leaders desire.

---

6. Willingness to Overcommit

The act of stealing bases in baseball is a valuable tool to increase the likelihood of advancing toward home plate, scoring, and winning the game. Yet, it is not without risks. To do it well requires good observation skills, foot speed, superb sliding techniques, a need to tolerate risk, and an ability to get a jump on the opposing pitcher. The best base stealers can also get into the opposing pitcher's head. If the player misjudges, leans too far toward the next base or home plate, or leaves too late, the likelihood of being called "out" dramatically increases.

Occasionally, even the best base stealer will over-commit and not have sufficient resources like speed and proper technique to execute the steal. Once in a while, the runner hesitates and doesn't have sufficient time to move to the next base or return to the original base. The hesitation/indecision results in getting picked off or caught in a pickle and run down, all of which the runner wanted to avoid.

Bad leaders are much like bad base stealers; they overcommit without sufficient resources to execute. They are likely to underestimate the resources required to overcome internal obstacles and the competition, much like a base stealer might underestimate the resources required to overcome the strength and accuracy of an opposing catcher's throwing arm.

> The bad leader's over-commitment to producing too much in too short a time with too few resources can profoundly demotivate those expected to make good on the leader's commitments.

In fact, over-commitments can cause anger, a loss of trust and productivity, and even justify giving up.

I first learned this concept in high school when I was a member of a top-ranked vocal choir. We were good because our director Mr. Melton was demanding yet pleasant, affirming, and able to produce excellence from our talents. Delta Records thought we were good, too, so they produced a Christmas album that contained some of our difficult pieces.

Then the choir participated in a choral workshop at Central Michigan University. There, an overzealous music professor forced us to perform a piece of music written by Dieterich Buxtehude. The song was beyond the choir's ability. When the professor pushed too hard, it led to total exasperation, a shutdown, and a walk-off. Singing the "Buxtehude" as he required humiliated us. It went beyond our skills, talent, maturity, and the time we had to learn the piece and perform it well.

I recall thinking that if I ever got into a position of leadership, I would never cause a similar meltdown, embarrassment, and disheartening defeat. Stretching the choir was okay but humiliating us by requiring us to perform a piece of music we couldn't learn in the allotted time was unacceptable. Mr. Melton showed himself a true leader when he publicly criticized the college professor for treating our choir in such a rude, demeaning way. From Mr. Melton I learned *good lessons* about capacity, resource allocation, and ways that good leaders step up and protect their people from others who demand too much of them.

A disheartening defeat like my choir experienced also occurs in workers when they are required to perform truly impossible tasks. Bad leaders will overcommit them without providing the funds, time, and additional people needed to complete a task well.

Bad leaders are irresponsible and unfair when they require optimum achievement without providing sufficient resources to do so.

It's like requiring a team to play baseball with insufficient players or no bats.

The indifference bad leaders show when they have overcommitted is among their most egregious characteristics. The "I don't care what it takes, just do it" attitude never builds confidence or *esprit de corps* among followers. Bad leaders overcommit to an action or deliverable at the expense of those who are charged with actually making it happen.

Good leaders sometimes ask their followers to stretch, expand, and move beyond themselves to achieve, but not to a point of likely defeat. Leaders that overcommit to a project or deliverable—especially at the expense of those charged with actually making it happen—are seldom able to regain the trust of followers who have long memories.

A good example of the balance required to adequately provision and motivate a team is shown in the history of the Lewis and Clark Expedition that occurred between 1802 and 1804. The Corps of Discovery, as it was called, is a great story of exceptional leadership, huge logistical challenges, and sketchy information. A lesser-known fact about the expedition was the planning that went into its preparation and provisioning. Although they didn't fully understand what the rigors of the trip would require, Lewis and Clark did not skimp on essentials. Food, tools to acquire food during the journey, scientific and medical supplies, weaponry, trading goods, and available maps and intelligence were accumulated. In the two-year adventure, only one man was lost and that was due to appendicitis early in the trip. They provisioned as well as they could, given the knowledge at hand. This enabled their successful exploration and cemented their reputations as good leaders.

History shows the Corps of Discovery to be a success because it had funding and the support of President Jefferson. It also had good leaders, men willing to follow, and an experienced guide, Sacagawea, who was retained *en route*. Certainly the Corps had to be spontaneous to acquire additional resources while traveling, but before they started, they had planned and acquired as many provisions as possible.

GOOD LESSONS:

- Good leaders are realistic and generally more accurate about resource requirements than bad leaders. They don't intentionally skimp or overestimate the resources needed.
- Be cautious while working for a leader who has a history of overcommitting to projects and initiatives without the resource allocations to fulfill

them, particularly when requirements for human resources are underestimated. It will never end in less work for you.

When you hear a leader say, "We can take on a new initiative with the same head count, financial, and time resources," beware that the leader might not include him/herself in the mix, and "we" means "you."

- Bad leaders become braggarts and overly optimistic about their group's capacity to bring a project in on budget and on time. Beware of the leader who makes a project sound too easy.
- As the primary resource, human beings take up the slack and compensate for other resource shortfalls when the over-commitments of bad leaders take effect. This pattern has long-term negative results.
- One way to determine the difference between good leaders and bad ones is to investigate the amount of unplanned resource use after a competed job and discover any excess resources are disposed of. Bad leaders hurriedly (and often needlessly) consume or bury resources. Good leaders return unused funds or resources. Bad leaders don't like to return resources, particularly employee FTEs, even for the greater good of the organization. They envision excess resources as rewards for their efforts.

Bad leaders have as much difficulty scaling down as they do ramping up.

- Bad leaders are likely to ramp up efforts and acquire resources for projects that will be career builders for them. They care about being in the limelight and seen as the prime resource for the project.

Bad leaders are not eager to reallocate their time and energy to projects controlled by others, deemed for the greater good of the organization, or not seen as career-builders for themselves.

- Achieving the correct resource balance can be a substantial challenge. Overprovisioning leads to waste, careless usage, and end of fiscal year splurges. Under provisioning leads to scarcity, competition, frustration, and fear that resources will be concentrated in the hands of a few ineffective and dispassionate leaders.

---

7. Willingness to Manage Problems Rather Than Solve Them

I always enjoyed the reaction of my students and advisees to the following statement. "The problem with being a good, problem-solving leader is that one gets successively harder problems to solve."

For some students this was a new idea, because they were mistaken in their notion that the higher people go, the easier the problem-solving becomes. Again, in reality, the higher people go within an organization, the greater the difficulty at finding solutions to problems. The problems that end up on the plates of the highest ranking leaders are the ones that have not been solved at a lower level and are the most difficult.

> Those at the highest levels of leadership are seldom called on to solve simple problems, because those problems have already been solved by someone in a lower position.

Other students and advisees were convinced that their workplace problems never really got solved; they just moved around to someone else or ignored altogether in hopes that the problems would just disappear.

As you rise on the organization chart, you will likely have additional human and financial resources to help solve difficult problems. The real difference in solving difficult problems at higher levels is that you have substantially less time to determine problem-solving strategies and durable solutions.

And I believe that problems don't often get fully solved. They only get managed to a degree that they have a less negative impact. Or, they are subsumed within bigger problems. Problem managers are not problem fixers. Problem managers may have the diagnostic and analytical skills to determine the source of a problem but not the moxie and discipline to fix it. Commercial markets do not allow problem managing to persist for long. They demand that leaders solve problems.

Bad leaders don't solve problems; they just make them appear less onerous.

Bad leaders occasionally appear to have solved a problem, but a problem is not fully solved if it is only moved elsewhere within the organization. *Shifting* **problems is not the same as** *solving* **problems.**

A corollary of shifting problems is the tendency to change the direction of a sinking boat (organization) rather than plug the hole that causes the boat to take on water and eventually sink. No amount of course changing will compensate for the effect of a hole in the hull. People who can indeed solve problems threaten the bad leader who only knows how to problem manage. The leader to whom those people present a threat is also the type of leader who will defy evidence and attempt to persuade followers that a problem doesn't really exist.

For example, a majority in the U.S. Congress refuses to recognize the federal debt as a problem because they don't have bold solutions to excessive spending or even the will to attempt to balance the budget. In American history, there are few (if any) better examples of an unwillingness to solve problems than this. It's likely the reason Congress's performance is rated so poorly. Citizens know that Congress will not solve the debt problem.

For bad leaders, problem solving lacks attraction. If they solve problems, they will run out of problems to manage and thus become expendable. Or, should they reveal themselves as disciplined problem solvers, they will shortly have more difficult problems to solve. That's also not an attractive alternative. Although unadmitted, this type of thinking is frequently found in highly bureaucratic organizations where breakout achievement and problem solving is scorned and where employee performance evaluation is marginalized.

I suspect you would much prefer to have a reputation for being a problem *solver*, not just a problem *manager*.

The difficulty with being a problem *solver* is that people who are identified as such threaten those higher in the organization who are only seen as problem *managers*.

I came across this type of thinking during a conversation with a family attempting to adopt a child. It seemed that if a family was evaluated, found to be acceptable, and a child located, an adoption could be completed. Then everyone would be happy, and the problem of giving a child a home would be solved for all concerned. But to my surprise and dismay, the problem may have been solved for the family and child but not for the state-managed adoption agency. If the child were adopted, there would be fewer cases to manage. So, wanting to preserve their jobs instead of solving the problem, the case workers managed it by stalling and preventing adoptions. Tragic!

GOOD LESSONS:
- Good leaders solve problems, then move along to the next challenging problem.
- Good leaders find solutions that fix problems permanently while not creating unintended negative consequence downstream.
- As much as possible, good leaders do not pass along their unsolved problems to their successors. When this happens, the incoming leader frequently blames the predecessor for the status of the organization and uses the argument as an excuse for not making positive progress and truly solving problems. When left unsolved intentionally or because of ineffectiveness, problems compound. Unfortunately, they become even more difficult for the next office holder or team to solve.

Be a problem solver but understand that, when you do, some folks won't like it. They will have less or different work to do and are likely to lose some of their power and control over people and resources when problems get solved.

- Bad leaders don't solve problems; they manage them, ignore them, or pass them along to someone else.
- One of the best questions to ask of potential employers is "What problems do you have that I can solve?" Their reply should give you a sense of what challenges them and also what you will likely face. This question will also clarify whether the organization is more concerned about managing problems or solving them.

8. Willingness to Use Conflicting Messages

A willingness to use conflicting messages can have negative consequences. For example, a semaphore signaler directs an aviator to land the plane on the deck of a carrier when she meant for the pilot to wave off and go around. Or you signal left with your car's turn signal, then turn right instead. Or you drive with your right blinker on but don't turn at all. These are examples of competing signals and conflicting messages.

In business, these behaviors are similar to the bad leader saying one thing to one group of people and the exact opposite to another. Some would call this person a two-faced leader. Others would call any leader who practices this type of behavior a lying SOB. Still others would call this type of leader absolutely normal.

Let's take the following statement and analyze it. "Ladies and gentlemen, I would like you to know that, under my leadership, we have had twenty-five number-one priorities."

You can parse this phrase in many ways. What types of people comprise the audience? Is the audience previously acquainted with the speaker? Is the speaker viewed as friendly, attractive, trustworthy, slick, tacky, humble, or manifesting hubris? Is the message understandable, persuasive, and consistent with expectations? What has this same person said prior to this statement?

What else will the speaker say or not say that supports her claims of having addressed twenty-five number-one priorities? What does she mean exactly? Has she been a leader for twenty-five years and had a different priority each year? Or, has she been in leadership one year and has had twenty-five differing priorities in just that year? If so, isn't this too many in such a short time? Most important, is there unity and agreement between what the speaker says and what the speaker does? Do her actions speak louder than what she says? Does the speaker show a willingness to use competing messages? Are her words and actions in competition? If so, is she bothered that they do not agree? Has the speaker sent a conflicting message unintentionally or intentionally?

Answers to these questions help create the profile, priorities, and message consistency of the speaker and the entity which the speaker represents. Analysis can center on consistency, believability, veracity, use of content such as statistical data, and form of delivery.

Good leaders trend toward intentionally *consistent* statements and actions, whereas bad leaders trend toward intentionally *inconsistent* statements and actions. They hope their followers won't notice, or if they do notice, they won't be alarmed by the conflicting messages.

Conflicting messages can have profoundly negative consequences. For example, my wife and I were nearly run over by a train while driving in Indiana. We had stopped at a well-marked crossing where the two-lane road we were traveling on intersected with a railroad. At the intersection, construction was taking place. Our car was first in line, and one of the construction workers was standing in the middle of the road directing traffic. Numerous signs made obvious that we were to stop and only to proceed as directed.

However, the construction guy kept giving an uncertain signal. He waved his hand and looked directly at the line of traffic behind us. While he was looking in my direction, he also appeared to be waving at somebody else. I was conflicted as to whether to remain stopped or proceed across the tracks. In my uncertainty, I stuck my head out the window and pointed to myself, as if to say, "Do you want me to move ahead?" He nodded his head and kept waving in my direction. I had what I thought was a clear okay to drive across the tracks.

But as I moved ahead and crossed the tracks, he went ballistic and shouted, "What are you doing?" I replied, "Exactly what you signaled me to do—cross the tracks." (Luckily, the train was not at the same spot, so no harm occurred.)

I became more animated in response to him and asked, "What in the world kind of signaling was that?" He explained that he was signaling to the train, not me. Still, he was looking directly at me, and I had confirmed what I thought he wanted me to do.

I've never forgotten that near miss. I have also learned that bad leaders can be really good at sending competing messages and that sometimes only luck stands between the bad message and career-damaging obedience to a mistaken instruction. Some circumstances demand absolute clarity of message and understanding.

From time to time, we hear of people living in geographical locations where warning signals for such things as tornadoes and tsunamis do not function, and consequently people die. On a more mundane level, when fire detectors and stop lights don't work, sometimes tragedies occur. Such situations demand delivering messages of certainty and utility.

Several acquisitions by major U.S. companies have resulted in substantial disputes and financial write-downs. Either sellers were inconsistent in what they said and did, or buyers were too eager to conclude their deals and failed to examine the truthfulness behind the seller's representations, or the acquirers believed (but did not verify) their investment counsel's opinions. Microsoft's purchase of aQuantive and Nokia and Hewlett-Packard's purchase of Autonomy are good examples of multibillion-dollar flops due to conflicting messages and unsubstantiated data.

> Bad leaders may send conflicting signals on purpose. You must be aware enough to perceive those signals and understand why they've been sent.

Why would leaders purposely send conflicting messages and mixed signals? Because they perceive a benefit from doing so. On occasion, anyone can slip and inadvertently send signals that seem to conflict, particularly with complex issues. Most often, this happens unintentionally. But intentional, continued statements meant to deceive in order to extend a relationship, program, initiative, ideology, or the status of the leader are highly problematic.

Bad leaders use deceitful public statements, off-hand interrogatives, and false representations because they cannot argue the issues or explain their decisions in truthful, straight-forward proclamations or communiqués.

Bad leaders display a willingness to engage competing messages and duplicitous strategies to entrap, embarrass, and destroy their enemies, competitors, and sometimes even their allies. They also do it as a means of enhancing their self-perceptions of superiority in position and intellect.

Leaders demonstrating these types of behaviors tend to get caught in their own webs, but they might blame others or bad messaging itself. Often, the higher the leader's position or status, the greater the allowance gap between what is said and what is reality. Ordinarily, this becomes less true for those lower on the corporate ladder. Moreover, those on the lowest rungs are seldom allowed the leeway to engage in the use of conflicting messages.

The unfortunate reality is that bad leaders, like bad politicians, are *expected* to have discrepancies between what they say they will achieve while campaigning for office and what they actually achieve while in office. And these inconsistencies don't seem to be a problem. The higher some leaders go, the more they are inclined to take advantage of the allowances they are given to mix their messages and be inconsistent.

GOOD LESSON:

- Good leaders maintain consistency among what is they say, what they mean, and what they do. For bad leaders, this isn't necessarily the case because inconsistency doesn't bother them.
- Good leaders explain and clarify when what they have said or done seems to conflict. Don't expect bad leaders to do this.
- If bad leaders attempt to clarify conflicting messages, the explanation is likely to be superficial. It is created to deflect attention away from them and on to other issues.
- Good leaders understand that willfully communicating mixed signals and competing messages should not be their practice, nor should they allow others to practice it.
- Bad leaders are willing to communicate conflicting, competing messages purposefully to keep employees, colleagues, constituents, partners,

and owners off balance, uninformed, and numb to detail. These actions become *de rigueur* for bad leaders. Although they might seem incomprehensible as productive and ethical long-term strategies for good leaders, they are not incomprehensible for bad leaders.

- You must pay attention, confirm, and reconfirm the consistency of the signals and messages being sent by those you believe to be duplicitous. This makes a good deal of sense in life and in the workplace when your career and livelihood are at stake.

- When new and better information becomes available, good leaders often "walk back" previous statements that are conflicting. They want consistency between their previous messages and their current ones.

- Bad leaders are less inclined to "walk back" their conflicting statements. Denying their own inconsistencies, they often state that what they said or wrote was misinterpreted.

- Using conflicting messages as a leadership strategy will eventually be seen by followers for what it is—falsehood and a willingness to be deceitful.

Bad leaders ask the question, "Do you understand?" Employees most commonly respond by affirming that they do, rather than admitting that they don't. They don't want to be seen as dull or lacking the ability to perceive what is being asked. Good leaders more often ask, "What do you understand?" It is a better means of providing needed clarification, achieving understanding, and opening a dialogue.

9. Willingness to Strike Back

When people discuss bad leaders, I often hear associations with a number of animals: rat, slug, weasel, skunk, toad, bat, crow, bull, ostrich, shark, ape, and leech among others. Not one animal comparison is complimentary.

I've wondered what behaviors and circumstances caused leaders to be compared to a particular animal or animal behavior. Few bad leaders have been described as butterflies, pandas, or bunnies. My personal comparisons include an arachnid such as a scorpion, a reptile such as a snake, or a crocodile because it's waiting to strike.

Working under such a leader is like the desert prospectors or determined ecologists who awaken to find a snake, perhaps a rattlesnake, has slithered into their sleeping bag. I can't think of a more horrible situation than to have a snake slithering around and over my body while trapped in my sleeping bag. I'm sure I would be too frightened to move for fear of being bitten. At this point, the snake has complete control. Risk and anxiety are high, and I'm facing an enormously unpleasant experience.

If you have lived or perhaps hiked in parts of the world where you need to beware of getting poisonous reptile and/or snake bites, then you have taken precautionary measures to protect yourself. Practicing a few rules like these can keep you safe: Be alert at all times; don't place your hand or foot in any place you can't see; shake out your boots before you put them on; have a snake-bite kit available and know how to use it; and sleep inside a well-sealed tent.

Feeling a snake in your sleeping bag is much like the feeling bad leaders create for their associates with their actions, attitudes, and willingness to strike out or strike back. Bad leaders tend to be like snakes. They lie in wait for someone or something to strike when they're threatened or when someone or something gets too close. Therefore, you need to take precautions to avoid being struck by them.

Many bad leaders tend to be a bit paranoid. They take problems personally and think that someone, something, or some group is purposefully causing them grief. Moreover, they often think that every problem is a human resource problem, and the best way to deal with that is to strike back and eliminate the person or group causing it.

> **Bad leaders are frequently fearful that they will be discovered to *not* have all the brainpower or solutions they've led people to believe they possess.**

Like snakes, they sometimes puff themselves up to appear to be more cunning and dangerous than they are. When confronted, they might seek to escape and find shelter.

Good leaders don't strike back in anger, but often bad leaders do so. Striking first or striking back is never an effective or beneficial leadership strategy. Preemptive striking against a competitor or market challenger is another matter.

Bad leaders tend to justify striking back by turning every oversight, challenge, or bump in the road into a war (or at least a skirmish). Because they perceive direct attacks, bad leaders think that every action taken to crush others is appropriate. This attitude tends to fatigue followers, consume financial resources, obscure mission focus, and waste valuable time. When they, their ideas, plans, initiatives, and products are one and the same, any questioning of these is an attack on them personally. Thus, an injustice to their ideas is an injustice to them.

Bad leaders tend to move in a progression from self-interest to self-centeredness to self-absorption. In that way, they move out of balance with those they lead and without passion for organizational mission.

If you think that striking back is primarily a fault in low-ranking leaders, you are wrong. High-ranking leaders behave this way as well, although one might expect more of them. Gamesmanship on this order is unattractive and unbecoming in any leader. Leaders who need to dominate and strike back are usually emotionally immature, insecure, and not likely to be effective in the long run.

In Victor Hugo's novel *Les Misérables*, Inspector Javert lets Jean Val Jean escape from custody and elude capture. Although Javert has been lying in wait to strike back and get even, he is unable to recapture Val Jean. Rather, he is dominated by his need to restore his version of justice and control Val Jean. Finally, Val Jean's freedom causes Javert to commit suicide.

Like Javert, bad leaders hold grudges. They may lie in wait for extended periods looking for the perfect time to strike back and unleash their venom. They may hold back for years, seeking just the right moment to strike out against people they perceive have wronged them or caused difficulty for them.

In contrast, good leaders display thoughtful, deliberative responses to affronts. Instead of retribution and punishment, they keep higher, greater, more redemptive moral purposes in mind. At times, good leaders need to react quickly and carefully. This certainly is the case in highly competitive business environments where the well-being or future of an enterprise is threatened. It's also true in the case of civil or military action when the sovereignty and longevity of a nation is in jeopardy.

In the face of threats, good leaders stay in fair balance with those they lead and do not begrudge others' opportunities to go away from the threat or receive attention and praise for doing so. Good leaders do not identify themselves so closely with their ideas and plans that when those are attacked or threatened, they cannot put them aside in favor of better ones.

GOOD LESSONS:
- Good leaders know how to defend their team members against attack.
- Good leaders don't "pick" fights.
- Good leaders minimize slights to their plans and ideas; they move along to more productive pursuits.
- Good leaders find it unproductive to hold a grudge or look for a chance to strike back.
- To be impervious to the threats of bad leaders, you must develop a thick skin.
- If bad leaders are waiting to strike back, help them strike at something unimportant rather than something vital.
- Give bad leaders praise when they have earned it. Don't purposefully steal their show or deny their claim to affirmations.
- Bad leaders are not likely to let personal affronts or criticisms of their leadership pass by without striking back. Many bad leaders lie in wait to strike back in order to get even with someone or something that has affronted them or their status.
- Bad leaders, like bad people, most often strike back against individuals and small groups rather than entire organizations. "Going Postal" is a euphemism for this behavior.
- Striking back often occurs when a bad decision or a weakness in a plan or idea has been made public or has otherwise been exposed. If bad decisions or actions of bad leaders never come to light, then they have little need to strike back or get even.

Bad leaders strike back when they think someone has arrested their power or prevented them from receiving credit for what they believe they are owed.

- Bad leaders will not tolerate being upstaged, but they cannot disclose that being upstaged has caused them to strike back. "Upstaged" is a theatrical term that means someone has stolen the show or taken away the limelight. Bad leaders, like egotistical actors, cannot allow this to happen.
- If bad leaders are upstaged or their real motives uncovered, they find a way to get even—even if it takes time and emotional energy away from higher priorities.
- Being around bad leaders who are ever alert for an opportunity to strike back is wearisome.
- Catching someone in a deviation, misstep, or error just to strike back is an unproductive waste of time and energy. Don't do it.
- Management by retribution is not the way to lead successfully.

---

10. Willingness to Prevent Consensus-Created Inactivity

Consensus is defined as general agreement, unanimity, solidarity, and collective opinion. Although each of these definitions has a generally progressive and positive tone, consensus-only decision making is ineffective when leaders need to make timely decisions in difficult situations. Relying *solely* on consensus to make decisions and provide forward momentum is a management mistake.

Often, consensus is thought to mean "a joint decision by a group of people to act" rather than "a group of people providing input and information upon which a leader can decide to act."

Consensus is often used as an excuse for indecision or a lack of bold decision-making by bad leaders. They are more interested in achieving group input—and good feelings—than tangible results. Decisions based solely on consensus often enable bad leaders to hide behind group decisions rather than being held accountable for the results of their actions.

Consensus leadership is process-oriented, not action-, outcomes-, or results-oriented. About consensus, England's former Prime Minister Margaret Thatcher said in 1981:

> **The process of abandoning all beliefs, principles, values, and policies in search of something in which no one believes, but to which no one objects; the process of avoiding the very issues that have to be solved, merely because you cannot get agreement on the way ahead. What great cause would have been fought and won under the banner: "I stand for consensus."**[27]

When taken to its fullest extent, consensus leadership means that no decision can be made until all leaders and constituencies agree. Consensus then becomes a recipe for organizational inactivity. It weakens leaders' roles and responsibilities for the outcomes of their decisions and the progress of an organization or business under their leadership.

When all participants have equal input and share equally in the decision-making process, then no single idea or argument is thought to be better than any other because the inputs to make a decision need to be agreed upon by all. When all decide, then little gets decided. When people must wait for consensus to act, then little action is taken. Decision by indecision occurs. A process orientation supersedes a results orientation.

Let me clarify the difference between consensus thinking and consensus decision-making. I've had the good fortune to have worked for two colleges affiliated with Quaker churches and traditions. I particularly like an approach they take to problem solving and the creation of policy and practice. When issues arise, they place the matter in the hands of the "Weighty Brethren," which is a collection of mature, wise individuals able to come to a decision. One of the Quaker practices that blends well into contemporary organizational management is the use of consensus thinking. It concentrates on achieving a sense of direction, recognizing the value of diverse opinions and group unity.

Consensus decision making is altogether different because it makes decision makers feel good about the process and less responsible for the outcome of the implemented decision. I've experienced the effects of consensus decision making and seen it increase the time frame for making a decision. It gives leaders an opportunity to walk away from negotiations and allow groups to discount the value of the dissenting opinion.

When all participants need to agree in order to move ahead, then consensus-based inactivity sets in. Good leaders do not let this occur; bad leaders encourage it because they are afraid of the outcomes of their own decisions. While unity and singleness of purpose is important, unity is not of *ultimate* importance. Productive and positive results are of greatest importance.

The phrase "All of us are smarter than one of us" seems to make sense to a superficial degree. This way of thinking is based on an input mentality and an assumption that leaders are not capable or cannot be trusted to make superior decisions by themselves. Group decisions are not always best because good leadership is about weighing the evidence, using sound logic, hearing diverse opinions, then deciding the best means to achieve a desired output. "All of us are smarter than one of us" is true to the degree that "all of us" can create greater volume of inputs but not necessarily superior judgments leading to superior results. More people making more decisions doesn't necessarily make for better decisions or make organizations more productive. Having more people involved doesn't make us smarter; having smart people involved makes us smarter.

Consensus-based decision making reduces the role responsibilities and accountability of the chief executive to produce desired outcomes. When everyone is responsible, then no one is responsible.

As a consensus mentality pervades upper levels of leadership, it also settles into most other levels of the organization where it will result in inactivity and lack of progress. Consensus-based decision making enables the individual or group to escape the responsibility of owning a decision and enhances plausible deniability. No one person can be individually responsible for a decision that was made by a group. This provides an "out" for bad leaders.

One of the original thinkers/writers/theorists of management was Henri Fayol, who created a fourteen-point typology describing management principles. Fayol's principles played a major role in defining the functions and responsibilities of management. They are as relevant today as when he first created them in 1916.

Of particular note are numbers two, four, five, six, and nine in regard to the arguments and commentary on consensus-based decision making.

Fayol's Fourteen Principles of Management

1. Division of Work – When employees are specialized, output can increase because they become increasingly skilled and efficient.
2. Authority – Managers must have the authority to give orders, but they must also keep in mind that with authority comes responsibility.
3. Discipline – Discipline must be upheld in organizations, but methods for doing so can vary.
4. Unity of Command – Employees should have only one direct supervisor.
5. Unity of Direction – Teams with the same objective should be working under the direction of one manager, using one plan. This will ensure that action is properly coordinated.
6. Subordination of Individual Interests to the General Interest – The interests of one employee should not be allowed to become more important than those of the group. This includes managers.
7. Remuneration – Employee satisfaction depends on fair remuneration for everyone. This includes financial and non-financial compensation.
8. Centralization – This principle refers to how close employees are to the decision-making process. It is important to aim for an appropriate balance.
9. Scalar Chain – Employees should be aware of where they stand in the organization's hierarchy, or chain of command.
10. Order – The workplace facilities must be clean, tidy, and safe for employees. Everything should have its place.
11. Equity – Managers should be fair to staff at all times, both maintaining discipline as necessary and acting with kindness where appropriate.
12. Stability of Tenure of Personnel – Managers should strive to minimize employee turnover. Personnel planning should be a priority.

13. Initiative – Employees should be given the necessary level of freedom to create and carry out plans.

14. Esprit de Corps – Organizations should strive to promote team spirit and unity.[28]

GOOD LESSONS:

You can't build a successful executive career on being known solely as a consensus-oriented leader, particularly if a consensus model produces inputs but not results and process but not productivity.

- You build a career on achieving positive outcomes, meeting missions, producing enduring results, and increasing profitability, not on talking about them.

- Bad leaders think that talking about a problem is all they need do to solve it. Not true.

- Sitting down and discussing a problem has no curative effects until a decision is made and action is taken to solve it.

- If consensus leads to individual inaction, group paralysis, and organizational stagnation, it should be abandoned. Senior leaders who solely depend on a consensus model to make decisions will reduce their skills and confidence in their abilities to make superior arguments and independent decisions that withstand scrutiny and criticism.

- Avoid making consensus your goal, as it leads to inactivity and voids accountability of yourself and/or your teams. Complete agreement should not be your goal; satisfied customers and constituencies should be.

- Decision makers must own their decisions or stop being decision makers.

- Inattention to the measurement of results, lack of goal attainment, and profitability are clear indicators of organizational inactivity based on over-applied and under-performing consensus.

- Consensus-based decision making should not replace (nor does it reduce) the responsibility of the highest ranking leader to make the most important decisions.

Take the opinions of others, arrive at a list of solutions and courses for action, and then decide. If your decision works, fine. If it doesn't, make another one that fixes both the original problem and the one you made. You can't wait for consensus-based inactivity to do it for you.

11. Willingness to Tolerate Organizational Imbalance

One of my friends balances loads for a living. In fact, he has done so for over fifty years. His is not the more common type of load balance associated with web traffic and technology, but the old-school type that manages the loading, unloading, and transporting of goods by container ships. If he tolerates an imbalance from port to starboard and from fore to aft, there will be dire results. The ship might list while still in port; its goods could float around in the Pacific; or the ship could sink. His job is literally to refuse to tolerate load imbalance.

Unfortunately, tolerating an imbalance is a common occurrence among organizations with bad leaders. An imbalance can occur when leaders hire only those who think, act, and look like they do. It can also occur when the "lookalikes" are allocated an unbalanced share of resources, while those who are different but among the most productive are starved of resources.

In this scenario, resources flow to those who have been granted "most-favored" status, and they are assigned the more pleasurable, meaningful, career-building work. In contrast, the least-favored employees, considered to be "non-players," are allocated fewer assets and assigned the least meaningful work. When leaders tolerate such imbalances, friction and resentment increase while respect for leadership declines. No one likes to get the short end of the stick, be dealt out of the deal, or denied an opportunity to prove their worth.

The willingness of a bad leader to tolerate imbalance is somewhat different from bad leaders creating imbalances to exercise their power to reward or punish. Tolerating and creating imbalances are both parts of a bad leader's playbook.

Bad leaders may purposefully create imbalances to disadvantage others and to advantage themselves and their allies. They may even attempt to rebalance what they have purposefully imbalanced just to demonstrate their leadership know-how. Imbalances can make others look incompetent, feel powerless, and achieve less. This becomes office and world politics and leadership at its worst. Avoid it.

An imbalance may also occur when bad leaders have an inordinate insistence on a particular strategy or tactic to achieve an objective from which they will not relent. Implementing a "most-favored" strategy could imbalance the organization by causing the reallocation of resources to less productive units.

The indifference to—or impunity with—bad leaders who intentionally imbalance organizations is among the most frustrating versions of bad leadership you can face. This is because the outcomes are predictably negative. Imbalances do not often result from chance. Rather, they appear when cunning leaders devise unbalancing strategies to direct attention away from what they really want to achieve—or from what could be even more destructive pursuits.

As my neighbor tells me, in the shipping business, an imbalance may not be recognized until certain environmental variables come into play. He loads ships to withstand storms that have not yet appeared and for conditions that have not yet occurred. Not until the storm arises does the quality of his balancing come to light.

My neighbor's work is analogous to the management of organizations: imbalances may not come to light until a storm occurs due to a sudden decline in revenue, the loss of key personnel, or the cancellation of a major account.

Imbalances show up in other insidious ways as well. I once worked for an organization that had among its accounting and budget managers a fellow I called the "Raider of the Lost Budget." As a good money manager/budgeter, I would squirrel away reserves to fund rainy-day opportunities at work. Several times, I attempted to access funds I had saved, only to find that what I had set aside had been "stolen" (my word) or "redeployed" (his word) to fund another department. In most cases, this fellow was a lousy manager who had overspent and had gone looking for funds to stabilize or expand his operations.

I was not only incensed that the accounting department had consented to the raiding but ticked off at the guy who had been rewarded for his overspending. I was never able to mount a counterattack to restore the funds, because the raid had taken place quickly and covertly. The pirated funds had already been spent. I didn't enjoy any benefits of his planned imbalance.

GOOD LESSONS:

- Bad leaders create and tolerate planned and prolonged imbalances even though they produce a preferred class of employee, deplete energy, create divisiveness, and diffuse unity of purpose.
- Bad leaders allow their organizations to get out of balance, and recovering from the imbalance is difficult. Think of it this way: If you have tried to handle an overloaded and unbalanced wheelbarrow, you know how hard the effort can be. The weight *is not* ordinarily the problem; the unbalanced load *is,* and it becomes unmanageable. Have you ever attempted to save an unbalanced wheelbarrow load from tipping over? Once it has started, you know it takes an enormous amount of energy and strength to bring it back in balance. Try as you might, it likely can't be rebalanced. So, too, is attempting to re-balance a team, business, or organization once it's out of balance. Enormous energy and resources must be expended by good leaders hired to do the rebalancing.
- Be vigilant concerning budget and personnel raiders, for they create imbalances and needless complications in your organization.

12. Willingness to Extend Earned Privilege to Abuse of Privilege

At some time, you may have been authorized to exceed the posted speed limit. I haven't. However, if I were instructed by state troopers to follow them at a speed higher than the limit, I'd give it a try—but only for the reason, time, and roadway on which I was granted the privilege. Nothing about our jobs, families, political affiliations, world views, or bank accounts have earned us the right to break the speed limit on a permanent basis. To do so would be to extend a one-time privilege beyond our authorization.

An earned privilege relates to special access, perks, opportunities, relationships, and information that accompany a position or status to which people have been appointed, elected, or have attained for themselves. The continued use of earned privilege can be based on good performance, an election, a single appointment, or a continuing appointment.

Earned privilege is also associated with a person having gained fame or notoriety. Basketball stars Magic Johnson and LeBron James probably don't need to buy tickets to see the Lakers play at the Staples Center in Los Angeles, but most everybody else does.

If someone has served a prison term and is released, then that person has earned the privilege of release. When immigrants become citizens, they earn the right to vote. Even a reserved parking place can be an earned privilege.

Certain privileges may be granted, not earned. A handicapped parking sticker, for example, may be granted to a person recovering from knee replacement surgery because she needs the privilege of a close, reserved parking space. If she allows family and friends to use her sticker when they don't actually need the close-in space, then she and they are abusing this privilege.

Abuse of privilege is the extension of a previously earned or granted privilege to a degree or purpose for which it was not intended. Abuse of privilege can occur at any level of the organization, not just at the lofty ones. When the privilege granted is extended as a means to show power or special status, misuse people, and take undue advantage, then abuse of privilege occurs.

Abuse of privilege often reveals people's or leaders' states of mind regarding their perception of their own status and importance.

Bad leaders tend to drift to a point where they think they deserve the status afforded to them. The status they think they've earned enables them to misuse the resources and people around them—although they'd never admit it.

Bad leaders will deploy "privilege" to create a certain status differential between two or more parties to elevate one party and devalue another. Sometimes this is called "putting them in their place" or "reminding them of their station."

A good example of abuse of privilege is seen in the 2006 movie *The Devil Wears Prada*[29] in which Anne Hathaway's character continually deals with the misdeeds and abusive attitudes of her boss, played by Meryl Streep. If you saw the movie, I'm sure you also felt the exasperation of attempting to compensate for negative and destructive behaviors of a lousy boss.

People can use almost any privilege poorly to satisfy their ego needs temporarily. The reverse is also true: People can use privilege to affirm their coworkers . You many have seen the grainy film clips of Supreme Allied Commander Dwight Eisenhower meeting with allied troops in Great Britain just a few hours before the D-Day landings started. In the clip, he arrives in an automobile, is saluted by soldiers, and returns a salute. He stands comfortably and says, "Smoke 'em if you got 'em." With this short statement, he levels the ego playing field, makes those with whom he's engaged feel comfortable in his presence, and quietly acknowledges what these soldiers are about to face. No ego, no status difference, just real comrades-in-arms.

Abuse of privilege takes place when success in one area is mistakenly and poorly extended to an unrelated field. Certainly, some people have expert knowledge in multiple fields, and people can develop such expertise. Some celebrities, however, misuse the privilege that their success in one field has brought them by acting as if they have expertise in another field that they've not studied.

I've always thought it curious that certain Hollywood entertainers who have accomplished a great deal "within their craft" are granted special status as experts in largely unfamiliar pursuits. Those might include environmental issues, the economy, and geopolitical affairs. I'm not bothered by whatever status is attributed to them by society but by what status they attribute to *themselves* by assuming they have this expertise. Because of their achievements in other fields, they extend privileges granted to them to become *de facto* spokespersons with influence beyond their expertise.

Bad organizational and business leaders who have more answers than questions also engage in this type of behavior.

Abuse of privilege also appears when would-be leaders inappropriately use company credit cards, planes, equipment, and human resources. They become troublesome when their vanity shows, and they use privilege to separate themselves from others rather than build unity. These people eat at the best restaurants when others are shorted on per diems, or they fly charter or first class when others are crammed into coach class.

These leaders rub the noses of fellow employees in their personal status and privilege. In contrast, most well-balanced employees know that earned privileges accompany most levels of leadership, and they understand appropriate usage.

One final example illustrates my point again. I once worked for a university where I needed fifty dollars from a petty cash account assigned to my office/budget for a short trip out of the state. I went to the cashier's window and asked for money against my signature. I was told that policy dictated that no one was allowed to receive an advance for any purpose until 9:00 a.m. It was 8:45 a.m. and my ride was at the curb ready to take me to the airport. Even though I was the president and CEO of the university, the cashier denied me the money.

I later determined that, although the cashier could have advanced the cash if she wanted to, she was more interested in demonstrating her power by hiding behind the policy. It was her one chance to use her power over me. She had no interest in accommodating my need; she cared about taking this opportunity to abuse the privilege her job provided. I wondered if she gave *me* this much grief, how much was she dishing out to students, faculty, and staff?

GOOD LESSONS:

- Good leaders don't let their earned privilege and status go to their heads. Bad leaders do.
- Good leaders appreciate the privileges they have been granted with their achievements and positions and maintain their balance in spite of the accolades heaped upon them. Bad leaders expect the privileges and accolades; they will leverage them as often and as ostentatiously as possible.
- Good leaders don't take themselves too seriously or over-capitalize on the power, access, and information that they have. Bad leaders do.

Before taking action, good leaders determine who or what is likely to be helped or hindered. They decide what message

they will send by exercising a privilege granted by their title, position, or responsibility.

- Bad leaders determine to what degree they can help themselves by the privilege of title and position. They have little regard to how they will be perceived by exercising it.
- When bad leaders can't tell the difference between earned privilege and abuse of privilege, other people notice. Although repelled, they will attempt to behave in the same manner if they lack proper character.

13. Willingness to Improperly Conduct Meetings

Among the many standards for assessing leadership quality is conducting meetings. I don't know of anyone who feels gleeful when required to attend a meeting, particularly when the person chairing the meeting is known to do it badly. A lot of really nice people conduct really bad meetings. Most of us have gone to meetings and have not been fully present. Emotionally or intellectually "checking out" of a meeting is something many of us learned to do in our high school and college classes.

Orchestrating a good meeting takes forethought, energy, and a willingness to make the meetings you chair worthwhile for all attendees. Certainly, there are many types of meetings—from staff meetings to exit interviews and everything in between. They all require a commitment to make them interesting, profitable, and valuable. Leaders do not want covert or overt resistance to attending the meetings they call and manage. But if there is resistance, it is probably justified.

I've noticed that a meeting anticipated to be bad usually has a person's name associated with it like "Brad's meeting" or "Anne's meeting." Sometimes the titles of meetings double up like "Brad's sales meeting" or "Anne's staffing meeting."

Some meetings are positively anticipated because of their topics such as annual bonuses. Some are not because of unwelcome topics such as employee evaluations or company reorganizations. Some meetings are anticipated because of the quality of communication, learning that takes place, or just the chance to hang with people one enjoys. Others are dreaded.

The agendas, topics, content, and orderliness make a difference in the quality of meetings. Good leaders know this and orchestrate them well. Bad leaders miss the opportunities that good meetings provide. That happens when they don't set the tone for their meetings by pre-determining what needs to be discussed, what doesn't need to be discussed, and who should or shouldn't lead the discussion.

If we were all evaluated only on the quality of dialogue and the positive outcomes of the meetings we conduct, we might all be in trouble. Even the best leaders don't get it all right all the time. This is not the issue. Rather, its leaders who systematically fail to conduct good meetings because of their willingness to settle for bad ones.

In the minds of many fellow workers, any meeting is a bad meeting and a waste of non- recoverable time. I'd like to think differently, but this is truth in far too many cases. It is the role of the leader to overcome this mindset.

Some people call good meetings bad when they didn't get what they wanted, weren't called on to show their brilliance, or were just having a grumpy day. You know who these people are. Don't be one of them.

Planning and conducting good meetings is hard work. If you need to achieve something important in a meeting, more thought and work must be put into it to achieve the desired outcome. Don't leave to chance getting the results you want.

Parkinson's Law states that the job expands proportionally to the amount of time allotted for it. If a job is allowed five minutes, it will take five minutes. If it is allowed five hours, it will take five hours.

Meetings are the same way. One of the ways you can compensate for Parkinson's Law is to schedule the meeting's length for a longer time than necessary. If you schedule hard stops to meetings and continually violate them, the word gets out. It is much better to schedule hard stops and use less time than scheduled. Participants greatly appreciate this. For example, if you schedule a meeting for an hour and a half and it takes only an hour, you give the time back to everyone. People notice it and love the mini-vacation. This simple decision goes a long way in the minds of people who attend your meetings and positions you as a thoughtful meeting leader.

Good, productive, and worthwhile meetings are not viewed as a waste of time or an intrusion into one's workday. If meetings do waste time, the organization's overall leadership is likely to be viewed the same way. The effectiveness with which leaders conduct meetings is a marker of the seriousness and manner with which they commit to other dimensions of their jobs.

This entire good meeting topic becomes even more complicated when work teams are located in different locations, cities, states, countries, and even hemispheres. Language, culture, and distance barriers create difficulties for which good leaders must compensate.

Most often, the bad aspects of a bad meeting outweigh the good aspects of a good meeting. Meetings can go bad due to any number of things. But they can go particularly bad when a chairperson doesn't have the discipline to stick to the agenda, talks a topic to death, or lacks the courage to reel in a colleague who is off topic. Attendees notice the level of engagement of other attendees. If the person who called the meeting emotionally checks out, they will too.

Bad leaders fail to realize that meetings should be more than a reporting and processing activity. They should feature a creative activity as well. A meeting as a creative activity is oversimplified when people say, "Let's get together and bounce some ideas around." "Let's toss some ideas against the wall and see what sticks." Or "let's pick each other's brains." Each of these partially gets to the need of producing creativity in meetings, but all of them lack the intentional planning required to conduct a meeting that is truly creative in its outcomes.

Seldom does forward-thinking creative activity take place in a meeting without a leader willing it to be so. This type of meeting is strategically and tactically planned. Certainly, spontaneous creativity can take place, but it more likely stems from a leader who orchestrates the environment in which that creativity occurs.

Good leaders are alert to those who purposely get off track and burn time, causing the real agenda items to be omitted. Oh, yes, these things do happen, and bad leaders allow it. If a meeting gets out of hand, if topics are not taken seriously, or if attendees are disengaged, a leader must either be bold and demand attention or shut the meeting down.

When you're in a meeting, do not ramble aimlessly by yourself or even with the few attendees who are still engaged. The non-engaged will let a struggling chairperson or attendee wander as far off topic as they care to, giving them time to tweet or respond to emails.

Bad leaders are often inattentive to fatigue. If something about the physical environment like heat or lighting is causing people to tire, fix those elements. If the topic or pace of discussion is causing them to tire, fix that as well. Having everyone stand and face away from the conference table while continuing the meeting will help reinvigorate everyone.

There are many terrific technical tools to help orchestrate meetings, but make sure the technology doesn't dominate or become a distraction. The tech must work for everyone in all locations. Don't allow bad conferencing technology to get more time and attention than a good agenda gets. The best things about tele-conferenced meetings are not needing to travel and being able to attend in your pajamas. But don't use teleconferencing as an excuse to *not* address difficult issues that might be handled better face to face.

There is no excuse for delays and screw-ups when scheduling meetings. There are many good meeting technology scheduling tools to help plan well and early. When bad leaders blame scheduling mishaps on their tools, look more diligently. Likely, more is going on than meets the eye.

Bottom line: If leaders fail to stay in control of the agenda or pace of the meeting, these elements will likely be taken over by others who have more intensity, an ax to grind, or an agenda of their own. When this happens, it is worse than not having a meeting at all.

GOOD LESSONS:
- Don't allow the quality of your meetings to be the sole test of the quality of your leadership.
- All good meetings should have informational and entertainment value. Plan for both.
- Good leaders set a positive tone for their meetings. Bad leaders leave tone-setting to others, and followers notice.

- Don't let your meetings become battlegrounds unless you intend them to be.
- Bad leaders expect others to carry the ball and make the case in difficult meetings.
- Good leaders take the responsibility of staying on task, even during difficult discussions.
- Bad leaders fail to organize and manage meetings that results in decisions, and followers notice.
- Bad leaders announce bad news in meetings badly.
- Good leaders announce bad news in meetings well.
- Only call meetings when necessary.
- When you call an "all hands" meeting, expect everybody to attend. Take attendance and make sure everyone knows it. If you are lax on the requirement to attend, it is assumed that you are lax on other things as well.
- Only call an "all hands" meeting when it's really needed.
- When regular meetings become too regular, they become stale. Don't conduct stale meetings on stale topics in stale locations.
- Good leaders should always know the outcome of a vote to be taken in a meeting before the meeting is held. If you don't have the votes you need, reschedule the meeting and find them.
- Always end a meeting on a positive and relaxed note, even if the meeting was difficult.
- Acknowledge what was or wasn't achieved with poise and assertiveness.
- It doesn't bother bad leaders that their mediocrity is on display during a meeting, even though it should.
- During meetings, good leaders don't punish others who have disagreed with them. Bad leaders punish publicly and feel justified in doing so.
- While in meetings, good leaders must be advocates of their own ideas and plans. They must not expect others to argue and advocate for them when they fail to do so themselves.

14. Willingness to Understate or Overstate Role as Influencer

I've written that bad leaders tend to *overstate* their role in success and *understate* their role in failure. Good leaders do not do this. However, leaders both good and bad cannot deny they have some degree of influence in the success and failure of their organizations.

Good leaders play their roles by developing influence with people and exerting control over things. Bad leaders play their roles by exerting control over people and influencing things…things being defined as the multitude of issues, circumstances and challenges faced by leaders and followers

Being a leader means being an influencer; these are inseparable. Followers are influenced by a leader's persona, human, conceptual and technological skills, and the quality and timing of decisions made. When these factors mesh well, it is noticed. If they don't, it is also noticed, and the leader's positive influence is diminished.

Having a positive influence is always at the core of a leader's responsibilities. This won't change.

Yet, one need not be formally appointed as a leader to have influence. Certainly, combining a position or title with influence makes a good package. However, when a formally appointed leader has the position and title but little influence, then role confusion occurs, and progress is likely to be affected.

Good leaders engage a full range of influence by their overt, covert, subtle, and obvious actions. Bad leaders generally overuse one of these types of influences to the detriment of progress and the people affected by the overuse. If leaders continually lean to one type of influence too much, it's like singing a song with a single note. It becomes repetitive and boring.

The role of influencer is one that a good leader desires to play. An influencer wants to positively affect behaviors and outcomes. It's like a basketball player calling for the ball to take the last shot or being at the foul line when the outcome of the game's winner is still in question.

These days, social and cultural influencers are having a greater role in marketing and product promotion than ever before. An influencer has become a coveted and good-paying position but not necessarily as a leader in a work setting or supervisory position.

The Urban Dictionary defines an influencer as a "makeup, hairstyle, or fashion blogger who is instafamous only on Instagram or buys 'followers' and 'likes' and gets free products from companies who fall in their trap of fake fame." It defines influence marketing this way:

> *Influencer marketing* **is a type of** *marketing* **that focuses on using key leaders to drive your brand's message to the larger market. Rather than** *marketing* **directly to a large group of consumers, you instead inspire/hire/pay** *influencers* **to get out the word for you.**[30]

Thus, an influencer is an individual who has above-average impact on a specific niche product. Influencers are normal people who are often connected to key roles of media outlets, consumer groups, industry associations, or community tribes. Such individuals are not simply marketing tools but social relationship assets.

Two of the explanations of an influencer noted above are of particular importance: that influencers have above-average impact and are social relationship assets. These characteristics are incredibly important to good leaders as well.

After all, no business or social organization wants to be led by leaders who have average or below-average impact. No search or job-hunting firm advertises for average or below-average employees. No athletic team wants average or below-average runners, hitters, or scorers. But there are bad leaders who will settle for average or below-average performance from their followers, because it is just too hard or costly to require above-average performance.

GOOD LESSONS:

- You can't lead people without influencing them, but bad leaders act like they can.
- Play the role of informal influencer until the positional power of leadership happens, if that's what you want.
- Some people would rather be an influencer than a leader. Why not be both?
- The better you are at positive influence, the better your chance to lead sooner.
- Good leaders are always concerned about the quality, impact, and durability of their influence.
- Influence can be either positive, negative, or null. Good leaders are dili-

gent in promoting and protecting their positive influence while eliminating any shadow of negative influence.

---

15. Willingness to Use False Narratives as Motivators

During my undergraduate days, a professor at my college decided to become a franchisee of a successful and growing fast-food restaurant chain. With a few partners, he put together the money, went through the training, and built the facility. This professor was responsible for locating personnel, so he looked to the college for a few full-time and several part-time employees. Because it was near campus, many of us saw this as a good opportunity for work. Also, we would be working with our best friends, getting paid fairly well, and eating as much as we wanted during breaks. That was a real chance to eat free, non-college food.

When the restaurant opened, there were more of us working behind the counter than customers in front of it. With this crew, it didn't take long to get ahead, and stay ahead, of the daily workload. When things got really slow, we had little to do but take longer breaks and eat.

This particular restaurant chain used a metric called "yield" to assess sales and profitability. Yield was the amount of cash in the drawer in comparison to the pounds of roast beef consumed. You get the picture! Given the overstaffing and no controls over how much we could eat, we employees were eating the place into oblivion. When the owners put eating controls in place, reduced the number of working hours, and woke up to their lack of yield, things turned bad. Many part-timers quit because they needed more hours. Most of those who remained lost confidence because it became evident our manager/owner/professor knew more about biology than leadership, restaurant management, and ownership.

To make things even more difficult, he became a leader intended followers would not follow. It all came to a head when this manager/owner/professor began to use a phrase so frequently that it became a term of derision on the entire campus. That phrase was "Stay with me now; you're the best man I've got."

In itself, this phrase could serve as a motivator and a relationship builder, because it identifies the listener as a special person differentiated from other employees. The problem began when he spoke this phrase to every employee. In a quiet moment, he would step up behind each of us and quietly whisper it. It took only a few days for him to say it to everyone, and it became a standing joke. I suppose it was his strategy to keep workers around after the cuts in hours and change in policy regarding how much we could eat. However, it did just the opposite. It undermined his credibility and authenticity.

The statement "Stay with me now; you're the best man I've got" was a false narrative. It did not achieve the level of motivation intended. When spoken to a single person at a specific time, it would have likely achieved its purpose. But when spoken to everyone, it lost its impact, and the person making the statement lost status. In this case, the phrase was, in time, a foreshadowing of organizational stress due to employee churn and a host of other things as well.

Learning that you are thought by a leader to be the best employee or the best player on the team loses its punch if every employee or team member is told the same thing, or if only one employee or player is told it too frequently. Being called the greatest, best, smartest, or even the hardest-working too often for too long eventually loses its effectiveness.

GOOD LESSONS:

- A motivating statement used too much for too long with too many people becomes false, and everyone knows it.
- Affirming statements can become false narratives, sounding good when first communicated but with time becoming just the opposite—demotivating and devoid of impact.
- Bad leaders use the same motivational narrative with such frequency and beyond its productive life span that an otherwise motivating statement becomes a false and unproductive narrative.
- Good leaders know how to use affirming statements tactically and strategically. Bad leaders use affirming statements politically.

Good Lesson Affirmation

There is no FEAR (Failure, Experience, Anxiety, or Roadblock) caused by a bad leader, from which I am not learning a good lesson.

Chapter 4.

Good Lessons: Refusal

1. Refusal to Take Responsibility for Financial Failure

The short phrase "on my watch" describes the period of time when one is on duty. It is used by good and bad leaders as a way of placing boundaries or parameters around what they want to achieve during the time they have ultimate responsibility. It has a naval connotation, as sailors were required to "stand at watch" for a certain period. So the phrase "not on my watch" means that during the time someone is on duty, certain things will not be allowed to happen.

Regrettably, perhaps shamefully, leaders may refuse to take responsibility for the financial performance of an organization during their watch. This applies to all types of organizations: for profit, non-profit, and government. When leaders deny financial reality and act as though spending more than they receive, not being profitable, or not balancing a budget has no substantive negative consequences, they abrogate their responsibilities.

When bad leaders refuse to take responsibility for financial failure, they fail to prevent it. Bad leaders may even fail to acknowledge that significant problems accrue from spending more than their organization receives. A failure to accept that great harm will happen shows their mistaken ideas about financial health, intransigence, and willful ineptitude.

> When bad leaders refuse to acknowledge or act to prevent financial failure, they admit that incremental financial decline is of less importance than the agenda they are advancing, even though their agenda could lead to insolvency.

For any organization, this is a bad place to be. Still, bad leaders fail to admit they are in a bad place nor do they show they ever want to get out of that bad place. They may say they do, but they lead as if they don't.

If leaders refuse to acknowledge their role in financial difficulties or deny that problems occur when financial goals are not met, then few positive things can be said about other aspects of their leadership. Leaders must get capitalization, profitability, and income and spending right. Without doing that, not much else will be manageable.

When bad leaders refuse to acknowledge the consequences of poor financial performance, they fail in their fiduciary duty by allowing the entity they lead to reach a point from which it may not recover. Moreover, bad leaders tend to rely on their status and charisma to influence others to ignore the negative consequences of their poor financial performance. In effect, they delude each other.

Because of recent government bailouts and easy bankruptcy, the sting of poor financial performance has become less threatening. Although most businesses will not get bailed out, like individuals, they will feel the weight of financial distress. That stress can be taxing, suffocating, and take years to correct.

Most good leaders are not interested in working through a recovery project or turnaround opportunity in which they will be financially hamstrung and lack room to maneuver. So, only two types of leaders appear to lead organizations out of financial doldrums and into recovery: 1) good leaders with a sense of rightness and calling as well as incredible skill and fortitude, or 2) weak leaders with a willingness to persist.

Good leaders know how and where to lead. They also know how to recognize and avoid disaster. They acknowledge the effects of poor financial management in word and deed. Because they understand that bad things will happen if they lead poorly, they intend to avoid financial problems as if they were avoiding rodents carrying the bubonic plague.

Good leaders do not refuse to accept responsibility for bad financial performance. They understand the necessary sequence of action to move from *causing* bad things to happen and *allowing* good things to happen. This sequence is as follows:

1. Acknowledgment
2. Responsibility
3. Accountability
4. Workability
5. Preventability

Preventing the negative effects of poor financial performance must move in this sequence: *acknowledging* that bad things are happening or will happen, *taking responsibility* for financial health, *becoming accountable* to a standard for good financial management and to those affected by poor financial performance, *creating workable solutions* to fix the problem, and *preventing* the problem from reoccurring,

Leaders who refuse to acknowledge that poor financial results create problems have no place to start in order to solve the problem. For them, no problem exists. By comparison, great leaders solve financial issues before they become problems.

The two final steps—*workability* and *preventability*—are essential to preventing the consequences of poor financial performance. Workability means that the proposed solutions actually function and produce the effects for which the leaders created them. Preventability means that the system has been changed so that negative financial performances and their consequences do not happen again

If businesses are not profitable or don't make more than they spend, they will eventually fail—unless, of course, they are too big to fail and are bailed out, bought, or change to better leadership. Unless individuals have trust funds, secure more credits cards, or rob banks, they can't spend more than they take in unless they go bankrupt, become disciplined, or start the sequence again.

Good leaders move through this entire five-step sequence and bad leaders don't. In fact, most bad leaders refuse to acknowledge the negative effects of bad financial performance because they don't have the will or solutions to prevent it.

Poor financial performance cannot go on forever, as a previous decline in the steel industry in the U.S. demonstrated. What was once the most thriving of industries was reduced to nearly nothing in recent decades. It lost the economic clout and influence it once enjoyed. People in northeastern Ohio and western Pennsylvania—particularly in Youngstown and Warren, Ohio, and the entire Mahoning Valley—are living the short- and long-term economic and social consequences of industry leaders' refusal to prevent financial decline. These leaders also ignored the signs that their industry was changing and new technologies and products were replacing steel. Thankfully, the U.S. steel industry is experiencing a significant renaissance as tariff and anti-dumping measures, better manufacturing technologies, fewer federal and state regulations, and better leadership are turning it around.

In addition to refusing to acknowledge the importance of financial decisions, some bad leaders also believe they can continually make *wrong* financial decisions and end up in the *right* financial circumstance. One major strategic correction, contract, or positive turn of fortune will not likely compensate for refusing to deal with the effects of continued poor financial performance.

Bad leaders have the tendency to believe that all it takes to achieve financial health is a few tweaks rather than greater management discipline, more investment capital, stronger personnel, inspired innovation, and more time. They need to not only project ahead but engage the process and rigors more diligently, using the resources they have in hand more productively.

Because financial decisions affect everyone in an organization, good leaders know that all people play a role in marketing, sales, and profitability. Therefore, everyone in the organization has a role to play in achieving financial health, although few bad leaders acknowledge this fact.

When people acknowledge their parts in achieving profitability, then each person is more cautious with expenditures and focuses on the bottom line. But when employees suspect that senior leadership refuses to acknowledge the effects of poor financial performance, they perceive their financial role and responsibility as being so small that their actions will not make a difference. Then they become careless with expenditures.

On the other hand, good leaders communicate that everyone must attend to the bottom line, regardless of the job assignment or budget management responsibilities.

Additionally, good leaders are wise to acknowledge good financial achievement and bottom line awareness publicly while privately reprimanding nonconforming financial results and any inattention to the bottom line.

Bad strategy, poor financial management, outdated products and services, and inept leadership are often identified as the primary drivers of crises and decline. But a number of default arguments make sense as well.

Some organizations and businesses are not sustainable because they have outlived their purpose or their customers. Technology advances might have moved beyond them. Some organizations can't seem to find the talent to thrive. Others move so far off track that no amount of repurposing, retooling, or redirecting can prevent further employee and ownership fatigue, decline, or eventual failure. Some entrepreneurial projects are dead on arrival and can't be brought back to life, regardless of leadership skill, amount of funding, slick marketing, or budgetary control.

Resolution to any of these crises requires that leaders get their heads out from under their arms, quit being quiverlippers, and become the type of leaders who refuse to deny the causes for and consequences of poor financial performance. This is where recovery is most likely to begin. Starting anywhere else guarantees failure.

Most people agree that bottom-line results must speak. To a large degree, the bottom line does say a lot about the financial and general well-being of an organization, yet it doesn't describe the whole truth about an organization. Because the bottom line is a snapshot for a given period of time, it does not and cannot provide the complete picture of what else is taking place at the macro- and micro-levels of the organization.

The bottom line is a good test, but it's not the only test of organizational well-being. Two additional tests are the degree of *reaction* that leaders have when not attaining organizational mission/vision and the degree of *denial* of negative consequences from their poor financial management.

GOOD LESSONS:

- Good leaders never rely on others to compensate for the financial shortcomings of their personnel, teams, or units. They pull their own weight and make their required contribution to profitability.
- Good leaders understand that they must be evenhanded when they enact austerity measures. They must also provide rewards for those who comply

and punish those who don't. To do otherwise is to punish those who comply and reward those who don't. Carve-outs and exceptions must not be tolerated, because they have enormous corrosive effects and will cause distrust of leaders, giving them reputations as petty, manipulative dictators.

- An essential skill in leadership and management is profitably by maximizing the resources at hand. Manage well with the cards you've been dealt, and don't wait until things get better. You can't continually blame the market, government, or your predecessors for current financial failure.

- Never lose the ability to borrow funds. When organizations are not creditworthy, then achieving stability and vitality via debt financing won't happen.

Never borrow money to buy coal. If you borrow to buy consumables or things that are not hard assets and they are consumed, they cannot be leveraged. The only thing left is the obligation to repay. Good leaders don't allow this to happen; bad leaders do.

- Don't work for anyone or become a partner to anyone who refuses to acknowledge the enormous negative consequences of poor financial performance—someone who is not concerned with achieving at least a balanced budget, breaking even, or making a profit.

- Every product and service must pull its own weight and not depend on another product or service to compensate for its failure. Good leadership divests or closes those functions that bring the health of the organization into question.

- Bad leaders don't willingly acknowledge that cash flow, however essential, isn't a long-term substitute for profitability.

- If the rewards for failure are equal to or greater than the rewards for achievement, no one will acknowledge the negative consequences of bad financial management or prevent them from happening.

- Bad leaders pass financial *problems* along to their successors and minimize the consequences on themselves. Good leaders pass financial health to their successors and minimize their role in good financial performance.

- The anger that followers express during times of financial difficulty is not necessarily directed at the crises. Rather, it's directed toward the bad leaders who created the conditions and climate for the crises to occur and/or continue.
- Financial difficulty seldom happens as an independent event; it occurs in a series of events produced when a climate for failure has been allowed to form.
- Organizations that find themselves financially squeezed are unlikely to be fixed by the same leadership that enabled their financial crises to occur.

Seldom does financial distress happen when someone doesn't see it coming. But frequently, those who see financial distress coming fail to sound the alarm for fear of encountering a bad leader who will deny it.

- Financial trouble—whether ramping up over time or occurring with the suddenness of an earthquake—displays a refusal by bad leaders to acknowledge the seriousness of pending or actual trouble. Thus, bad leaders do not prevent it from occurring or cure it when it does.
- If leaders fail to plead for financial success, they fail to lead.
- Bad leaders default to blaming everything or everyone but themselves for financial distress. Good leaders get realistic, show boldness, and engage human and financial resources in the wisest, most profitable ways possible.
- Companies with high market capitalization and low profitability early in their lifespan are the most easily managed and also the domain of the least able leaders. With maturity, these companies will need stronger, more bottom-line focused leaders to succeed.

2. Refusal to Create Direction, Momentum, and Detail

Perhaps you have heard these phrases: "Without a clear destination, any will do" and "we don't know where we are going, but we are making good time" and "the devil is in the details."

Independently, each of these phrases foreshadows behaviors that are often missing or underdeveloped in bad leaders and lacking in the organizations they attempt to lead. In the first phrase, the themes are clarity and destination. In the second, the themes are direction and momentum. In the third, the themes are personality and detail. Each phrase emphasizes core principles essential to effective leadership and organizational success.

Customers, employees, and society in general have high expectations that proper direction, discernable momentum, and sufficient detail will be inherent in every entity with which they interface. This is because customers, employees, and society in general desire integrity and genuineness in their institutions.

As integrity and genuineness cannot be ignored, so too direction, momentum, and detail cannot be ignored by leadership. They are expressions of integrity and genuineness. If leaders refuse to provide direction, momentum, and detail, they default on their responsibilities.

Good leaders do not need reminders that each of these short phrases represents a requirement. To fail at any one of these steps is to fail at them all because they are interdependent. Bad leaders do not take this to heart, nor do they set in motion appropriate strategies that make the three work in harmony.

In fact, bad leaders claim that they lead equally well in articulating direction, establishing proper momentum, and providing compelling details. But their followers know differently.

Society expects greater access to and clarity from non-governmental and business organizations, because they don't perceive to be getting them from impenetrable, unresponsive, bloated, and poorly managed governmental organizations.

Due to abundant information, sunshine laws, and quick access, whether public or private, organizations are now held to a higher standard for detail and exactitude than at any previous time. Vague plans and uncertain initiatives just don't cut it. Leaders are required to provide exacting detail and enormous specificity in order to achieve buy-in. Citizens and employees are not easily persuaded. Followers don't automatically follow. For example, what compelling argument and detail would it take to persuade you that building a new airport near your neighborhood was a good idea?

Not only does the detail about the airport need to be voluminous, but it also needs to be persuasive. Cultural expectations require not only that exacting detail is made available for analysis, but also that a specific, demonstrable link exists between the detail and a desired outcome or a tangible benefit. Gone are the days when a leader is allowed to provide sketchy plans containing few details.

At one time, people were more trusting, less skeptical, and had fewer ways to check on the veracity of what the leader was saying or asking them to believe. Today, with instantaneous access and messaging, people can parse, scrutinize, analyze, criticize, plagiarize, publicize (an old-school word), and distribute a leader's words to the world before comments, speeches, or pitches are made.

Bad leaders refuse to articulate detail and specific plans, but they are good with generality and producing good feelings. Bad leaders don't provide the details because they can't. Bad leaders fail at making "how to" goal statements and end-result statements because they don't want to be held accountable for the claims they make and the initiatives they promote.

Good leaders understand that bundling clear direction, proper momentum, and exacting detail provides a higher degree of acceptance and adoption than if any one of these components were missing. Without compelling detail, leaders have little chance of moving their organizations in the direction or at the pace they desire. If leaders cannot or will not provide detail, then they give away the fact that they really don't know the ultimate outcomes they want to achieve.

Details are incredibly important to customers, constituents, voters, and students. Without them, the very people you want to please may be those who feel cheated by your product or policy when they see it in its final form. For example, like other parts of the U.S., Seattle has horrible traffic congestion. The South Lake Union area of the city has needed a solution to traffic congestion for a long time. This neighborhood has undergone massive redevelopment and is now the home of Amazon.com and the Bill and Melinda Gates Foundation among others. The primary access points are I-5, Mercer Street on the north, and Denny Way on the south. Seattle Center and the Space Needle are immediately to the west.

Before redevelopment traffic in this area was a real mess, and during redevelopment it got worse. People agreed that the streets needed improvement. So the city and State of Washington determined they would expand and reroute Mercer

Street. This project took several years and tens of millions of dollars to complete. The new Mercer Street is only about a mile in length. When it first opened, it was actually comical because drivers were unacquainted with the signage and unaccustomed to the new roadway. Of course, the news media were on the scene interviewing frustrated drivers and officials from Seattle Department of Transportation (SDOT). While watching the TV interviews, I nearly fell out of my chair when one of the SDOT people finally acknowledged that the traffic was worse than it had been before the rebuilding. Then she said the new configuration was never intended to decrease congestion.[31] Incredible!

After the city and state spent tons of money, and people endured years of dislocation and inconvenience, traffic didn't get any better. Why was the project undertaken, if not to aid traffic flow and reduce congestion? Perhaps the real goal was to frustrate drivers so much that they would quit using their cars, walk, take the bus or trolley, or ride their bikes. Without a compelling end game in mind, this project became a classic case of having no destination, so any would do.

Good leaders are candid and truthful about the goals they want to reach, the direction in which they want to go, the momentum they want to achieve—all of which they argue with compelling, persuasive detail. However, if a leader or a leadership team can't provide complete detail from start to finish because it is simply unknowable, then they must use progressive vectoring.

Progressive vectoring is my term for a strategy for getting somewhere rather than nowhere, getting started rather than stagnating, enabling progress, and controlling for the fact that no one can foresee all the twists and turns the future holds because NOORTS will arise, even with exquisite initial detail.

So, if leaders can't get from A to Z directly, then they should go from A to the next clearly knowable status point (B), and vector to (C), then (D), then eventually get to Z, the desired, known final destination.

Progressive vectoring gets organizations where they want to go. Of course, this pathway presupposes that leaders have locked down a clear destination. Without a destination in mind, progressive vectoring is just wandering around. So, to avoid wandering around, leaders and organizations have to pay attention to vision and mission statements. Still, these are sometimes too ethereal to generate buy-in because they are too general and lofty. Goals and objectives, although more easily understood, require the greatest compelling detail.

To some degree, people are correct in their view that top leaders do vision and mission statements better than they do tactical planning or operations. High-level leaders are expected to articulate the big vision but leave most of the planning, details, and execution to others. Yet, they must be fully aware of what progress is being made toward the mission—in addition to closely monitoring resource expenditures.

For most competitive environments, this approach only partly works because followers expect more than general ideas, plans lacking salience, or outcomes set by detached, disaffected leaders. Employees are often skeptical because they've heard lofty statements and strategic plans that didn't create direction, momentum, or results. Followers have been disappointed too many times. They are tired of inaction and platitudes; they want their leaders to roll up their sleeves and engage in the tactical work with them.

Good leaders are increasingly expected to take the responsibility to communicate *what* will be done, *why* it should be done, *how* it will be done, and *how* success or failure will be measured. Participatory decision making has a large, important role to play in all of this. But at the end of the day, followers increasingly expect real leaders to step up, do what they are paid to do, and do what they say they are doing: leading and achieving.

Bad leaders are mistaken in their belief that burning through resources means progress. Because they fail to create cogent, meaningful metrics and systems to measure results, any pseudo-progress will suffice.

Good leaders are better at closing the gap between stated goals and real goals than are bad leaders. Stated goals are related to public relations and image statements, while real goals demand resource expenditure to achieve.

One of my favorite movies depicting bold leadership and precision to attain goals is in the 1998 movie *Saving Private Ryan*. Harv Presnell, playing General George C. Marshall, makes the following statement, then follows it with another definite and powerful command about what is to be done to find and extract Private Ryan.

I have a letter here, written a long time ago, to a Mrs. Bixby in Boston. So bear with me. "Dear Madam: I have been shown in the

files of the War Department a statement of the Adjutant-General of Massachusetts that you are the mother of five sons who have died gloriously on the field of battle. I feel how weak and fruitless must be any words of mine which should attempt to beguile you from the grief of a loss so overwhelming. But I cannot refrain from tendering to you the consolation that may be found in the thanks of the Republic they died to save. I pray that our heavenly Father may assuage the anguish of your bereavement, and leave you only the cherished memory of the loved and lost, and the solemn pride that must be yours to have laid so costly a sacrifice upon the altar of freedom. Yours very sincerely and respectfully, Abraham Lincoln"[32]

The scene continues by General Marshall saying that a team will be sent to find Private Ryan and "we will get him the hell out of there." Three of the Ryan brothers had been killed in action, and the general was not going to allow the fourth to be killed as well. Great compassion, rationality, and leadership was expressed in that scene. General Marshall's sagacious decision and action statements were so precise that they could not be mistaken by the downstream chain of command.

When I first saw that scene, I was struck with the clarity of the statement and the compelling purpose of the strategy. The rightness of the action was not in question, nor was there any underestimation of the resources required to save Private Ryan.

Although other officers attempted to dissuade General Marshall from sending a team to find Private Ryan, General Marshall indicated clearly what was to be done, period...end of discussion. General Marshall not only showed decisive action, but an internal sense of the compelling rightness and morality for finding Ryan.

Not all members of the extraction team saw the merits of their mission. Some saw only the risks. However, the value was understood by Tom Hanks's character and expressed clearly when he said in his dying moments to Ryan, "Earn it." There was unity of purpose between the minds of General George C. Marshall and Hanks's character Captain Miller to execute the plan, although they were not in direct contact. The purpose and larger objectives of the mission were understood and actionable. There was undeniable moral significance of the mission. There was undeniable clarity to the command.

In addition to enjoying the movie for its characters and action, I found the central theme of knowing what one is to do, in spite of the risks, was wholly refreshing. It was also uncharacteristic of bad leaders who do not display a command presence or provide mission clarity.

GOOD LESSONS:

- Good leaders provide sufficient detail so their plans will not be misunderstood or their people unable to support them.
- Good leaders' detailed arguments will include accuracy, consistency, and realistic achievability.

Bad leaders have difficulty grasping the implications of a crisis and articulating compelling solutions to avoid or end it. Crises are seen by bad leaders as opportunities to promote their agendas and to hail themselves as messiahs or avengers.

- Not receiving a clear, compelling directive from a leader can be an enormously off-putting to those waiting to follow. Leaders should be willing and able to articulate clear objectives, establish forward momentum toward those objectives, and secure the commitment of followers through precise detail. Most bad leaders fall short of these basic, minimal requirements for good leadership.
- Many leaders act as though compelling mission clarity that's sufficient for personnel to act in spite of the risks is unnecessary. Emotional speeches are not enough to compensate for a lack of mission clarity, weak arguments, and questionable motives.
- Don't depend on bad leaders to produce actionable directives if they cannot articulate desired goals.
- One should not expect a bad leader to create a vision so compelling that personnel will set aside other important tasks and support it.

- When bad leaders refuse either to stand behind or to abandon their own proposals and arguments, they project their emotional and intellectual weaknesses and cause doubt among followers.
- Followers expect leaders to make a commitment, "lead out," and get in front of their own proposals rather than delegate those tasks to others who then will take the flack and shield leaders from challenges.
- Good leaders don't leverage the tragedy of a crisis for their benefit. Bad leaders may be slick or shrewd in doing so, but they are not morally justified by doing it. For a bad leader intent on self-promotion, bad news is good news for them.
- Bad leaders who purposefully cause delay, routinely withhold resources, intentionally fail to provide details, and willfully keep others in the dark prove to be counterproductive to the very initiatives that they espouse. Their actions speak louder than their words.

3. Refusal to Admit Bias

Bias often has a negative connotation, but in fact, it also has positive attributes. For example, I enjoy reading what various U.S. states say about themselves by their state mottos and license plates. They are not hesitant to promote the features and benefits of their states. In fact, they have a clear bias and want others to know about it.

Arizona—The Grand Canyon State

Arkansas—The Natural State

Idaho—Great Potatoes

Kentucky—Unbridled Spirit

Louisiana—Sportsman's Paradise

Maine—Vacationland

Massachusetts—The Spirit of America

Michigan—The Great Lakes State and Pure Michigan

New Hampshire—Live Free or Die

My favorite is from Montana—Last of Big Time Splendors

These slogans project a state's positive bias about itself, a unique geographic component, or a feeling or a philosophy that the state embodies. The states aren't likely to make comparative comments such as "Oklahoma. It's nearly as good as Texas" or "Idaho has some pretty good potatoes" or "Washington has more rain than any other state."

A high-ranking official in Kansas said that Kansas had more shoreline than any state in the union. It was a bold claim and inaccurate, but it also didn't lack in bias toward what the official thought was a competitive distinction. It's better if a bias is true, but that doesn't stop the travel and tourist boards from stretching their claims. Consider West Virginia's slogan—Almost Heaven.

Mottos communicate how citizens and tourist boards feel about their states and those states' attributes that set it apart from all others. They admit a bias, just like I admit my bias for the following:

1. Boeing planes
2. Jif peanut butter
3. American-made products
4. Strawberry ice cream
5. Michigan State University Spartans
6. My wife
7. My children
8. My grandchildren
9. College students

I use the word "for" to mean I am a dedicated advocate of Boeing, Jif, and strawberry ice cream, etc. Also, notice I don't use any comparatives such as Airbus planes or Skippy peanut butter to state my preferences. And, it's not that I'm against Airbus, Skippy, or chocolate ice cream, but I prefer Boeing, Jif, and strawberry.

As a word, bias has a negative connotation for some people. It might even mean "unfairness" or "lack of even-handedness." Substitute the word "preference" for bias, if you have a bias against "bias."

Determining the biases of bad leaders is quite difficult. They intentionally tend to obscure their preferences and commitments, and in doing so, make it hard for followers to follow.

In general elections, people get tired of candidates bashing one another and indicating what the other person was for or against. Most would rather have candidates state what they are "for," what they intend to do, how they will achieve their agendas, and how citizens will be able to measure success. If they do a good enough job of informing people what they stand for, voters can discern for themselves the policies each candidate opposes.

Do you recall the scene in the 1994 movie *Forrest Gump*[33] in which Forrest quits running back and forth between the west coast and east coast? He abruptly stops, says he is tired, and heads for home. His entourage is then placed in a quandary. When Forrest ran, they followed, because he had a bias for running, and they thought he had a greater purpose in doing so. When he quit running, they didn't know what to do next. You could see the questioning looks on their faces as if to say, "What should we do now?"

To some extent, this is what followers of bad leaders wonder all the time. When leaders have a bias, followers can react, relate to, and follow their leader's bias. When the leader doesn't have a bias, though, what do followers do?

If a leader has a bias for action, then followers are most likely to have a bias for action. If a leader has a bias for inaction, then followers are most likely to a bias for inaction.

Bad leaders don't want to reveal their biases (if they have them) because they will need to defend those biases. In doing so, they become accountable for the positions they have taken in defense of their biases.

Bad leaders tend to believe that their unbiased or non-committal views are virtuous. They also tend to think an overarching benefit to *not* making up their minds exists, so they attempt to lead using neutrality.

But continuous neutrality makes negotiating and progress difficult. People appearing to be non-biased also appear to be elusive, detached, and ill-informed. Their refusal to take a position and defend it causes organizational chaos and missed opportunities. It's just like elected officials who vote "present" or "maybe," rather than "yes" or "no" on an up-or-down vote. They don't want to be pinned down; they won't defend their vote; nor do they want a definitive "yes" or "no" vote to establish the direction of their voting and follow their political careers.

This is not a sign of superior knowledge or taking the moral high ground; it is vacillation and weakness. If followers are paying attention, they should recognize it as such. In this instance, a bad leader's vacillation is like soap in a tub. You know it's there because of the smell and bubbles, but it's difficult to see, takes a while to find, and tends to slip away easily.

Admitting to bias has lost its value; it's been replaced in many organizations by the belief that the business will somehow unsettle customers about the true identity of the organization and what it wants to achieve if it admits bias. The manufacturing, banking, and insurance industries, as well as many others, are afraid to admit their biases for serving customers, making a profit, and producing quality, in-demand products and services. Their principal goals should *not* be giving to a charity, sponsoring a cancer walk, or supporting the local high school football team—as worthy as these secondary goals may be.

Most businesses are created to separate consumers from their money by providing goods or services of comparative value. Nothing is wrong with this goal if each party engages in fair exchange to everyone's advantage. Some organizations are afraid that, in admitting their biases, they will offend or turn off potential customers. These types of organizations are the ones whose leaders say, "We can't be all things to all people." But that is exactly what they do by not admitting bias for the way they conduct themselves and how they produce goods or services.

As bad leaders fail to admit their biases, they admit their belief that the organizations they lead are no better than any others, that their products are no better, or their missions are no more worthy of support than any others.

If, in promoting their neutrality, bad leaders do not admit their biases for their products, services, or their people and processes, they will attract little support for their leadership.

I've always felt uncomfortable sitting in an opposing team's cheering section. My wife and I once attended one of our son's critical basketball games, and we arrived late. The place was packed. For some reason, the only seats were among the fans of the home team. We learned a lesson. We weren't obnoxious, out of order, or impolite, but we were out of sync with the fans of the home team. We didn't get harassed to any great degree, but we did find seats for the second half among more friendly fans. We complimented the local fans on their support for their team, whether the team was behind or ahead. There was no mistaking their admirable bias.

Bad leaders tend to fear offending those who have an opposing point of view, and those who challenge them. They ride the fence, because they don't see the value in committing to one side or the other. It's also because they are overly concerned about the criticisms of others, and because they lack confidence in their own decisions.

Intent on being unbiased, bad leaders don't provide definitive support for the initiatives of others. They are uncomfortable with action plans that call for authoritative decisions and lasting commitments. These leaders make up their minds to remain unbiased, letting others make decisions and bear the consequences of those decisions.

For this type of bad leader, being unbiased trumps all other values or contributions they could make. They are of little, if any, value as allies.

Great enterprises are not built by the unbiased.

How much better to say, as good leaders do, "I am making a decision. I believe it to be the right one, based on the data in hand. If it is not the right decision, we can fix it downstream."

Achieving firm, lasting commitments or "lockdowns" from bad leaders is quite difficult. They tend to concentrate on being noncommittal. They even attempt to build their personal brands around their non-commitments, although they are seldom willing to admit doing it. Perhaps you have seen those who turn "wavering" into an art form. Unfortunately, it can be modeled by others in the organization as an effective strategy to emulate.

Bad leaders tend to hide behind their indecision due to emotional and even career protection. They are unusually averse to being found "in the wrong" or following ineffective strategies. Failure to be biased for the proper things leads to personal and organizational identity confusion.

The refusal to admit bias creates a false sense of objectivity that supersedes other good management practices. Being unbiased does not make one superior in judgments, morality, or actions. If you are truly *for* your company, say so; if you are truly *for* your employees, say and act like you are. If not, leave.

One way that companies and organizations show bias for themselves, their products, or their services is to create a consistent message in their branding—colors, fonts, and logo. To illustrate, one of the higher educational institutions for which I worked had a number of mixed messages regarding its branding. The institution had been transitioning from college to university status. There are no hard-and-fast rules for such transitions. For some institutions, the transition can merely mean a change of the stationery and web address; for others, it can mean a fundamental change in structure and direction.

This particular institution had made the change in name and status many years earlier, but leadership had not taken the initiative to tell the city and state to change its name on traffic signs. Some signs read "college" and others read "university," thus allowing confusion about the institution's status.

The same was true about its official colors. I observed thirteen different combinations and colors on various athletic uniforms. (This was well before the days of multiple color combinations of uniforms. See Nike and the University of Oregon athletic programs.) When I inquired about this, I was informed that each team wore the shade of color and font its leaders thought were most attractive. No unified font or color existed. This was so unlike other universities where the base colors for uniforms and branding never change. In fact, a university promotes much of its identity through its colors, font, and logo. A lack of inattention and persuasive leadership allowed this inconsistency to occur and continue. Leaders were afraid to admit and act on their biases for even such things as university colors.

Similarly, registered logos and trademarks, fonts and colors of companies seldom change. When they do, solutions are well researched and market tested. Not so for bad leaders. They waver in their opinions and don't see the symbolic and practical nature of speaking with a single voice in something as important as company or university colors, logos, and signage.

As in the university example, no virtue exists when being unbiased leads to chaos and an unwillingness to work toward competitive distinction. I've noticed that those leaders who are least likely to be biased about what they have been tasked to do are the ones who also have a false sense of what being unbiased produces. Often, being unbiased is a virtue; but having bias is especially vital to producing competitive distinction.

If bad leaders imply (through the cloak of being unbiased) that their company's products or services are no better than those of their competitors, that the company lacks anything exceptional or unique, then they are the wrong leaders. This test applies to countries, non-profits, and educational institutions as well.

Leaders have the responsibility to extend their company's bias for action, R&D, superior products and/or services, and what it does better than all others. Leaders must promote these things repetitively and passionately, not deny them by being unbiased. If leaders think they are no better than their competitors, this behavior is easily unmasked and sends a chilling effect throughout the organization.

> Most people become discouraged when they realize their leaders are not acting as cheerleaders for the entities they are supposedly serving and promoting. Such behaviors send an internal virus throughout the organization that infects the willingness and tenacity of employees to persist.

GOOD LESSONS:

- Good leaders understand that their followers expect them to be biased in favor of the company, its people, and its products or services.
- Good leaders take well-researched, rational positions and defend them as superior.
- Good leaders admit their biases and use them to promote a competitive distinction.
- Good leaders understand that there is cultural sensitivity to the use of the word "bias," but they engage it in a positive fashion to become discrimi-

nating in their choices and actions while not engaging in discrimination of people.

- Good leaders take a stand and defend the rightness, merits, and what they believe to be the ultimate success of their initiatives.
- Adopting a noncommittal stance is not a good way to build great companies and institutions, but bad leaders think it is.
- Bad leaders, if they are biased at all, are biased in favor of quick, inconsequential, and superficial solutions to nagging problems, but they won't admit it.
- Bad leaders minimize the arguments and personhood of those who oppose their destructive biases, but they won't admit it.
- Good leaders have learned from bad leaders that the myth of neutrality causes distrust, malaise, and identity confusion.

4. Refusal to Use a Reverse Gear

Several years ago, my wife and I were traveling with our sons to Steamboat Springs, Colorado, where we have spent many extraordinarily good times both in the summer and winter. Late one snowy night, we were traveling to go skiing and were approaching Steamboat on highway 40, just to the south and east. To get to Steamboat from the SE on highway 40, we were forced to go over Rabbit Ears Pass, which has both an east and a west summit. At about two in the morning, we were between the summits in the middle of a huge snowstorm. We had whiteout conditions, and travel was slow, tedious, and dangerous. As with many paved mountain roads, there are frequent sections with additional uphill lanes. They serve to increase safety, reduce congestion, and aid heavy vehicles on the climb.

We were proceeding at no more than fifteen miles an hour in this nearly continuous whiteouts. The only things I could see to keep on the road were the reflective snow poles along the sides. As I was hugging the right lane and following the snow poles, I didn't realize I was also traveling in the outside lane of one of the uphill three-lane sections. Additionally, I didn't see the signage that indicated to move left because the three lanes would soon become only two.

Much to my great surprise, I drove headlong into a ten-foot snowbank. I looked at my wife and sons, and they had the look of "my, what a mess you've gotten us into!" We could not stay stuck there in the snow for fear of being hit from behind. But there was no possible way ahead because the snow was too deep. The only solution was to slowly and carefully back up while using the same tracks that got us into the snowbank.

I have never been more thankful for a reverse gear in my life. We got out of the snowbank and slowly crept over the west summit down the hill into Steamboat Springs. I did notice we were the last westbound car over the pass, and the eastbound lanes closed just as we passed. I later learned that the white-out conditions were caused by winds of more than one hundred miles an hour.

I have reflected on this Rabbit Ears Pass experience many times and felt thankful that our SUV had a reverse gear. I had to back up to get out of the trouble, and I learned a good lesson.

All too often, bad leaders tend to not use a reverse gear. Instead, they keep pressing ahead when they shouldn't. Often leaders are so intent, as they should be, upon reaching objectives and goals that they don't notice they have lost their way. As a result, they're heading for personal and organizational disaster.

Every well-managed entity has an appropriate pace and rhythm. Going too slow is sometimes as bad, or worse, than going too fast. Shifting into reverse from a dead stop is far easier than shifting into reverse at high speed. Slowing down, stopping, then shifting into reverse is a tactical decision that bad leaders often see as a bad strategic move.

Often, bad leaders fail to assess their direction, progression rates, or resources being consumed to drive ahead, so they refuse reversing. Reversing is too harmful to their egos and the self-perceptions they have worked hard to establish as proof of their good leadership. Bad leaders hate going into reverse even when doing so is realistic and justified.

The inability to use a reverse gear and back out of a harmful situation is a characteristic of bad leaders. These are the leaders who, because of an internal need to be seen as having used their superior judgment in charting a course, have too much invested in a decision or direction than to use a reverse gear.

When good leaders see that the way ahead is blocked, they don't try to jam ahead. They know reversing is sometimes essential to long-term progress, so they set their pride aside and go from "D" to "R." If they need to back up, they do so intentionally, correct their course, and press on.

Successfully using a reverse gear repositions an automobile or corporation to more ably progress toward their long-term goals. Good leaders know the difference between the persistence required to work through difficulties and the unwarranted ego and self-perceptions that cause bad leaders to press ahead when it is unnecessary or dangerous.

Leaders who have had the courage to re-evaluate progress, shift into reverse, and then continue forward earn far more respect than those who refuse to use a reverse gear and move capriciously ahead to the company's doom. Perhaps their fear of losing momentum overrides the company's need for caution.

When shifting into reverse, good leaders are not forsaking core principles and values but ultimately working to move more efficiently in the right direction at an increased speed. Reversing direction is not a permanent strategy but a tactical correction to stabilize, minimize risk, cut stress on resources, and then move ahead more ably.

Business and military history is filled with leaders who saw themselves as so grandiose and heroic that their egos would not let them use reverse gear. By pressing ahead, they would not only lose battles, but sometimes wars. In the Battle of the Little Bighorn in June, 1876, the action of Lt. Colonel George Armstrong Custer is a prime example of this type of refusal.

Organizations get into difficulty when leaders are so vested in the pressure of maintaining their personal egos and the company's image, however erroneous, that they cannot emotionally afford to be seen as going in reverse—even temporarily. Bad leaders reject the thought and deny the need to reverse course, while good leaders with teachable attitudes use whatever means necessary to get out of trouble. That includes going in reverse.

GOOD LESSONS:
- Good leaders know that shifting into reverse is a repositioning strategy.

- Good leaders know that going in reverse is not a permanent replacement for going forward.
- Good leaders know it is better to face forward and look at where they are going rather than where they have been.
- Riders, like employees and shareholders, become more nervous the longer it takes for leaders to move to reverse and stay in reverse.
- Bad leaders are mistaken in their fear that going in reverse will become a permanent solution.
- Refusing to go in reverse to get out of trouble indicates immaturity, impatience, and a lack of inventiveness.
- Using reverse gear is not a sign of weakness but of superior judgment, resolve, and willingness to engage a short-term tactic to meet a long-term strategy.
- Good leaders know it takes more concentration when going in reverse than going forward. That's why they don't do it for long.

5. Refusal to Loaf Creatively

To most people, creativity and loafing don't seem to go hand in hand, but in fact, they are strongly related. Most bad leaders don't *creatively* loaf; they just loaf. What's the difference? Creative loafing is planned and productive idleness.

Good leaders learn how to loaf creatively and productively, and they can draw substantial benefits from doing it. Bad leaders don't loaf creatively because they don't see the knowledge, insights, and understanding that the proper kind of loafing can provide.

Bad leaders are known to loaf, but not creatively.

The history and etymology of the word "loaf," as you might suspect, comes from the idea of mixing and kneading flour and various ingredients to make bread. Loafing is to form into portions or blocks to be baked. Yet, another definition is to idle away time.

After the Industrial Revolution, loafing became identified with nonproductive time and nonproductive people who are non-energetic. People who are idle produce nothing. But good leaders know that productive idleness exists and is highly useful.

Some of the best managers/leaders set aside time to loaf creatively because it sharpens their emotional intelligence and perceptions. If can also deepen their knowledge about how people use and talk about the products and services their companies provide.

Creative loafing is a less sophisticated form of observational research than ethnography. Ethnography is a form of observational research in which researchers spend large amounts of time observing groups of people and identifying behaviors specific to each group. An organization might use ethnographic techniques to identify how potential customers spend their time, how lifestyle choices influence buying and product use, and how consumers access and consume services. The setting for the research may be the workplace, home, a leisure activity, or a variety of other locations such as shopping malls and airports.

I often try to make the most of my time and sharpen my observation skills while waiting in airports. After the emails, texting, and phone calls have been done and I don't want to read or write, I attempt to guess the country of origin, state of residence, vocation, primary motive in life, state of mind, or destination by observing the actions, attitudes, and appearance of people passing by. This then provides the data upon which we might engage in a conversation.

In many ways, this is similar to the process used during creatively loafing. Good leaders go out of their way to more creatively interpret the information they have, get new information from others, and use what they have gathered to create productive engagements.

A leader's refusal to creatively loaf can mirror an unwillingness to acknowledge the benefits created by coming out from behind the desk, purposefully walking around, and anticipating discovery. Creative loafing also sends the message that a leader is willing to learn and be led. Yes, it's good to be seen as a "creative loafer" by employees. And, it's bad to be seen by employees as just a "loafer." There is a huge difference between the two.

Ken Blanchard picked up on this theme in the *One Minute Manager.*[34] Other authors regarding management and leadership have written about management by walking around and using short segments of time to learn and gain perspective.

For leaders, getting out of their primary setting for a few minutes to make observations will alter perspectives and increase the spirit of discovery.

Leaders who are too busy to speak in depth with their customers, employees, and fellow workers are clearly too busy to express their humanity. They see no benefit in touching hands and hearing the hearts of people they attempt to lead, influence, and sell. This imperialistic, detached, and thus untouchable leader would consider "creative loafing" to be silly and non-productive.

GOOD LESSONS:

- Great benefits accrue to those who become experts at creative loafing. It becomes a standard practice to increase awareness and exposure to people and ideas that make organizations relevant.

- Good leaders carve out time to creatively loaf. This requires a reprioritizing of their time and focus, but it seldom fails to produce insights and energy.

- For bad leaders, loafing creatively is just too much work.

- When bad leaders have the need to see themselves as busy (and others see them busy, too), they are less inclined to practice and derive value from creative loafing.

- Creative loafing causes bad leaders to reflect differently on their self-importance and the criticality of their presence, so they are unlikely to practice it.

Creative loafing has both a process value and a product value, but it should not be practiced merely to escape conflict and avoid decision making.

- When practiced well, creative loafing sends a message about the good leader's willingness to learn and be attentive, accessible, and visible. When not practiced, it sends a message about the bad leader's unwillingness to learn and be inattentive, inaccessible, and invisible.

- Good leaders use creative loafing to *increase* human interaction, not *decrease* it.

- While creatively loafing, good leaders capitalize on and leverage what they have learned through human interaction.
- If you are too busy to loaf creatively, then you will miss the short-term energy, enhanced relationships, and long-term benefits created from this practice.

---

6. Refusal to Acknowledge Role in Success and Failure

The words mistake, miscalculation, bust, blunder, mess, screw-up, flub, flop, blow-up, strikeout, glitch, accident, and error all describe some form of failure.

There are various degrees of failure: e.g., complete, partial, big, or small. There are percentages of failure: e.g., 50 percent or 75 percent. Failures are created by bad timing, faulty data, misreading of the market, over-aggressiveness, and presumption. A lack of talent and proper execution, misappropriation of resources, underfunding, and/or simply a bad idea are often cited as having roles in failure. Degrees or partial failures provide the best cover for ineffective leaders.

Good leaders tend to understate the role they play in success while bad leaders tend to understate the role they play in failure.

Partial failures are sometimes partial successes, depending on who's making the assessment. What the data indicated, what was achieved, and what was not achieved is left to interpretation. Federal unemployment rates are a good example. If unemployment is ten percent, then it also must mean employment is ninety percent. This statement is not necessarily true or untrue. Which percentage is considered the best measure of the health of the economy—that is, the number of people working or not working. The answer depends on the interpretations, the interpreter, and the complexities of the data collected.

Using a traditional "CYA" strategy is the first option for a leader who refuses to take responsibility for failures. Rather than launching an investigation to determine what went wrong, bad leaders are likely first to determine who is responsible for what went wrong, then point an accusing finger rather than immediately start triage.

Bad leaders may attempt to deflect attention away from their role in failure or attempt to minimize the failure's effects. Of course, bad leaders initially look to those other than themselves or their teams as explanations for failure. They may also default to a no-fault mentality that says no one person or thing is responsible for the failure.

After triage, good leaders are inclined to point to their own roles and what they did or didn't do that created or accelerated the failure. They look first at their own behaviors and decisions as possible reasons, then to other people or systems as reasons for failure.

Bad leaders are likely to attribute failure to a lack of resources, saying that if more resources were available, then failure would have been averted. "More" is always the cure for their failures.

Good leaders tend to think that failure was caused, not by a lack of resources, but by a misuse of resources, lack of diligence, and poor execution.

Bad leaders affix failure to blame and blame to a lack of resources. In contrast, good leaders know that failure does not always result from lack of resources but probably from interrelated systems problems.

Bad leaders would rather determine who is responsible for failure than how it occurred or how to overcome it. They rarely offer assurance that an appropriate solution will prevent the same problem from reoccurring. But placing blame does not fix problems.

Many public figures such as celebrities, athletes, or politicians can say they have taken full responsibility for a failure in their judgment, comments, or actions, and they quickly skate away with little consequence. Failure related to your job performance is another issue and not nearly so easy to avoid, especially when you need to confront it on a regular basis. If the failure is not just an indiscretion or temporary weakness but could develop into a career-crushing stigma, then not only taking responsibility but also guaranteeing it won't happen again is essential.

Bad leaders seldom, if ever, fully commit to an initiative that cannot be blamed on someone else if it goes wrong.

Supreme Allied Command General Dwight Eisenhower is an excellent example of a good leader who took responsibility for potential failure. *Before* the D-Day landing took place, Eisenhower took full responsibility for failure so that others who may have been implicated in the decision would not bear the criticism if the invasion failed. Eisenhower "manned up" in case the invasion failed. He got ahead of potential criticism for failure.

However, when the invasion succeeded, Eisenhower gave the credit to others and minimized his contribution. This is just as it should be with great leaders but is rarely the case with bad ones. I speculate that if D-Day had failed, Eisenhower would have never stated it was a lack of resources that caused it but said it was bad timing and a lack of planning and execution on his part. Questioning the effort of his troops would never have entered the mix.

If the initiative/idea/plan/product is successful, a bad leader will take the praise. If not, a bad leader will point the finger at someone else. Refusing to take responsibility for failure and blaming others are profound character flaws that have a profound negative effect on morale. Being unjustly blamed for failure is an enormously difficult experience. When a bad leader refuses to take accountability for a failure and implicates an innocent party, it is particularly despicable. Unfortunately, this behavior is to be expected.

GOOD LESSONS:

> If you caused the mistake, miscalculation, bust, blunder, mess, screw-up, flub, flop, blow-up, strikeout, glitch, accident, or error, then take responsibility and fix the problem. If the failure is not your fault but you get blamed for it, make your position known and defend yourself responsibly knowing the person or group who caused the failure will refuse to do so.

- Bad leaders won't skin their own skunks; they are not likely to take responsibility for or fix the disasters they cause.
- Good leaders put organizations in the center of the road, go in the right direction, and stay out of the ditch. They keep organizations doing the right things and avoiding the wrong.

- Bad leaders put organizations on the shoulder of the road close to the ditch and going in the wrong direction. They keep organizations doing the wrong things instead of the right.

- Good leaders want to discover and solve the problems that led to a failure. They seek to instruct the people who lacked the insight, knowledge, and leadership skills that allowed failure to occur. These leaders understand that a best strategy is to not ignore or denigrate those accused of causing the failure but to help them ensure the failure won't occur again.

- Bad leaders are attracted to retribution against those who caused a failure, but they are not likely to admit it. They may wait a long time for a chance for retribution, particularly if the failure reflected badly on their performance and status. They are likely to withhold their attack until a time when it will have the greatest impact on those who caused the failure. They neither forgive nor forget.

- Good leaders get in front of possible failures. They anticipate that something could go wrong and will work to prevent it. And if, by chance, a problem or portion of an action was not or could not have been anticipated and prevented, then a good leader will recognize the failure, own it, apologize for it, and fix it.

- If you are responsible for a failure, admit it, and forget it to the point of not being haunted by it. Then compensate for it through other relevant successes.

- Seldom is a single failure a job- or career-ending occurrence, but bad leaders can make it so if they are committed to finding fault and placing blame.

- Good leaders create the means of re-establishing their credibility and status after a failure, but bad leaders won't take the time and energy to do so. Either they will not engage in the recovery process, or they will exit.

Many highly successful people have decisions and deeds somewhere in their history that achieved less than stellar results, but they took responsibility for them and achieved compensating successes.

- Good leaders know that the wisest time and energy ever spent is to reconfirm all technology and safety systems, ensure a positive customer experience, and guarantee launch readiness. If a product, plan, or system cannot be fully vetted before rollout, good leaders are alert to the first sign of trouble and resolve it prior to a crisis happening.
- Sometimes do-overs just can't happen. When a bad leader refuses to take responsibility for failure, even do-overs can't set all things right. Good leaders assume responsibility and move ahead toward a new, more desirable reality that ensures the quality of the redo and corrects the failure it was created to fix.
- Good leaders concentrate on *preventing* failures. Bad leaders concentrate on *denying* failures.

Good leaders, although understanding of those who have caused failure, are cautious to fall on their swords for the sake of proving their own charity and empathy.

- Good leaders never expect others to fall on their swords or metaphorically take a bullet for them if they fail. They do this for others.
- Bad leaders expect that others will fall on their swords and metaphorically take a bullet for them when they fail, but they won't do it for others.

---

7. Refusal to Take Responsibility for Organizational Culture

Bad leaders do not fully understand (or in some cases partially understand) their responsibility for creating and maintaining their organization's culture. Either they haven't thought much about it, or they mistakenly think that somehow the type of culture they desire will just create itself. It doesn't.

Good leaders know that the organizational culture they want is not left to chance or to develop by itself. Rather, it is a conscious act of creation and requires continuous diligence to maintain.

234

resetting

I once heard it said, "Culture is growing up not knowing what Velveeta is." That is a different interpretation of culture altogether! However, culture is formed by the characteristics of a class or group, enlightenment and excellence of taste acquired by intellectual and aesthetic training. It can also refer to the typical behavior of a group or class of people. The terms "pervasive atmosphere" and "organizational climate" are somewhat synonymous with culture and used as such within most organizations.

Without deliberate efforts to create an organizational culture, it will create itself. Some organizations take the "*Que sera, sera*, whatever will be, will be" approach to it. Bad leaders don't take seriously the fact that group and/or organizational cultures will either develop by design or by default. However, molding a culture intentionally is easier than remolding one that has created itself.

If you don't act with intention to create the organizational culture you want, then you will get the culture you *don't* want. Good leaders do not shirk this creative activity. In fact, really good leaders determine what type of climate they want before they develop a business strategy, vision, or mission statement.

It makes no sense to let organizational culture form by default, because the cultural climate will supersede everything, including tactics and strategies. Like a shadow that follows or a form that molds, the pervasive culture of an organization will make or break its success.

Often, one hears of new leaders stating that their first order of business is to "change the culture of failure and defeat." The phrase "change in the culture" is used many times in reference to failing businesses, losing teams, and the federal government in Washington, DC.

I recall overhearing conversations that centered on issues of policy and corporate culture among employees at Starbucks, Boeing, Amazon.com, Chipotle, Home Depot, Bank of America, Raytheon, and others. The comments were both positive and negative. I couldn't help but overhear their conversations. Occasionally, I asked if they had intended to include me. What ensued was some interesting dialogue and learning about organizational culture.

I was greatly surprised at what some employees said, either because they didn't think anybody was listening, or because the culture of their places of employment allowed them to say whatever they wanted, whenever they wanted.

The immediate culture determined their degree of freedom to express their views, whether the openness to speak was approved or unapproved by company policy and culture.

Organizational culture ends up being whatever it is allowed to be. It determines what appropriate behavior is and is not, what will be tolerated and what will not.

From large corporate offices to start ups in warehouses to elevators and board rooms from Beijing to London and from LA to NYC, one simply needs to listen to what employees say to each other in off-hand conversations. That's how to determine the cultural profile and ethos of their organizations—whether planned or unplanned, formed by design or by default, fertilized and watered, or allowed to grow unattended.

If you pay attention, a pattern of communication and employee behavior will quickly emerge that is a either a reflection or a repudiation of a company's corporate culture as it is announced to the world or posted in prominent locations.

Regardless of size or status, every corporation, NGO, or government has a discernible, palatable, culture that was either designed deliberately by good leaders or left to grow organically and unattended by bad leaders.

Bad leaders tend to let the organizational cultures design themselves. Good leaders don't. The enduring, enriching, goal to achieve positive organizational cultures are thoughtfully created and carefully nurtured.

Corporate cultures are likely to evolve over time as conditions and people change, but certain "core value" absolutes—such as quality goods and/or services and customer- and employee-centric innovation—are not likely to be modified capriciously.

Corporate cultures can also develop around unanticipated, unusual themes, opportunities, and practices. Consider Lambert's Café in Sikeston, Missouri, and also in Ozark, Missouri, and Foley, Alabama. The café's corporate culture and consumer image includes throwing bread rolls to customers. "Lambert's Café is the Home of the Throwed Roll."

Yes, the entire ethos of Lambert's is tied to throwing baked goods, and they make it work. Their customers drive great distances to enjoy its country cooking and catching the rolls!

Why We Love It: We can't help but appreciate the gusto with which Lambert's employees toss bread at us. And it's not just a wimpy little lob; they pitch those rolls clear across the dining room. Sometimes you just need to loosen up and appreciate a silly tradition. And the roll is...quite good. Super hot, super soft, fluffy, melt-in-your-mouth bread.[35]

Regardless of how it began, Lambert's has made throwing the roll its public image. But under that image is a culture of serving good food and helping customers have a memorable experience.

In many organizations, great differences exist between their stated goals and their real goals. The real goals are those they expend resources (PECIT) to achieve. Their stated goals are for their websites, Facebook pages, funders, and shiny print pieces. They want their various constituencies to believe those stated goals.

Bad leaders don't seem to be bothered by discrepancies between stated goals and real goals or stated cultures and real cultures. Good leaders, on the other hand, spend a great deal of time and energy closing any gaps between real goals and stated goals, and between actual cultures and desired cultures.

GOOD LESSONS:

- The better the leaders, the more energetic and diligent they are about the design and continuance of the culture they desire.
- Good leaders determine by design rather than by default what type of organizational climate will produce the intended results, whether financial or missional.
- Good leaders don't delegate their role in building corporate culture. Rather, they understand that their actions, attitudes, and modeling help form and interpret the culture.
- Bad leaders lack the interest and diligence to play formative roles in creating a planned corporate culture. They think that their actions, attitudes, and modeling only marginally affect the culture they want. They're wrong.

- Bad leaders just hope for the best culture; good leaders take responsibility and actions to ensure the culture they want.
- Because bad leaders would rather move along to more "important" stuff, they fail to acknowledge that few, if any, more important responsibilities lie before them than to design, articulate, and lead toward the desired culture.
- Creating an enduring and relevant organizational culture is a matter of passion, focus, and will rather than a matter of time or chance.

You can become known, build your brand, and be compensated as an incredible leader *if* you learn the lessons of building, maintaining, recreating, and/or reforming organizational cultures.

- Good leaders start building their personal brands as good leaders in their micro-responsibilities, small groups, and teams by successfully learning what good leaders do and bad leaders fail to do regarding corporate culture.
- The leader who learns the nuances of corporate culture that enable goal attainment will get opportunities to set them in motion repeatedly.
- If you want a certain type of culture or tone within your organization, you must clearly state what you want, add what will enable it, and eliminate things that don't—all while understanding that you will need to attend to it.
- The type of corporate culture you want doesn't always require big promotions or large financial expenditures. It can be realized by simply letting someone overhear your conversations about how much you appreciate employees' efforts and how proud you are of them.
- Good leaders carve out resources to fund competitive activities that help create the organizational cultures they desire. They take extraordinary measures to create or improve organizational climates that enable mission achievement. For example, I once participated in an activity in which members of our faculty were placed into teams to play Whirlyball. This afternoon Whirlyball event was an excellent culture- and team-building activity because it was competitive and put us in an unfamiliar context with people we had little opportunity to build relationships with.

Although some of the "stuffy" faculty members questioned the efficacy of Whirlyball, the majority perceived it to be an enjoyable activity that helped build an organizational climate. Bad leaders won't make the effort to try Whirlyball or a similar culture-building activity.

---

8. Refusal to Provide Covering Fire

The term "covering fire" has military and combat overtones, but it also applies to business and organizational settings. Covering fire is the protection provided by your team members and/or your leader when you attempt to change your position, gain a strategic advantage, or take new ground as in combat.

Bad leaders underestimate the stress and potential harm that can occur when followers perceive that their leaders don't have their best interests in mind and don't provide covering fire. They often fail to shield their people from unwarranted criticism and exploitation, forcing their followers to take on the fire themselves.

You know when a good leader has your back and provides covering fire. Generally, you feel relief knowing that when you move ahead with new arguments and initiatives, your leader's covering fire could save your corporate life.

On the other hand, if you or your ideas have ever been exposed to attack and in need of covering fire, you know how being uncovered and unsupported feels. Realizing you are on your own because your leaders are uninterested in your dilemma is an extremely unpleasant experience.

Refusal to provide covering fire means a leader perceives there is "too great a risk and too little reward" for engaging the incoming opposition. Bad leaders fail to provide covering fire because they believe the expenditure of resources is too great to justify taking action on behalf of others. Still, spending resources to provide covering fire for themselves and their ideas is justified to them. For this reason, refusal to provide covering fire may indicate that a new direction, initiative, or product will likely die from lack of leadership support—not because it was badly designed or unable to be successful.

Additionally, bad leaders fail to provide covering fire if they're more interested in punishing those at risk or attempting to get even for previous offenses. Reasons for not providing covering fire arise from inter-organizational fighting and company politics. Moreover, bad leaders might flaunt their disinterest by choosing not to provide protection and by placing their people at risk.

A willingness to provide defensive countermeasures to protect an idea or people from incoming fire is among a good leader's key duties. Bad leaders tend to rationalize away duties that require protection. The concept that "we take care of our own" is foreign to the bad leader who is unwilling or unprepared to provide covering fire.

When employees and fellow workers learn they will not receive covering fire while attempting to advance, they experience tremendous demotivation. Their feelings of loss and betrayal can lead to abandoning the cause for which they initiated the advance. Good leaders anticipate the need to provide covering fire and will *move toward* the engagement. By comparison, bad leaders *move away from* most engagements requiring covering fire.

Good leaders provide covering fire to shield good ideas from deterrents and those who intentionally create opposition. It also prevents a feeding frenzy of opposition while building strength, *esprit de corps*, and group identity.

Using covering fire exceptionally well separates the good leader from the bad and the great leader from the good. No historical or current leader is considered great who has not demonstrated a clear record of providing timely covering fire. They have used it when it's likely to do the most good. Their timing needs to be nearly perfect, because they want their teams to achieve as much as they can *without* cover to strengthen their own leadership skills, maturity, and success.

When U.S. President Franklin Roosevelt took office at the height of the Great Depression in early 1933, he had already set in motion a large number of historic policy additions and changes to federal law. These aimed to reduce further stagnation and lead the county toward economic recovery more quickly.

Whether you agree with his New Deal or not, you can see that Roosevelt provided covering fire and backed those he appointed in order to advance his policies. He used his power of covering fire and the clout of his office to achieve his stated goals fast.

Leaders who have the ability but not the willingness to provide covering fire face more negative blowback than leaders who don't have the ability or status to provide it.

Followers do not expect to receive covering fire from a leader who can't deliver it, so they will be more cautious when it comes to taking risks. Far more discouraging is having an unrealized expectation that covering fire will be provided. It is better to deliver covering fire when it's *not* expected than to not receive covering fire when it *is* expected.

Bad leaders tend to justify their lack of covering fire by saying they didn't think it was needed or they couldn't deliver it. This position is of little solace when team members have poured their hearts, souls, and minds into a project—only to have it unsupported by covering fire they thought would be present when needed.

Those benefitting from covering fire feel great relief. The first time I felt that relief occurred when I was a child. I enjoyed riding my bike to my friend's farm several miles out in the county. My parents would drive the car there while I rode. I had fun riding, except for the huge, mean collie dog that hated little boys passing by his yard on bicycles. In fact, he hated and chased *everything* that passed by. The first time I rode by, I feared being eaten alive, so I developed several strategies to get by the dog safely. If I attempted to sneak by quietly or quickly, I would get attacked. I even threw water balloons and rocks at him as I raced by. But nothing worked until I finally figured out a solution. I timed my passage by the dog's yard at precisely the same moment my dad drove by in the car. The dog chased after dad's car, not after me. What a sense of protection I felt when my dad provided covering fire!

I kept that experience in mind when, in later years, I could provide covering fire for my coworkers and those in my employ. I often did it for my senior managers and VPs when I knew they were under time pressure or needed a few hours of research and prep time for important activities. And I would occasionally have them offload work to me to handle on their behalf. These actions benefitted them and me as well. When I temporarily stepped into their shoes, it gave me opportunities to develop fresh insights. Never did I feel they had taken advantage of the covering fire I provided.

Receiving covering fire is a rewarding, encouraging experience. Failing to provide covering fire for colleagues, fellow workers, or employees when needed is cowardly.

GOOD LESSONS:

> Covering fire doesn't always require a crisis. Good leaders might inconvenience themselves for the sake of others by sharing the load.

- Bad leaders seldom, if ever, provide covering fire by taking the criticism aimed at their people or at ideas their people express.
- Some covering fire never becomes known except to those who received it. Good leaders don't expect to be acknowledged for doing so, while bad leaders expect to be noticed and praised for covering fire (if they ever provide it).
- Good leaders anticipate the need to provide covering fire but never to the point of followers allowing themselves to be ill-prepared to advance their ideas, arguments, and initiatives.
- Although not paternalistically, good leaders expect that their followers will need their covering fire as they draw fire from those who are critical of innovation and others who are content with the status quo.
- Providing covering fire for your people and their ideas lets them know you have their backs and will draw criticism away from them.

9. Refusal to Steadfastly Engage Performance Evaluations

No one I know gets euphoric when it's time to conduct employee performance evaluations. Like going to the dentist, performance evaluations need to be done; but people can find a lot of better things to do instead.

Supervisors dread the interruption that conducting formal employee evaluations cause, except when their own evaluations are tied to the integrity of the process and could have compensation implications for them. At that point, how they feel about the process becomes less tedious.

Some managers attempt to humanize and enhance the process the best they can, but even they and their 360-degree evaluation groups prefer doing other activities. HR experts and their firms are paid great sums of money to make the appraisal process more redemptive and productive. But, try as they might, few evaluators are ever really content with the evaluation process.

Better forms, metrics, processes, and even inventiveness seldom achieve higher expectations and better results. In fact, rarely is there sufficient time or energy to conduct first-rate evaluations that assess, diagnose, and implement strategies to benefit those being evaluated. And, as you know, conducting performance appraisals is hard work when done well.

Even for those who achieve A++ ratings with promotion and compensation attached to the evaluation, the process is often clumsy, suboptimal, and only marginally productive.

Employee performance evaluations (EPEs) are frequently viewed as interruptions to core functions and a supervisor's prime responsibilities. This view of EPE is ordinarily perceived by less able leaders because they don't consider the benefits to exceed the cost of conducting the EPE. Part of the reticence to conduct EPEs is the inherent guilt that evaluators experience when they don't conduct properly planned or well-timed evaluations or when they discover employee deficiencies they must address but don't have the resources to remedy.

Bad leaders might use EPEs as opportunities to get even, punish, and put employees in their places. On occasion, they might use the process itself to control and intimidate employees. They also use evaluations to justify their decisions to not act, to isolate, to exile employees to lesser posts, or to place them in positions that force them to exit the organization.

The leader who doesn't take EPEs seriously might do so because of an organizational ethos of non-concern or a lack of appreciation for the ongoing value of employee development. It could also be a *de facto* statement about replacement employee availability and current employee expendability.

I learned of a supervisor who gave a performance appraisal form to his employees and told them to complete it any way they wanted. He would sign it and pass along the results, thus confirming the employee's comments and categorizations. Everyone knew this to be a phony process that enhanced no one professionally.

However, it did minimize the stature and trustworthiness of the leader in the eyes of others.

The seriousness with which supervisors conduct EPEs often indicates their personal commitment to those they lead and how seriously the organization takes its responsibility to help employees arrive at and go beyond standards. Employees know their immediate supervisor is serious about training and development when they get the commitment of senior leadership to fund training and address deficiencies discovered in the EPE.

Those looking to change employers or those seeking their first professional job after from college or grad school should inquire about the EPE process. If the potential employer equivocates, then the forewarned job seeker should be cautious about the company's commitment to employee growth and development.

Even the best leaders aren't thrilled about conducting EPEs *unless they see a direct relationship between assessment and improved employee performance.* Properly assessing performances can be gut-wrenching, especially for those with whom the supervisor has a good relationship.

To properly evaluate those who are marginally good or bad is far more difficult and emotionally taxing than evaluating those whose performance is clearly exceptional or sub-par. The obviously bad ones can either be terminated or reassigned. It's the highest ranking employees who require the greatest care because they are the most promising, productive, and retainable. They are also the ones most attractive to other employers or likely to exit to start new ventures. These employees need nurturing, motivation, and progressively more challenging assignments, but they also require more sophisticated EPEs.

Many well-intentioned companies have spent large quantities of resources on high-potential employee programs (HIPO) with only marginal success. When the output of HIPO programs are examined, HR professionals don't always agree on their efficacy. They have only limited ability to move HIPO employees to full potential or workplace loyalty. It's similar to farm league baseball teams that need a lot of players in the pipeline to produce one or two big-league stars. It's an expensive but necessary process in player development that comes with high expectations for finding top-rated personnel.

GOOD LESSONS:

- The better the leaders, the more positive their mindset and commitment to conducting proper employee performance evaluations. This commitment bleeds through to other dimensions of their leadership, and their associates easily perceive it.

- Taking a serious interest in the development of one's team members yields rich dividends, including a high regard for the leader who has taken the EPE process as a primary leadership responsibility and uses it to enhance the skill sets of those they supervise.

- Bad leaders see EPE as an unpleasant ancillary activity, not a core responsibility or interest.

- Good leaders inform employees of their status at times other than during formal evaluations. Intermediate informal performance reviews are essential to determining whether employees are performing on task and on time. Then, when employees face the formal evaluations, wholesale corrections don't need to be made, and they will not be surprised by the evaluation's results.

- Good leaders check previous evaluations to determine if any progress toward the objectives has been met. Bad leaders tend not to look back beyond the most recent EPE for comparison.

- Good leaders communicate the importance of EPE. Employees tend to take the evaluation more seriously or less seriously depending on the leader's commitment to and regard for the appraisal process.

Good leaders persuade their followers that EPEs are essential as a means of enhancing performance and satisfaction, not as a means of punishment.

- Beware of the leader who engages EPEs carelessly, openly criticizes the process, and discounts its ability to move employees toward goal attainment.

- Bad leaders tend to let deadlines for evaluations sneak up on them and then rush to get them concluded. If they can offload the EPE task, they will.

- Bad leaders tend to use EPEs as tool to highlight their own bias for or against employees.
- Bad leaders use EPEs as a means of intimidating or punishing employees particularly if they have crossed-swords or disagreed on tactics or strategies.

10. Refusal to Make Decisions

The quality and timeliness of a leader's decision-making is often the supreme test of leadership competency. Few standards are held higher than these. And few things confound and frustrate followers more than a leader's indecision. The quality of a decision is often viewed the same as the accuracy of a decision. That is, the quality of a decision is based on the accuracy of the decision to achieve what it is meant to achieve. Good leaders make decisions in accurate and timely ways.

Bad leaders delay decisions because the desired outcomes of a decision are not fully known or knowable. But outcome quality is not determined by the *amount* of data; it is determined by the *accuracy* of the data. The supreme test of great leadership is making good decisions while not having all the data, knowledge, or time to obtain it.

Not making a decision can be a result of an inability, refusal, or unwillingness to not make it. Not deciding due to fearing the outcomes is the default position for many bad leaders who lack insight, foresight, and courage.

Often bad leaders/supervisors state that they can't make a certain decision because the data needed doesn't exist or isn't available. When indecisiveness is the leader's default behavior, it is noticed and becomes both a point of frustration for coworkers and a huge impediment to smooth operations. An indecision is like a dam of built-up debris that restricts the flow of water behind it.

Delayed decisions are not always better decisions. They often morph into non-decisions. If a decision is delayed or not made due to lack of knowledge, then it's necessary to create or discover that knowledge ASAP. This discovery needs to be specifically assigned with a time terminus to a person or group who will be held accountable and rewarded for its creation.

There is nothing wrong with a responsible leader delaying a decision if big or important pieces to the puzzle are missing. But bad leaders frequently stall, not because data is missing, but because they don't have the will to make a decision.

If leaders deliberately delay in order to frustrate and unnerve their followers, this behavior is manipulative and self-seeking. It builds neither community nor *esprit de corp*. What it does build in followers is distrust.

The term "indecisive" is often used to describe leaders who can't bring themselves to make a decision. It's a descriptor no leader wants, yet this type-casting is difficult to overcome once established. Fear of failure and criticism is often its source.

Not all single acts of indecision by a leader turn into career breakers. But if an important decision is delayed due to duplicity, a display of positional power, or a means to frustrate subordinates, the indecisive title will stick.

Often, bad leaders don't make vital or even mundane decisions because they just don't have the courage to act. Instead, they blame a lack to data rather than their own indecisiveness. When this occurs, they are prone to need subordinates to stand with them in the indecision.

Having all the data doesn't always mean a superior decision will be made. Often there are missing pieces of data, but timing demands that an immediate decision be made. If so, make the decision and move ahead. If it is a bad decision, it can be fixed or reversed downstream, when more data comes available. If it is a good decision, then let it stand.

The refusal to make a decision with only the data at hand provides insights into bad leaders who believe there is more merit in delaying a decision than making it now. This is often true. But many times, delaying a decision due to lack of data doesn't mean a higher-quality decision can be made later. Don't assume that more data later will lead to a better outcome.

The real problem is that decisions sometimes need to be made in concert with other decisions, or in serial order. A delay at one stage might bring everything to a halt.

The following example illustrates how a lack of reliable data—not necessarily more data or data driven by emotion or politics—can have enormously negative consequences.

Sir Winston Churchill has often been viewed as one of the greatest leaders of all time, particularly as the political and military leader of Great Britain during World War II. Early in Churchill's career, he was First Lord of the Admiralty. It was at his insistence that the ill-fated second front was opened during WWI.

The Battle of Gallipoli took place in early 1915 as British and French ships came under heavy fire attempting to pass through the Dardanelles Straits. A land invasion soon followed with disastrous results. Suffering heavy losses, allied troops began evacuating in late 1915. The blame for the massive defeat was laid squarely at the feet of Churchill, along with insufficient intelligence regarding the terrain and a lack of ground-based resources and support. There were 480,000 allied troops engaged, more than 250,000 casualties, and 45,000 deaths.[36]

Following the defeat at Gallipoli, Churchill came under enormous criticism. He resigned his post, enlisted in the army, became an infantry officer, and was wounded while fighting on the western front in Europe.

The Gallipoli disaster followed him during WWI and was used against him for the remainder of his political life. However, it was this stinging defeat and its repercussions that enabled him, in part, to be a determined and successful leader during WW II.

Good leaders make decisions based on all the information they have at the time the decision needs to be made. Often, they don't have all the data they would like, but they decide anyway—in light of the data they have rather than the data they don't—and with respect to the consequences if a decision is not made.

Data doesn't always queue up in desirable ways or on time, but when a decision is needed and waiting won't make the decision any better, make it. To do otherwise weakens your influence with followers and colleagues and makes your organization arrhythmic.

GOOD LESSONS
- Good leaders don't continually hide behind missing data as an excuse for refusing to make a decision.

- Bad leaders delay or don't make decisions in a timely fashion because they can't envision the good results of their decisions and tend to think only of the negative.
- Convinced they are the only person capable of making a good decision, a conceited leader will ignore or discredit the value of input from others. Followers take note of this.
- Often a well-timed, well-executed B-Class decision immediately is better than an ill-timed, poorly executed A-Class decision later.
- What's the best time to make a decision? When it is required and when all necessary data is in hand pointed toward an optimum outcome.

11. Refusal to Become a Datapreneuer

If you were to ask a cross-section of my former MBA students what single business concept, illustration, or value they recall from our time together, I'd predict a high percentage would choose my phrase, "Trust the Data."

That means in wise and timely decision-making, we have to let our weight down and believe that the data upon which we make a decision is trustworthy. If we can't trust objective data, what can we trust?

Today, I'd like a do-over. A great deal of untrustworthy, unverified, unverifiable, tainted, politicized, and weaponized data is present. As stated elsewhere in this book, individual data points make up data; aggregated data makes up information; information should lead to knowledge; knowledge should lead to wisdom.

The better way to say this is, "Trust the data, only if it can be verified as trustworthy."

If you use bad cherries to make a pie, you get a bad pie. If you use bad data to make a decision, then you get a bad decision. Simple, but profound. Good leaders know it; bad leaders disregard it.

One of the errors of young and/or inexperienced leaders is that of believing the data too soon. I'm not suggesting you develop a deep-seated cynicism or even skepticism, but adopt a cautious attitude toward what you have been told or have seen in the data.

Using data wisely is a mantra I now teach; it means using it to become a "datapreneur" by monetizing data.

In his book, *The Billion Dollar Byte,* Deva Justhy created and defines the term datapreneur. It is a new way of looking at how tech and non-tech workers as well as organizational leaders use and monetize data. Like all entrepreneurs who move resources (PECITs) to higher levels of productivity, create innovation, and cause marketplace disruption, datapreneurs move data to a higher level of productivity.

Justhy writes that datapreneurs:

> ". . . **take the initiative to harness the power of data for value creation. Datapreneurs are knowledge workers who 'just don't work with data'; they create value with data as they look for ways to unlock new value through increased revenue, improved compliance and greater efficiency."**

In Justhy's view, "This makes them next-level business strategists . . . who take responsibility for creating economic value through data."[37]

Sometimes you can trust the data more than you can trust the person interpreting the data for you. I'm not writing about the self-evident things, like a professional or college football team that has a horrible win-loss record but does charitable things for its host community. They are considered a bad team because they are 0-10 and have only won three games in the last four years. All win-loss data can be objectively interpreted in only one way. Even if the coach says the team is gaining momentum and the players are becoming respectable citizens, the data makes the case that the team is bad.

In most cases, data is objective, neutral, and unbiased. It is when data is viewed only via subjective eyes and interpreted through prejudiced minds that data should not be trusted. Employees and business owners who have been around a long time and are emotionally mature should be able to correctly read the data; others less so.

Data monetization is defined by Gartner Research as:

> . . . **using data for quantifiable economic benefit. This can include indirect methods such as: measurable business performance improvements, beneficial terms or conditions from business partners, information bartering, productizing information (i.e., new information-based offerings), "informationalizing" products (i.e., including**

information as a value-add component of an existing offering), or selling data outright (via a data broker or independently).[38]

This is an all-encompassing definition, but it is the key element is using various types of data in ways that produce economic value, meaning cash for yourself or others.

There are at least two forms of data monetization: 1) self-generated personal data, which is the easiest and sometimes least expensive form to generate, and 2) artificial intelligence (AI) or algorithm-generated data.

As an example, Amazon.com knows exactly how much each customer is worth based on individual profiles and purchasing habits. The company is monetizing search and purchasing records, and that shows up in its capitalization value and Jeff Bezos's net worth. Amazon.com is, indeed, run by datapreneurs who monetize both self-generated and artificially-generated data

In a digital world, this is the only way business is done. The problem comes when monetization of data is not done well due to shortsighted leaders. It is also a problem when data is monetized illegally.

Two more examples of datapreneurship are Facebook and Google, among many others. They monetize data, which is voluntarily created by consumer/users, and then sell it to third and affiliated parties.

Taking data generated in one sector for one purpose and repurposing that data has been occurring for a long time. Ever get on a mailing list for one catalog or non-profit charity and suddenly you're flooded with other catalogs or charitable giving opportunities? These groups are repurposing and monetizing your data.

Datapreneurs find hidden value in data, extract that value, and monetize it. This is a learned skill that some leaders never learn, and good leaders learn well.

Extracting value is exactly what I want you to do as you think about the concepts in this book. If you didn't initially see value in it, you would not have even picked up the book! So, seek to find value, extract it, and become a datapreneur as well.

Finding value and extracting value are two different things. Good leaders can find value in people and opportunities unseen by bad leaders. For example, my wife and a handful of college professors observed some intellectual value in me that others had not seen. The information/data was right in front of the others, but they didn't see it. Because of my personal experience, I have chosen to purposefully, consciously, and aggressively look at people and opportunities from the point of view of value and extraction.

Extracting value can be done in many different ways. I can research information about taking a trip to Iceland, but if I didn't file it away for when I went to Iceland, I haven't extracted value. If I never go to Iceland or don't extract value from what I have read, my reading was a waste of time.

Monetizing data is a targeted form of extracting value from data.

Without doubt, the transition to and reality of a digital world has resulted in inconceivably massive amounts of data. Knowledge is based upon aggregated data. The amount of raw and by-topic aggregated data that creates knowledge is too enormous to even be known.

Knowledge can be extracted from data but never monetized. Take, for example, a student who graduated from college with a major in philosophy, art history, or romance languages. No doubt earning this degree took time, money, and commitment. But creating value by monetizing the data and knowledge the student learned will not be achieved unless a job is found that uses the data learned to create monetary value.

Having data and knowledge and monetizing that data and knowledge are two different things. To be sure, there are computer programs, such as electronic stock trading, that monetize data, but it takes humans to design the majority of these systems to do so. However, the type of monetization I'm writing about stems from a conscious effort of leaders and followers to take the data at hand, create knowledge from it, and produce monetary value.

Most people have knowledge created through aggregated data that they will never use and thus never monetize. They wish to get paid for what they know. Rarely do companies and organizations monetize or optimize all the data they have. Doing so requires a major change in mindset for them while creating substantial career opportunities for those who are becoming datapreneurs.

GOOD LESSONS

- Become a datapreneur. It's the next big career opportunity.

- Use only data you can trust through verification; to do otherwise is to risk your career.
- Using big data badly isn't much different from using little data badly.
- Don't believe the data too soon or place too much trust in it without realistic caution.
- Trusting data means distrusting opposing data.
- Creating monetary value from data that others haven't seen can position you extraordinarily well—and quickly.
- Transitioning to the reality of a digital world has resulted in inconceivably massive amounts of data. Knowledge is based on aggregated data; the amount of raw and by-topic aggregated data that creates knowledge is too great to be fully known by any individual. But good leaders learn to monetize the percentage of knowledge that can be realistically known. Be one of them.

12. Refusal to Play Role of Mediator and Lead Reconciliation

Unless it is purposefully chosen as a college major or career path, few leaders or supervisors have received formal training as mediators. However, this skill will be called upon to resolve conflicts and disputes. If you are good at mediation, opportunities might occur more often than you would prefer. It's better to become a mediator via a planned career path than be called on to do it as a default responsibility.

There are many reasons why leaders would refuse to play the role of mediator. Foremost among them is the idea that, during a mediation, no one wins, including the mediator. If a dispute occurs, one side or one person feels he or she got the short end of the decision. That person might feel the dispute should never have been brought to leadership.

If the dispute happens between two immediate reports, the leader can take one of four routes to find resolution. (Note: I'm not referring to disputes between labor and management, or within a collective bargaining situation, or formalized arbitration. Rather, it's the remediation of a problem, dispute, or misunderstanding between and/or among the members of the same working group or team.)

The leader can:

- Ignore the need or request for mediation.
- Refuse to engage.
- Hire an outside mediation professional or bring in an inside HR resource.
- Ask a non-conflicted third party from within the work group to serve as a mediator.

By ignoring "it," I mean the need and direct request for mediation of a problem between individuals or between opposing groups of individuals. In this case, the need for mediation and resolution is clear in the minds of those involved but not in the mind of the bad leader.

Bad leaders either purposefully don't recognize a problem or, seeing it, don't think it requires a mediated solution. Moreover, they may also determine the process of mediation would be more emotionally painful and disruptive than letting the dispute continue. Their hands-off inaction will not resolve the dispute, but it will cause followers to confirm that they don't have a "go-to" leader they can depend on to resolve disputes.

If, on the other hand, a leader does engage as a mediator and helps resolve a dispute, it's likely to be perceived that somebody won, and somebody lost. At times, this cannot be avoided, and a good leader can live with this perception. No leader should play favorites and take one side over the other in the mediation.

However, a bad leader is more likely to mediate in a way that allows the disputing parties to feel like they both won. The fact is, when both parties feel as though they have won, they will also feel they have both lost at some time. With this perception, they are likely to feel cheated by their leaders and disillusioned by the mediation process.

A good leader will be aware of a dispute, or potential dispute, and act to achieve a resolution before mediation is ever requested or required. Anticipating and then defusing a potentially explosive dispute before it becomes a disaster will be noticed and appreciated by those involved.

A bad leader will not have enough foresight or boldness to address the conflict until forced to—perhaps by their superiors. By this time, the conflict could be so deep seated that a breach of trust occurs and negatively affects workflow and relationships.

GOOD LESSONS:

- The best leaders will anticipate potential conflicts and act before they get severe. Bad leaders don't see, hear, or learn of conflicts until they become disruptive.
- A good leader works both behind the scenes and in clear view of those involved in the dispute and defuses the conflict before it gets worse. A bad leader delays until the dispute becomes critical and reaches a point when mediation and reconciliation are impossible.
- A bad leader is likely to disregard or refuse to orchestrate a mediation for conflicts evident to others but which have little effect upon the leader.
- A good leader knows his/her people well enough to detect potential conflicts between or among them and doesn't wait for things to "just work themselves out."
- Disputes tend to be denied or ignored by bad leaders, not resolved.
- Good leaders are balanced in their approach to dispute resolution and will strongly stand behind a decision once made.
- A good leader has the skill to detect the difference between a false conflict and a real conflict but will act to resolve them both.
- A bad leader may act as a mediator of conflicts caused by others but also ignore conflicts worthy of mediation caused by him or her.

13. Refusal to Prevent or Mitigate Cybercrime

To whom does the role of cybersecurity fall? Everyone. The attitude that we don't have the type of information that has value to thieves just doesn't cut it. Some cybercriminals do what they do just to create disorder and feel the thrill of having power. They have a "just because I can" attitude, like the guy called

"Mayhem" on the All State Insurance Company TV commercials. It's his job to cause turmoil, chaos, and personal anxiety.

Every organization must be confident it has taken all reasonable steps to assure that if attacked, systems are in place to detect threats and mitigate them if they have begun. This requires that every employee has received information about cybercrime and how it would affect their organization should an attack occur. Also, every employee should receive proper and frequently updated training regarding the prevention of cybercrime. These policies don't create themselves; they are the result of good leaders intentionally taking responsibility to create and enforce them. Bad leaders do not see the urgency of taking steps to assure data security or training employees to prevent and detect threats. For them, this is a job to be done by IT or someone other than themselves.

Many organizations put proper policies, guidelines, and procedures in place only after a data breach or cyberattack has occurred. Or they might do it after media reports are released or when insurance companies require cyber-safety measures.

Take, for example, the use of your personal data for bad purposes by nefarious criminals. Cybercrime is a form of negative or inappropriate data monetization.

Cybercrime is estimated to have cost the world economy as much as $600 billion in U.S. dollars in 2017, according to the Internet Society. Forbes.com projects the cost of cybercrime will reach $2 trillion in 2019. And according to Cybercrime Ventures, cybercrime damages may reach as high as $6 trillion by 2021.

A March 6, 2019, report titled, "The Ninth Annual Cost of Cybercrime Study" by Accenture concludes:

> **In an ever-changing digital landscape, it is vital to keep pace with the impact of cyber trends. We found that cyberattacks are changing due to:**
>
> **Evolving targets: Information theft is the most expensive and fastest rising consequence of cybercrime. But data is not the only target. Core systems, such as industrial controls, are being hacked in a dangerous trend to disrupt and destroy.**
>
> **Evolving impact: While data remains a target, theft is not always the outcome. A new wave of cyberattacks sees data no longer simply being copied but being destroyed—or even changed in an attempt**

to breed distrust. Attacking data integrity—or preventing data tox-icity—is the next frontier.

Evolving techniques: Cyber criminals are adapting their attack methods. They are targeting the human layer—the weakest link in cyber defense—through increased ransomware and phishing and social engineering attacks as a path to entry. An interesting devel-opment is when nation states and their associated attack groups use these types of techniques to attack commercial businesses. Attempts are being made to categorize attacks from these sources as "acts of war" in an attempt to limit cybersecurity insurance settlements.[39]

GOOD LESSONS:

- Bad leaders don't stay on top of potential cybercrime threats, because they believe their data is just not that important. Good leaders don't make this mistake.
- Bad leaders do not take seriously their leadership role in preventing cybercrime. Good leaders do.
- Bad leaders encourage employees to be only as smart as the bad guys. Good leaders require that employees be smarter than the bad guys. If their people are not technologically able to be smarter than the bad guys, they demand that someone somewhere in the organization is.
- Good leaders are continually vigilant to potential cybercrime attacks. Bad leaders don't take cybercrime seriously, because they mistakenly believe that most other matters with which they deal are higher priorities.
- Bad leaders continually underfund cybersecurity measures. Good leaders make sure that cybercrime prevention efforts are well provisioned.

14. Refusal to Provide an Escape Route

Soon after boarding a cruise ship or airliner, instructions are given that start with the phrase "in the event of." Cruise ship companies and air carriers are required by federal and international law to instruct passengers about what they should or should not do "in the event of" an emergency. These instructions are intended to be obeyed, because the consequence of *not* obeying them might result in physical harm, death, or jail time.

A planned escape route is ordinarily a part of the instructions.

Safety and escape procedures have become such a commonplace part of our lives that we often overlook them. From riding an elevator to escaping a fire in building, arena, or retail space, we are instructed on how to escape potential dangers.

Moreover, signs are posted along roads and within residential areas that provide warnings and instructions for dealing with floods, fires, tornados, earthquakes, tsunamis, lahars, haboobs, and more. These rules and protocols assure the safe passage of all persons aboard within a defined space or while in a certain geographical terrain. Whether the warning message is provided vocally, with signs, or in audio and/or video formats, it doesn't diminish the urgency of doing the most appropriate thing in light of a serious event.

One of the most graphic "danger" messages I've seen is along U.S. Highway 24, just west of Colorado Springs, Colorado. It has both a text and a graphic image that indicates what your response should be if a flash flood comes down the canyon. It says, "Climb to Safety."

A southern rock band from Georgia, Widespread Panic, recorded a song with the title "Climb to Safety" by Jerry Joseph. Some lyrics of this song make sense for the purpose of this discussion:

> **You can hear it coming**
> **like a train out of control**
> **surely leaves you wondering**
> **exactly where your ticket goes**[40]

Good leaders, unlike bad ones, provide a route out of a difficulty, and they often help their people climb to safety. Climbing to safety as an escape route always requires more energy than falling back. The alternative is to do nothing. This choice doesn't require any resources or expenditure of energy immediately, but eventually the consequences of doing nothing will require multiple resources.

Some problems at your job and in your career are predictable; you should remain alert and see them coming. Other problems are unpredictable and likely to surprise you, even when you *are* alert.

Good leaders create contingencies for as many adverse situations as they and their teams can. Bad leaders don't think ahead or plan escape routes. Rather, they think that adverse events likely won't occur, so no escape route needs to be planned. Or, they think that planning an escape route far ahead of the event will cost more than the resources required to fix the problem after it happens. This approach provides cover for the leader, but it doesn't give much comfort to the follower. As the song says, "Surely leaves you wondering exactly where your ticket goes."

There is a big distinction between what good leaders do and what bad leaders don't do in providing escape routes. This relates not only to matters of physical safety but to emotional and financial safety as well.

A well-planned escape route provides colleagues and employees with an alternative to suffering through the effects of an adverse event. It doesn't always need to be a big escape plan to make a big difference. Over my career, I have seen a few small escape plans end up providing great results.

Take, for example, a circumstance that could have gotten out of hand resulting in hard feelings and a potential dislocation. I once served with a capable university administrator. He was well respected and loved by the academic community through his long, positive history with the institution. He and I had applied for the same job, but I landed it. He was a real gentleman about the outcome, but I knew the time would come when we might not see eye to eye. When that day came years later, I already had an escape route planned from a potentially negative circumstance.

He wasn't the kind of person who would have been impressed if I provided some sort of financial reward as an escape route from conflict. I knew I needed to come at it from a different direction. As a scientist, he had a deep interest in keeping track of weather and weather patterns. (This was before temperature and other weather-related data was available on one's phone or via the Internet.) So, I bought him the finest home weather station I could find. It only cost a few hundred dollars, but it made a big impact in our relationship and our effectiveness working together.

Another time in a different setting, I had an assistant manager of one of my properties who was newly married. He and his spouse didn't have any comfortable furniture for their apartment. His job was physically and emotionally taxing, and I knew he needed a comfortable escape. So I bought him a premium-label reclining chair and had it delivered. This chair provided a temporary escape from his highly demanding job. He noticed the high quality of the chair and also realized I was aware of his need to escape the stress of the job. His having an escape route paid dividends for both of us and the business.

Most often, it doesn't take much to provide a personal escape route for frustrated and/or overworked employees. But it does take some thought to get it right.

Followers are relieved to know their leaders have their best interests in mind. They have thought carefully and developed contingency plans/escape routes and off ramps that create employee satisfaction, ensure momentum, and secure the organization's future.

Escape routes are pertinent to the following situations: What happens if we lose our biggest customer or contract? What happens if our primary supplier goes out of business? What happens if we lose our funding or the bank calls our note? What happens if we lose key employees or are the target of a takeover?

These are all real concerns for which an escape route should be planned and ready to be executed in case they occur.

Creating an escape route is not a waste of time. Good leaders do this well. Plus they don't sit around worrying that adverse events might occur. They are far too busy to worry but not too busy to create escapes routes. In this way, they exhibit forethought and competence.

Good leaders seldom, if ever, ask the question "what if" as bad leaders do, but they engage in the mindset of "nevertheless."

This difference in perspective is a dead giveaway between good leaders and bad leaders. Good leaders exude the confidence that communicates to their followers this message: "Whatever crisis comes our way, we will, nevertheless, overcome it."

They do not panic when adversities happen, because they know they have a escape route in addition to the personal acumen to overcome. Followers notice and deeply appreciate this kind of leadership when things become difficult.

GOOD LESSONS:

- Many bad leaders don't have the interest or energy to plan safe escape routes, and their employees and coworkers know it.
- Because they need to deal with small problems of their own making, bad leaders can't find the time to create escape routes.
- Good leaders can detect disequilibrium and threats, but they will have already created escape routes.
- Good leaders, like good sailors, know there are stormy times when the best escape is to put their organization, its people, and themselves into the wind and hold steady.

---

15. Refusal to Recognize the Cost of Value Production

Here are a number of idioms: You can't build a house out of thin air; you can't pull a rabbit out of a hat; you can't make something out of nothing; you can't squeeze blood out of a turnip.

These all have a common theme, namely that it's difficult to produce something without an initial level or degree of resources, something to build on, or someplace to start. But a lot of bad leaders think you can. Notice I've written "think *you* can" rather than "think *they* can."

This leadership flaw is similar to Willingness to Overcommit found earlier in this book. But it differs in this regard: In order to produce something out of nothing, having nothing is not the place to start. For example, if one has nothing to eat, it's not hard to start and maintain a diet. The task of producing value requires the drawing of resources—personnel, capital, equipment, information, and time—from somewhere or someone else.

The cost-of-value production or cost to produce value is the theory that the price of an object or condition is determined by the sum of the cost of the resources that went into making it. The cost is comprised of all resources—personnel, equipment, capital, information, and time—and might include taxation, less any government taxation concessions that benefit the business or a community entity. Thus, the cost of a produced good is equal to the sum of the cost of the inputs used to produce that good. It includes interest charges on any debt financing and/or opportunity loss from otherwise investing or depositing the funds used to produce the good.

The precise part of this definition that applies to this leadership refusal is the cost of the inputs used to produce that good. "Good" can be viewed several ways: as a *commodity* such as shoes or cars, as a *value* such as truth and honesty, and as a *good experience* such as a vacation or long weekend. Each one of these implies some good can be derived if there is some resource through which the good can be produced or experienced.

Refusal is noticed when leaders state, "All we have to do is . . ." Thus, they quickly demonstrate shortsightedness regarding the degree of difficulty and the number of resources it will take to produce the good or desired outcome. For example, if you want to take a trip but the resources for taking it are not available, then the money budgeted for essentials such as food and clothing must be tapped to fund it. Something or someone must provide the cash or credit if the trip is to be experienced.

Certainly, there is a substantial difference between well-established, well-funded organizations and others that have fewer resources to produce value, but the principle is still the same. Bad leaders often refuse to recognize the resource costs of producing value. It's bad enough when this behavior manifests itself occasionally, but when it becomes standard operating procedure, it can produce a serious lack of trust and even deep resentment. Furthermore, bad leaders who create overly competitive political and fiscal environments most often look to meet only their budgetary needs. By refusing to recognize what it cost to create value they don't advance the greater organization.

Moreover, this refusal exposes not only a deep lack of regard for the people assigned to produce the value, but also an insular distancing and denial of what resources are required to create the desired objects or conditions. When this reality is brought to their attention, bad leaders often become obtuse.

GOOD LESSONS:
- Human capital is the resource that bad leaders most commonly overlook when they want to produce value.
- One can't expect the Thomas Edison Junior High School basketball team to defeat the Golden State Warriors pro team. A bad leader/coach would fail to recognize the emotional and physical costs of having this expectation.

The refusal to recognize that it costs people something to produce value is evidence of a leader who lives in a dream world—someone who has a tendency to exploit people, overstate capacity, and deny what it takes to deliver goods.

- When good leaders expect their teams to create value, they provide the required resources and get on the development train with their people.
- Bad leaders disregard the need for the resources sufficient to create value. They are unlikely to get on the development train, but they expect their people to do so.
- If bad leaders were held accountable to the same production standards to which they hold their people accountable, a great deal more value production would occur.

Good Lesson Affirmation
There is no FEAR (Failure, Experience, Anxiety, or Roadblock) caused by a bad leader, from which I am not learning a good lesson.

Chapter 5.

Judging Wisely:
Setting Yourself Apart

H aving considered the fifty-two leadership lessons, we should now think about the profound dilemma created by the cultural *aversion to* yet the *necessity of* evaluating the actions, attitudes, and performance of those considered to be bad leaders.

Distancing yourself from bad leadership behaviors and toward good ones requires making judgments about what bad leaders do that's *bad* and what good leaders do that's *good*. Wise judgments regarding these distinctions will set the course to advance your career with greater alacrity than that of your peers.

Because judging others is a minefield, you might ask, "Why would an argument be made for judging others?" The fear of being labeled "judgmental" has become a social certainty and the statement "who gives you the right to judge?" is commonly heard. This statement is more easily made by those *not* facing the obligations of conducting formal evaluations or making hiring and placement decisions.

In western, social, business, and political cultures—particularly in the U.S.—individuals have become afraid to evaluate bad as bad and bad leaders as bad leaders. Many have become fearful of making assessments, because they're afraid others will evaluate them according to the same standards by which they evaluate.

However, this fear is unfounded and counterproductive to good management practice. Pointing a finger at another person who can point a finger at me is a good thing: it makes both of us accountable for our actions, attitudes, and performance outcomes. This reciprocity makes what we do or don't do at our places of employment really matter. Being overly polite, unwilling to assess, and non-offensive to a point of absurdity is no substitute for wisely evaluating performance. This is particularly true if that performance is detrimental to an organization or culture.

The fact is, human beings aggressively judge almost everything and everyone we encounter, although we deny it and resent it when we feel we are being evaluated as lacking or not benefiting from the judgment. When we are assessed in a fair, timely, positive, affirmative manner, being evaluated is less of a problem.

Being judgmental is not a positive characteristic; *exercising sound judgment* is. It's essential to any social group such as families and businesses that discerning, thoughtful people make judgments to prevent chaos. Assessing the performance of bad leaders is required for organizational stability and success, but this is not the same as being judgmental.

As you move up and through the corporate structure, you will need to prudently and courageously assess the performance, attitudes, and actions of others. An ability to adroitly discern and pass fair judgments on the performance of others is a necessity for advancement. The person who can display superior diagnostic judgments, create solutions to amend deficiencies, and increase the capacities of both individuals and groups will be of great value.

> Overcoming the fear of evaluating others is a requirement for good leaders. Gaining positional power, personal authority, and high financial compensation is based on the accuracy of your judgments. High-ranking leaders don't get there by judging people or opportunities badly.

When they're not evaluating other people, most people have no issue with making judgments. For example, some food is both good and bad—good because it looks or tastes good but bad because it isn't healthy. Some food becomes bad when consumed in great quantities but not as bad when eaten in moderation. Some food that looks bad also tastes bad, but some food that looks bad can taste good. Some food consumed too often or too late in the evening can become bad.

Some food that's too spicy or hot in temperature can be bad and even dangerous. Some food consumed raw is good for you, and some raw food is not.

So, if you can determine that some food is bad, you can assess—without guilt or reticence—that some leaders are bad for you, your employer, your culture, and your government.

You have the right to call a bad leader bad because the leader's performance justifies the descriptor. And you do so because the bad leader has produced outcomes that have personally affected your performance or future and the health of your organization. You also have the obligation to call bad leaders bad because they don't measure up to established, objective standards for sound leadership.

All performance-related assessments should be based on a balance of objective standards, subjective observations, and direct experience with the person being evaluated as well as direct knowledge of the outcomes produced by the person being evaluated. Leaning on one index too much or too little leads to a less-than-truthful evaluation and skews it positively or negatively.

The bias against assessing is partially based on the fear of judging falsely or being accused of it. Proper judgments are truthful, not prejudicial or based on falsehood. Fair persons make fair judgments based on truth. The truth always leads to more truth and organizational order whereas falsehood leads to untruth and organizational chaos.

A part of our aversion to judging is the fear that we will become systemically judgmental and act with wrong motives. Being viewed as *judgmental* is not a descriptor to which anyone should aspire. By comparison, being a *wise, fair judge of character and performance* is a descriptor to which everyone should aspire.

The actions and attitudes of leaders are less likely to be judged harshly if followers trust them to put the followers' interest ahead of their own and ahead of fuzzy goals and entrenched ideologies. Followers know when they have lost out to these.

When evaluating vapid, vacuous, and consuming leaders, a good perspective is that of a teacher who just can't say that a written response on an examination is wrong and leave it at that. The teacher must communicate better ways to answer questions or make a point. Failing to specify what is most correct is not acceptable or even a fair response. When patient teachers make judgments about assignments or written responses to questions on tests, they know they will likely need to participate in the solution or help students come to standard.

Judgments have both objective and subjective elements. Even some yes-or-no, true-or-false questions have shades of rightness or wrongness inherent within them. Take, for example, the work of a meat inspector. If an inspector judges a side of beef to be unfit for human consumption, would that same side of beef be unfit for consumption by dogs and cats? Would it be okay to give it to someone who was starving? These questions don't prevent inspectors from making a judgment about human consumption. Rather, they are required to judge based on their responsibility, and that responsibility gives them the right to say good or bad, fit or unfit.

Judging work performance doesn't always mean that something negative will occur. Not all judgments made in courts of law convict; some exonerate.

However, without the threat of judgment, all behaviors and achievements become acceptable and cannot be assessed to be superior or inferior to any other. This argument primarily belongs to the ineffective leader, unemployed philosopher, or disingenuous social worker. In the real world, consumers, markets, and good leaders make definitive distinctions.

One problem with evaluative judgments is that they develop into philosophical arguments rather than issues related to performance and job suitability. In the workplace, an "I can't judge" philosophy is nonsense. No moral superiority is gained when a leader or a follower wholly adopts an "I can't be the judge" position. This is a breach of leadership responsibility, a form of escapism, and a recipe for failure.

Some judgment calls are easily made. Take, for example, a three-point shot in basketball. If a player is within or on the specified line and makes the shot, two points are awarded. If a player is beyond that line and makes a shot, three points are scored. Sometimes it takes a video replay to make a call definitive, forcing the refs to make a judgment based on the rules. That judgment has implications for the final score and which team wins.

Humans are less likely to behave badly if they know that other humans or electronic devices will monitor and assess their behavior. Consider what happens when people drive dangerously or above the speed limit and suddenly spot a police car. They are likely to hit the brakes, slow down, and drive differently. They know that an officer of the law might pull them over, apply the legal standard to them, and write a citation.

Judging the *inconsequential* things in life is easy. However, assessing the *consequential* things—such as the performance of national and international leaders without political bias—is enormously difficult. Judging a product or service as "bad" is wholly acceptable; so is asking for a refund or replacement. Yet determining that a person has performed badly is considered outrageous and socially unacceptable.

This is nonsense. People do better to evaluate only those things of true consequence and let things of little or no consequence slide by. The worse the leader, the greater the likelihood that the truly consequential will be ignored in favor of focusing on inconsequential issues.

Occasionally, you must exercise your responsibility to judge, but unlike in a court of law, you do not have the right to condemn. You achieve no benefit whatsoever of harboring ill will, resentment against, or loss of emotional energy to bad leaders. So, go ahead, you are free to evaluate. You may not have the positional or formal authority to judge, but you have the moral obligation to evaluate a leader's performance and character, particular in matters relating to theft or misuse of personnel and other resources.

If bad leaders have proven themselves to be bad through their attitudes, actions, or inactions, then you have the right to judge them accordingly.

You may be fully justified in *judging* a bad leader as bad, but you are not justified in *condemning* a bad leader for being bad.

Enduring "crap" from bad leaders can be difficult, but far more onerous is watching a bad leader's behaviors, attitude of non-responsibility, and outright failures affect your coworkers whose demeanor and productivity you respect. And when a bad leader affects the well-being of those you love, especially the members of your family, you have earned the right to assess that leader as bad. To assess a leader as bad is to exercise discernment and wisdom but not to enable a posture of condemnation or superiority on your part. The focus should not be on your act of judging; it should be on the leader's performance.

You can determine a leader to be bad and never bring it to the attention of superiors. Or, when necessary, you can carefully and justifiably disclose a leader's degree of badness without being a snitch or "ratting" on him/her.

If you have identified a leader as bad, chances are others have as well. If it weren't for the leader's poor performance as measured by objective standards, you would not need to make any disclosure. This becomes *disclosure without guilt*, because it is true, justified, and precipitated by the performance of the leader. However, if you cannot disclose a bad leader's performance without pettiness, whininess, or a get-even mindset, you should not do so. Only make such a disclosure if you can do it at the proper time with maturity and cogency.

Sometimes disclosing bad leadership is unnecessary. Over time, bad leaders often reveal themselves through continued bad judgments and decisions other people bring to light. Sometimes, though, bad leaders will self-amend unproductive actions, attitudes, and behaviors to create the best resolution possible.

Most wise, clear-thinking people will conclude that bad leaders produce unwanted results. In response, many bad leaders will argue profusely to cover for the suboptimal results their attitudes and choices have created. However, denying that bad outcomes are the result of bad decisions and poor execution does not invalidate the facts or minimize the role that wise leaders should play in fair evaluation.

Accurate, fair-minded judgments regarding a bad leader's attitudes and actions can provide emotional release. It can also serve to counter the personal and group frustration created when a bad leader attempts to hide negative outcomes behind a non-responsibility argument. The non-responsibility excuse for negative performance—"it's out of my hands"—is unacceptable. In fact, it's just plain cowardice and reveals a failure to *own* negative results.

Using the non-responsibility argument fools no one, but bad leaders use it frequently when things are going badly. When they're going well, though, the non-responsibility argument disappears, because most bad leaders like to be first in line when praise and bonuses are handed out. Yet, they are nowhere to be found when their bad decisions necessitate austerity measures.

Although you may have been deeply wronged, forgiveness is the best remedy for your short- and long-term emotional and career health. It's best to forgive bad leaders for their deleterious actions while exercising caution in any ongoing relationships and interactions with them.

Depending on the nature of the bad experience, you might find forgetting and forgiving equally difficult. Still, the act of forgiveness will release you from your internal turmoil. Pledging that you will learn *good lessons* can hasten the forgiveness process and place the hurt in proper perspective.

Forgiveness brings you freedom from the havoc and ongoing rehearsal of the difficulties endured. It also releases you from the desire to lie in wait for an opportunity to get even. Looking backward is a waste of your time.

As a means of learning *good lessons,* it's best to keep a "forgive and remember" perspective. "Forgive and remember" is a cautionary remedy to existing in an emotional state in which the bad leader has *de facto* control over your life and ongoing career.

Moreover, it's good to "forgive and believe" that the cards the bad leader has dealt you will evolve into *good lessons,* applied knowledge, and eventual wisdom. These will be beneficial rather than detrimental in the long term.

Given these two perspectives—"forgive and remember" and "forgive and believe"—the bad leader's competency, attitudes, actions, and performance will be evaluated appropriately and likely negatively. The bad leader's performance and attitude can be placed within the context of the Good Lessons Affirmation. In this way, condemning the bad leader doesn't become the focus of your response.

Good leaders must overcome the fear of negative judgments. They should not fear judging people negatively, knowing they will work out, reduce, resolve, and eliminate those issues that caused people to receive negative performance judgments. Because good leaders assess fairly and not harshly, they need not fear criticism as bad leaders do.

By comparison, bad leaders do not fear judging others negatively or harshly, because they are *not* concerned with resolving and reducing negative performance—unless it reflects badly on them.

Life is too short to enable bad leaders to influence your well-being. Learning *good lessons* helps you to rise above their spin—to find ways around them, above them, beyond them, and in spite of them.

Some bad leaders are good people who just can't lead. Some bad leaders are just difficult to follow, because they lack moral character and general effectiveness. Bad leaders should judge others fairly, prudently, and circumspectly, but they often lack the moral character to do so.

Six *good lessons* fall out of the role that good leaders play in making proper judgments. They are:

1. Good leaders have the willingness to recognize and promote truth in their evaluations.

2. Speaking truth to good leaders will accelerate your career.

3. Speaking truth to bad leaders may jeopardize your job but hasten your career.

4. Identifying a leader's disinterest in making proper assessments and establishing objectivity bring their moral authority into question.

5. Evaluating yourself by higher personal standards than you use to evaluate others will build your credibility and moral authority. Doing so will irritate bad leaders.

6. Judging should not be an end in itself but a means to accelerate personal progress, career development, and organizational success.

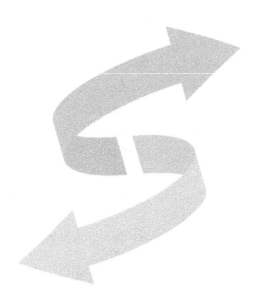

Chapter 6.

Looking Ahead

1. Determination to Unburden Oneself

The following three topics can be considered some of the highest hurdles preventing one from becoming a good or a great leader. These three need special consideration because they are often the source of many of a bad leader's behaviors and inadequacies. Once they have been detached and released, then the likelihood of achieving leadership and management distinction is substantially increased. They are:

- Ability and willingness to unburden oneself of the need to be a "know it all."
- Ability and willingness to unburden oneself of the need to always have/get one's way.
- Ability and willingness to unburden oneself of self-absorption.

The process of unburdening begins with admitting these three are certain to reduce leadership effectiveness and personal likeability. It all begins with a resolve to do so, then it leads to monitoring one's behavior to make sure that re-burdening never occurs.

Think of it this way: For professional bicyclists such as those who ride in the Tour de France, unburdening themselves of even the slightest weight is a must. Anything that might slow them down, impede their performance, and increase their times is thrown aside. Empty water bottles and energy bar wrappers are tossed. They unburden themselves of even the smallest weight, because they self-monitor and realize that a one-ounce weight when carried over one-hundred-fifty kilometers can accumulate to twelve-and-a-half pounds. They are so in tune with riding competitively, they can feel the slightest excess weight and act to unburden themselves of it.

It is highly unlikely that people will become effective leaders if they don't unburden themselves of these three disruptive behaviors. These three are often minimized and not taken seriously. They are thought to be only minor blind spots or personality flaws, but they are not. They can limit or even prevent job and career success.

Many leaders carry into their jobs and relationships a need to be a know-it-all and always get one's way. This could be the result of internalizing years of overly high expectations. Parents, siblings, teachers, professors, coaches, spouses, children, supervisors, board members, shareholders, investors, and the marketplace are often sources of these needs.

The need to be a know-it-all is an overcompensating response to the self-perception of intellectual inadequacy. It is often observed in leaders who are hyper-busy, overcommitted, and intent on proving that they, indeed, know it all.

The phrase, "My way or the highway" is again a threatening example of the need to always get one's way. It is also strong evidence that the person making the statement hasn't gone through the unburdening process.

This isn't about the generalized pressures we face due to our responsibilities. It is about the burden and emotional heaviness these particular needs and inclinations cause. The commonality among them is the lack of self-awareness, one's self-made status, and the unwillingness to own them, regardless of any external expectations. Blaming others for one's need to be know it all, to get one's way all the time, and be self-absorbed has a limited shelf-life. It should not be the excuse for *not* unburdening oneself of them.

Bad leaders are often severely unaware of their need to be a know-it-all and have their way all the time. They are self-absorbed. If you work for this type of leader, you perceive these behaviors better than they. And, for you, they are impossible to ignore. Creating "work arounds" to compensate for their needs is even more difficult.

Many times, bad leaders mistakenly believe they need to be brilliant, data-informed, knowledge-competent, and invariably correct in all statements and decisions—without exception. This is not the case. Just because a leader doesn't know it all and doesn't have dazzling solutions, it doesn't mean the person is inadequate and should be devalued. The problem doesn't lie in the follower, but in the leader who needs to be seen as all-knowing and spectacularly good at solving all problems. This creates a huge burden from which both the bad leader and their assigned followers need to be freed.

Once bad leaders unburden themselves of these misconceptions, better relationships, higher productivity, and improved work-life balance will occur, along with emerging pleasantness, authenticity, and transparency. All of these are evidenced in the lives and work-related relationships of great leaders.

You usually feel a sense of relief when something you didn't want to do has been taken off your plate and reassigned to someone else. You didn't want to chair the committee on Company Celebrations or create the standards for Bring Your Pet to Work Day.

Lifting a duty or onerous obligation should bring you a sense of temporary unburdening. Yet, the unburdening of one's need to always be right and get one's way should be so profound that one's optimism, performance, and even one's character should change. This is a big deal.

As data, information, and knowledge continue to expand at an ever-increasing rate, it is folly for anyone—no matter how smart, erudite, or clever—to think they can keep up. And now, with artificial/augmented intelligence (AI) analyzing and creating even more data, the task has never been so impossible. That means the attitude that one knows it all cannot be a reality.

When a leader or manager is referred to as a "know-it-all," it is a state-of-relationship statement rather than a depth-of-knowledge statement. It is pejorative and meant to communicate that the person is not as smart as he or she thinks.

Most people don't think they are "know-it-alls," but often, others think that they think they are. In any event, unburdening one of thinking or acting as a know-it-all is not only good for a leader but for all who work with and for that leader.

I don't know of a better way to fall out of positive relationship than for leaders to communicate through words or impressions that they have superior knowledge, thus making themselves superior people. Ever heard of the "kiss of death"? This is it.

The late Dr. Dennis Kinlaw stated, "There is no greater slavery than that which insists that you must have your own way . . . in every situation. Nothing in the world destroys human relationships more quickly and completely than this bondage to one's own wishes. This tyranny pollutes marriages, friendships, and parent-child relationships."[41] To that, I add work and job-related relationships.

There are big differences among *self-interest* (a good thing) and *selfishness* and *self-absorption*, which are not. What I have observed in the behavior of suboptimal leaders is a tendency to move beyond self-interest. Often, it is a form of success that fuels their transition from self-interest to selfishness and finally to self-absorption. When people reach the self-absorption stage, everything is indeed all about them. When leaders become self-absorbed, they may not notice the transition, but others will.

Self-absorption is so common in the workplace, entertainment, sports, and politics that it has been a theme of many TV comedy and drama shows. Prime character examples are Homer Simpson of "The Simpsons," Sheldon Cooper of "Big Bang Theory," Frasier Crane of "Frasier," George Costanza of "Seinfeld," and Mandy Baxter of "Last Man Standing." The commonality of these characters is their inability to get over themselves and see their immediate and greater world through the eyes of others rather than only their own. They, like many bad leaders, are insufferable.

Self-absorption is troublesome enough when found in TV and movie characters, but it can be devastating in the lives of those we work with and/or report.

Unburdening oneself of the need to be a know-it-all, the need be right all the time, and self-absorption are positive steps toward being emotionally mature and becoming a successful leader. It takes awareness and willingness to achieve these.

2. Leadership in the World of Big Automation

Recently, I've been conducting research concerning automation and robotics. My interest in what's labeled as A/R (automation and robotics) has not been limited to how A/Rs are being engaged in the telephony, retail, entertainment, health care, logistics, and the military sectors. It has also been extended to the automotive, education, and aerospace-manufacturing sectors.

The majority of my research time has been spent in addressing these questions:

1. How are organizations, workplaces, and humans being affected by A/Rs?
2. What human and leadership characteristics will need to be carried over into the data-led A/R world?
3. What happens in organizations when A/Rs replace humans?
4. What happens to human relationships when work shifts to A/Rs?
5. What will we need to learn about leading well in a world increasingly managed by A/Rs?
6. What do good leaders do in the A/R environment that we can emulate?
7. What do bad leaders do in the A/R reality that we should avoid?

The range of emotions concerning automation and robotics runs deep and wide throughout society. Some view it as a means of making mankind's status on earth more manageable and sustainable. Others view it as good, but they view robots as a threat to employment and life in general. Emotions and reality sometimes coincide, sometimes not.

In just a few years, A/Rs have morphed from industrial/manufacturing robots to collaborative or light-industrial robots, service and humanoid robots, and automation in the operating room, the pharmaceutical company lab, the skies, roads, classrooms, warehouses, and roads. A/Rs have arrived in a big way!

From basic manufacturing jobs to automated business processing and management (ABP/ABM) to drones and autonomous vehicles, A/Rs are here to stay, with many more applications to come. A/Rs don't create and, in most cases, don't run themselves. They need humans. The question is, how badly do we need A/Rs? And how will we engage A/Rs to serve our human purposes?

A/Rs that do what humans don't want to do seems to make sense. However, A/Rs doing the things humans don't want *them* to do is a whole other matter.

The reality of living in an automated world—and what it will take to produce the systems to live in an automated world—have profound consequences. For example, while in Dubai, I rode on the world's longest, most automated train. It was an enjoyable, fast, and safe experience. I didn't think much about what it meant for the train to drive itself. But when I returned home, I did think about what it would mean—safety- and security-wise—to fly in a fully autonomous plane or ride in a fully autonomous car.

Painted on the inside of the dome of the U.S. Capitol is what is called the Apotheosis of Washington. The word "apotheosis" is not common, but it can even be found in the urban dictionary. It means the elevation or exaltation of a person to the rank of god. It is defined as an ideal example, epitome, quintessence.[42]

The Apotheosis of Washington fresco was painted in 1865 by the European artist Constantino Brumidi. In a classical style, it depicts George Washington rising to the heavens. Two female figures, Liberty and Victory, are next to him. There are six groups of additional figures representing war, science, maritime, commerce, mechanics, and agriculture. Benjamin Franklin, Robert Fulton, and Samuel F.B. Morse are in the science section. Robert Morris is in the commerce section, and the McCormick Reaper is in the agriculture section.

Each of these individuals played a role in the business and commercial development of the United States in steam power for transportation, communication, finance and agriculture. They formed the foundation of the U.S. economy at the time. Of interest to me are the transatlantic cable (communication), the bag of money (finance), and particularly the McCormick Reaper (manufacturing).

The McCormick Reaper, invented in 1831, is considered the first semi-mass-produced mechanical farm implement capable of dramatically reducing human physical effort. At the same time, it increases productivity of land and the efficiency of harvesting wheat. It is said the reaper could, in one day, ream as much quantity as six farmhands. Furthermore, the reaper could harvest approximately ten acres a day while a single farmer would max out at about three acres. It primitive example of automation was a first for its time.

The McCormick Reaper was horse-pulled and mechanically driven, not powered by gasoline or electricity. Yet, in several respects, it was a form of automation in the sense that it reduced human physical labor, consolidated farming functions, saved time, and increased productivity enormously. These are, in most respects, the same benefits being created by today's automated and robotic systems.

Automated and robotic systems have been integrated into culture over many years, and we have barely noticed them. We interface with and depend on automation on a regular basis, but we seldom think about how our lives are affected by it. Elevators and escalators, stop lights, railroad crossing gates, automated doors, self-checkout at the local grocer via bar code, and automobile turning signals are all automated conveniences. More recently, our banking and financial transactions, how we learn, and how we consume water and power at home are part of an automated system. How the products we use are manufactured, our pharmaceuticals are produced, our cookies packaged, and our surgeries performed are partly, if not totally, the result of automation and robotics. Soon, drones will deliver our pizza and packages.

3. Sapience and Sentience

It is hoped that automated and robotics systems will be faster and smarter at performing mundane, repetitive tasks far better than humans.

We also want A/Rs to be more sapient like humans. "Sapient" means having and displaying great intelligence. However, we don't want them to be more sentient. "Sentient" means having and displaying emotions. That is, we don't want automated and robotics systems to have emotions or a sense of moral rightness. It is supposed that all sorts of apocalyptic disorder will happen if A/Rs become sentient.

Sapience will indeed get us to better and smarter functionalities while sentience will lead to chaos, because it's exclusively human . . . for now. Yes, we want SIRI and Alexa to think and do for us, but we don't want these services to feel emotions or store everything we say.

4. The "Can I"/"Should I" Dilemma

Current automated and robotics applications show some degree of sapience. Without it, applications would not be automated or robotic. Having and expressing great intelligence is expected from A/Rs and some humans, as well. But A/Rs are not currently (or in the immediate future) able to be sentient, to have feelings and emotions. Having intelligent A/Rs is one thing; having emotional A/Rs is quite another. Herein lies an enormous dialectic. How sentient should A/Rs be?

Research in AI, machine learning, and neural networks are attempting to create the data, connectivity, and processing power of A/Rs to answer the "can I?" and "should I?" questions. Intelligence coupled with electro-mechanical devices answers the "can I?" question. Yet, A/Rs cannot yet answer the "should I" question.

"Should I" responses include more than intelligence. They involve actions derived from emotions and based on inputs of a social, psychological, physical, and even a spiritual nature.

I consider it a leap of gigantic proportion for A/Rs to answer the question "should I?" For example, if an autonomous vehicle (an A/R application) had to make a choice between hitting one child or hitting two senior citizens in the same roadway, what choice would it make? Would it hit one or two? The sapient autonomous vehicle (AV) would be programmed to avoid hitting "everyone," but that is not the choice.

The forced choice is one based not only on sapience, but also on sentience. The "can I/should I?" dilemma is a difficult issue to reconcile for even the highest functional levels of autonomous vehicles. It may never be solved, because it is a moral issue. Moral issues, for now, are the exclusive domain of humans.

Furthermore, most humans are not opposed to computers, automated systems, robots, and AVs that are highly intelligent. But they are, and likely will continue to be, opposed to computers, automated systems, robots, and AVs that are emotional. Creating and programming an automated or robotic application to make moral choices is in itself a moral choice. It would be viewed as a highly irrational activity in the minds of many humans. How much better to have human and A/Rs having and displaying great intelligence and leaving the moral choices only to the humans. This would be, in my opinion, a good example of an appropriate division of labor.

If sentience affects rational decision-making processes for humans, and A/Rs cannot or should not be sentient, then sentience must come from another parallel, complementary, and safe source. Superior leadership is that source.

5. Who's in Charge in the A/R World? Give Back and Take Back Role Confusion

Within the developing universe of A/Rs is the autonomous vehicle domain, and within this domain is the autonomous car sector. Autonomous cars are also referred to as self-driving or driverless vehicles. Autonomous cars were first and more recently envisioned as a means of reducing vehicle fatalities, accidents, injuries, and financial losses.

Like most A/Rs, autonomous cars and delivery trucks manage themselves through data derived from what they see and sense and what they are programmed to do. This reduces performance variables to *potential* actions or reactions. Fully autonomous vehicles—called Level 5—are completely self-driving. They are not driver-assisted but driver-replacing vehicles. Level 5 is what AV companies are attempting to create, but it is a difficult technological standard. AVs at levels 1 to 4 are not fully autonomous, but they are also not immune from answering the "can I/should I?" questions and other sentience issues.

The "can I/should I?" arguments for all levels of AVs are substantial. When the "must do" standards are added, as expected by consumers and government, the task of creating Level 5 vehicles is enormous.

Because AVs are not smart enough to do all the driving and piloting actions themselves, they may at times need to release control to an occupant/driver. Give-back anxiety occurs when that occupant/driver is forced to take back managing control of an AV. This feature is not pertinent to Level 5 AVs, because they are not designed to "give back" or "take back."

Role confusion can occur for both the AV and the occupant/driver when a take-back command is given. This requires a level of alertness and confidence by that person to quickly take over the driving. This functionality defeats the purpose of the AV in the first place.

A substantial problem is created when an AV encounters an environmental circumstance it does not recognize and for which it cannot immediately create a solution and communicate it to the appropriate electromechanical systems. The AV must then determine if it should continue to seek a solution for the anomaly or hand off the driving responsibility to the occupant/driver. When the AV abandons itself and moves from self-controlling to other-controlling, what then?

It is the *handoff* that causes role confusion. It's like a relay team of runners when a baton is passed or dropped; the anxiety peaks when the handoff occurs, not during normal running,

So you might ask, "When I am in charge and when am I *not* in charge?" The transition from one role to the other (or to no role at all) is confusing. It is particularly so for those who have no formal training in the multiple roles as a rider, driver, or participant in riding in or piloting an AV. The roles change when system fail. It's as if the AV says, "We are in a critical situation that I can't solve, so you (rider) take over."

Role confusion further increases when a passenger is required to take control or give back control but doesn't know which systems remain engaged and for which systems he or she is responsible.

For the unknown future, role confusion will remain a huge obstacle to widespread adoption of AVs. Any confusion caused by "take-back" and "give-back" commands lies at the heart of AV user/owner trust, usage, and purchase rates.

Current AV technologies are based on a threat-avoidance philosophy. All vehicles, pedestrians, bicycles, and other dynamic inputs are seen as impediments to be avoided. Why? Because their absolute intentionality cannot be assured.

Most autonomous vehicles' sensing systems are nearly as capable as humans'. But there are one-of-kind variables that autonomous systems may have not previously seen and for which they have not be programmed. They might not be able to respond. For these situations, sentient decisions will need to be made.

So, who's in charge in an A/Rs world—automated systems, robots, or humans? The answer is, *All of them!*

The need for good leadership in an autonomous world will not decline or go away. Assuming that having more robotics will require less human interaction is an error. The A/R world will require leaders to teach and supervise even more, not less.

It appears that several recent airplane crashes occurred because an automated system was defective, and that pilot training and skills were not sufficient to compensate for the defect. This leads one to conclude that the greater the workplace integration of A/Rs, the greater the need for human-supervised training.

How many layers of automation will it take to remediate anomalies? How long will it take to find humans capable of fixing them? The need for human intervention is not ever likely to cease. There will continue to be a need for leaders capable of recognizing that humans must be involved, too.

6. The Road Ahead

What type of leaders will be required in an autonomous world?

First, it will take those who understand both the limits of autonomy and the limits of humanity. Second, it will take leaders who are skilled in determining what humans do best and what robots do best. This requires moving well beyond traditional requirements for good leaders to have excellent human, conceptual, and technical skills. They will reach a skill level where they have to grasp what these three mean in a new A/R context.

In an autonomous world, more decisions will be made *for* humans, but crucial moral decisions will continue to be made *by* humans who are prepared intellectually and emotionally to make them. Just as there are limitations for humans, so are there limitations for A/Rs, now and into the future. It will take good leaders to understand, differentiate, and explain these changing realities.

The parallels between leadership effectiveness and organizational efficiency in the soon-to-be AV and A/R worlds and the characteristics of good leaders to build community in the present one are similar and changeless.

The characteristics include:
- Trust building
- Vigilance
- Wise use of time
- Threat avoidance
- Warmth
- Depth of knowledge
- Depth of learning capacity
- Responsibility for building physical and emotional safety
- Sapience
- Sentience
- Ability to determine human intent

7. Too Small for Your Britches and the Role of EI in Good Leadership

Being too big for your britches is an idiom referring to a person who has become emotionally too self-absorbed and conceited. It refers to people who have become full of themselves, arrogant, over-confident, snooty, and haughty. Other synonyms are being smug, disdainful, pompous, brash, opinionated, and insolent.

This is not the type of person one would care to date, marry, or work with. The phrase "too big for your britches" doesn't refer to a person's physical size or soma type, but rather to his or her state of being as perceived by others.

Rarely, if ever, do leaders who are too big for their britches know it, nor is it evident in their state of awareness, their approach to work, and how they lead their subordinates. Yet, some bad leaders have—in word, deed, and self-perception—become too big for their britches.

On the other hand, some bad leaders have become too small for their britches. That means the job responsibilities and complexity have grown larger than the talent and capacity of these leaders.

Many bad leaders have positions that are beyond their capacities. Moreover, their responsibilities are too great for their educational backgrounds, temperaments, and experience level. The social dimensions of their jobs require more than they have to offer.

Furthermore, being too small for one's britches has less to do with bad leaders' Intelligence Quotient (IQ) than with their Emotional Quotient (EQ), also known as Emotional Intelligence (EI). Being too small for one's britches has more to do with personal, social, and organizational ignorance springing from a lack of emotional intelligence than how intellectually smart someone is thought to be.

Emotional Intelligence (EI), or a lack of EI, has become a means of explaining why individuals and families are either functional or dysfunctional. EI also accounts for a great deal of the success organizations achieve through the people who manage them.

EI first came into public focus in 1995 via the research and publications of Daniel Goleman. His book, *Emotional Intelligence,* was the popular genesis of EI. Goleman defines EI as: "the ability to identify, assess and control one's own emotions, the emotions of others and that of groups." [43]

The next step, emotional competence, is: "a learned capability based on emotional intelligence that results in outstanding performance at work."

The combination of EI and IQ is strongly believed to be the key factor in high levels of personal and career achievement.

Goleman and others generally conclude that success in life and occupation is not just a result of high IQ but also the extent of one's EI. In fact, EI may be a stronger indicator of leadership success than IQ.

Most bad leaders do not have sufficient EI to lead successfully. This deficiency appears in most of the inabilities, willingness, and refusals mentioned in this book.

Goleman's EI model focuses on these five ideas:

- Self-awareness – being able to know one's emotions, strengths, weaknesses, drives, values, and goals and recognize their impact on others while using gut feelings to guide decisions
- Self-regulation –controlling or redirecting one's disruptive emotions and impulses and adapting to changing circumstances
- Social skill – managing relationships to move people in the desired direction
- Empathy – considering other people's feelings, especially when making decisions
- Motivation – being driven to achieve for the sake of achievement

Each of these is considered more of a learned competency rather than a trait injected at birth. They tend to be learned over time, if learned at all.

How is it that a lack of emotional intelligence shows up in the behaviors of bad leaders more than an abundance of emotional intelligence is noticed in the behavior of good ones? What a leader lacks in emotional intelligence is often more obvious than the emotional intelligence a leader has.

As a comparison, people who have bad breath or BO often don't know it because no one has told them, or they don't have the self-awareness or self-correcting behaviors to amend what is offensive to others. They lack EI.

EI is often the means of determining a good course of action and/or an ill-advised one.

I have occasionally considered hiking either the Pacific Crest Trail (PCT) or the Continental Divide National Scenic Trail (CDT). Both trails run through the

U.S. from Canada to Mexico. The PCT is 2650 miles; the CDT is 3100 miles. I suppose some people have hiked both trails completely. I know of several who have hiked portions of them but not all of both. The most I've done is thought about it.

I've walked a few miles of the PCT in Washington, Oregon, and California but haven't walked any of the CDT. To do so takes a great deal of physical skill and emotional resolve. Successfully hiking one trail is likely to create the confidence to hike the other. However, I don't currently have the confidence to do either.

I have enough self-awareness to keep myself out of situational problems. If I were to start the PCT or CDT, I'm aware enough to know that my chronical age and general physical fitness is against me. Self-awareness/EI keeps me from thinking I could do the walk easily. (I don't know if *anyone* could walk the PCT or CDT easily.)

If I were fit enough and motivated enough to make an attempt, I'd be sure to have good situational awareness by not starting the hike in the wrong place, at the wrong time of year, or in the wrong state of mind.

Bad leaders don't have the self-awareness inherent in emotional intelligence to know that they are lacking in any respect of the fifty-two lessons in this book. The result of this lack is organizational malaise and personal dysfunction—that is, they don't know what they don't know. By comparison, good leaders know what they don't know and are willing to admit it while seeking to learn what they don't know. This is emotional intelligence.

It is the emotional intelligence of leaders that enables them to fit well in their britches. Bad leaders are too small for their britches, because they are "small" emotionally and because they lack the EI to produce likeability and effectiveness.

Eighteen-year-old David Holsten from Coeur d'Alene, Idaho, received national attention for his emotional intelligence and foresight when he earned $35,000 in four days by plowing snow in Seattle. When I saw the news report about him and what he had achieved, I shouted, "Atta boy!"

How did David show EI, insight, and situational awareness? He was in Seattle when a snowstorm approached, and he owned a pick-up with a plow. He saw an opportunity. In Chicago, Denver, or Salt Lake City, a large snowstorm isn't a big deal. These cities have the snow-removal equipment, personnel, and know-how to deal with snow. Seattle doesn't.

So Holsten made the best of a bad situation and began to plow snow. While plowing it, he had the EI to charge extra hourly rates considering the magnitude of the storm and how few people had snowplows. This is a classic supply-and-demand case. Further, Holsten had the moral compass to give twenty percent of what he earned to his home church.

I have a dear friend who holds the title CBE (Commander of the British Empire) awarded to him by Queen Elizabeth II. Several times, he was named Industrialist of the Year in Great Britain and is a confidant to the monarchy. He is a brilliant thinker, businessman, entrepreneur, and turn-around artist.

Every conversation with him is fascinating and exhilarating. I've taken my university students to his home in England. He also spoke at one of my presidential inaugurations. When he conversed privately with my sons, I told them to listen intently because I consider him a compelling, winsome, and wise person.

A frequent theme of our many conversations is what he called "awareness." Our conversations started before EI emerged, but I now realize he was talking about awareness as a component of EI.

EI is never acquired instantaneously. It begins as one chooses to acquire it—by monitoring oneself, observing others, and analyzing situations and relationships. EI develops episodically and with experience and maturity. Good leaders take seriously their role in crafting their EI, then influencing others to create it within themselves.

Inc. magazine published an article by Justin Bariso titled, "13 Signs of Emotional Intelligence."[44] They are essential to providing EI informed leadership in the A/R world. They are:

1. You think about feelings.
2. You pause.
3. You strive to control your thoughts.
4. You benefit from criticism.
5. You show authenticity.
6. You demonstrate empathy.
7. You praise others.

8. You give helpful feedback.

9. You apologize.

10. You forgive and forget.

11. You keep your commitments.

12. You help others.

13. You protect yourself from emotional sabotage.

I suggest you work to gain EI. It will augment your IQ and help you form your CI (Cultural Intelligence) also gain SI (Spiritual Intelligence). With EI and SI as well as learning *good lessons*, you will be well prepared to lead in the A/R world.

8. Lessons Regarding Passion

When you google "passion and careers, passion and jobs, or passion and leadership," your search will return several hundred million hits.

Passion for your life, work, and career has a central theme based on the contemporary definition that is similar to romantic love. However, the original Latin root word for passion is *passio,* which means *suffering*.

So, finding passion for one's job and career is based on a willingness to suffer in order to achieve them. This is a hard, unromanticized approach but far better than flippantly saying, "Find your passion and do it."

Finding your passion is not easy for everyone. This pursuit requires thought, discipline, a willingness to learn, EI, CI, and SI. However, this type of passion/suffering is worthwhile, because it leads to a sense of identity, purpose, and fulfillment.

For this reason, you should find a job or career for which you are willing to strive and suffer, if necessary. Find one for which you are willing to set other good things aside. Find what you are naturally gifted to do, what you really like to do, and what you are willing to suffer through to achieve. This is not likely to occur in your first job or even your second or third. Both good and bad leaders and good and bad jobs can help you establish a direction and eventually find your passion.

Many times you determine what you want to do by determining what you don't want to do and by critically examining what you have already done. This approach calls for an adventuresome spirit, a strong work ethic, and a sound foundation in people management, flexibility, and your willingness to learn *good lessons*.

One of the underlying themes about passion and work/career is that when you find it your work won't seem like work. Your work will be generally pleasurable and fulfilling and when it isn't your passion will get you through the rough times.

What often stands in the way of achieving work-related passion are the negative experiences brought about by bad leaders. Who has not heard another person say, "I really loved the work and the people I worked with, but the leaders were so bad, they killed my passion"?

Good leadership builds and enhances your passion. Bad leadership minimizes or can even kill your passion.

Look for the leader who helps others find and realize their passions.

Become the leader who helps others find their passions.

Find the good leader who is willing to help you achieve your passion by entering into suffering with and for you.

Become the good leader who willingly suffers with followers to help them find their passions.

Bad leaders will not use the suffering definition for passion. They will not strive or suffer to achieve with their followers, nor will they suffer to help others realize their passions.

9. Lessons Regarding Covenant

Throughout this book, many distinctions have been made between good leaders and bad leaders and between which leadership behaviors should be emulated and which should be avoided. Issues, such as transparency, truthfulness, and approachability, have distinguished good leaders from bad leaders. But the foundational component upon which the best leaders lead is *relational covenant*, which is highly desired but seldom achieved.

Covenant is defined as an agreement, promise, compact, and pledge of fidelity. Its effectiveness is based on candor and genuineness between parties. Covenant lies at the intersection of all of the best qualities of leadership, and it is the predominant characteristic bad leaders are missing. Great leadership is expressed through covenant, and covenant leads to great achievement. Bad leaders have no desire to be in covenant with those they lead unless it is beneficial to them.

Imbedded in a covenantal relationships is the concept of exchange. Within the concept of exchange is concept of fair exchange. Within the concept of fair exchange are the concepts of loyalty and commitment. (See Inability #2)

Bad leaders lack in fair exchange. Good leaders have an excess of fair exchange. Bad leaders take more than they give, but good leaders give more than they take.

> Through covenant, good leaders have mutual agreement with followers to serve the needs and interests of each other and to advance the agenda to which they have agreed. Bad leaders demand that followers meet their needs and interests and adopt their agenda without covenant.

Covenant cannot be created out of thin air but must be based on a preponderance of other positive leadership attributes. Even good leaders can't expect to move to covenant immediately. Rather, they must prove themselves able and trustworthy by their attitudes and actions and by the progressive openness of followers to enter into covenant.

When bad leaders are out of covenant, followers know it and are not likely to persist in pursuing the leader's agenda. When good leaders remain in covenant with followers, followers are more likely to stay engaged and move toward mutually established goals.

Followers look for leaders with whom they can create covenant, and good leaders look for followers with whom they can create covenant. Covenant sustains relationships, teams, and organizations when they encounter difficulty and defeat.

Any lack of covenant exposes bad leadership. It's because bad leaders don't seek covenant; they seek control.

Bad leaders display animus toward those they lead. Moreover, they reveal personal unsettledness, internal churn, and a lack of moral clarity. They act as though they are uncertain of their ability to lead. Their lack of conviction regarding the direction in which they want to lead creates organizational unsettledness and internal churn.

Covenant is not built on indecision of direction.

With covenant among leaders and followers, issues such as mutual sacrifice, goal attainment, and shared experience take on greater meaning and durability. Covenant is built by a longer, deeper view of human nature and value. Good leaders value human beings; bad leaders value human beings only if they are productive and contribute to their leader's agenda. When human beings fail to do so, they become expendable.

Followers want to be in covenant with good leaders but do not want to be in covenant with bad ones because at the core of the matter they perceive that the bad leader does not have their best interests at heart. Bad leaders have other things at heart: their own well-being, status, or an agenda that they think is greater and nobler than the people they attempt to lead.

Following leaders who don't want to be in covenant is difficult, because they treat people as though they are "flatties." The term "flatty" is the name for people who are treated or viewed as one-dimensional objects with no depth of awareness or knowledge. They are people bad leaders consider undeserving of full care or esteem.

Bad leaders only see people as flatties, as if there wasn't anything beyond a face or a body. You can feel like a flatty at the DMV, a drive-up restaurant, or a super-market checkout. You are just another person to be processed, with no humanity, vitality, or depth, and certainly not within covenant.

By comparison, good leaders treat others as multi-dimensional—that is, they are more than what they see, more than meets the eye.

Covenant has within it the feeling of intimacy and endearment.

Good leaders endear themselves to followers. Bad leaders endear themselves not by their character and work ethic but by the power of the potential benefits they offer to their followers.

Good leaders show covenant by their genuine respect and care for the people with whom they serve. Bad leaders care only about how their followers can help them advance their own agendas.

Good leaders enable followers to perceive and understand their intrinsic value. Because bad leaders don't embody this message, followers don't flourish in those environments.

Good leaders project that followers may look out for their own best interests while bad leaders project that followers are helpless to do so without paternalistic oversight.

Covenant is built on the demonstration of enduring commitments. Good leaders work through issues and disagreements; bad leaders work to remove issues and disagreements by eliminating those who present opposing perspectives.

Covenant is not expressed in self-centeredness. Recall that the phrase "my way or the highway" is often used to express the worst in bad leaders. They avoid covenant because it requires mutual accountability and it makes them feel uncomfortable. They prefer compliance and dominance.

A leader's willingness to model covenant and lead through covenantal relationships are the ultimate leadership skills. Yet, it is not based on over-familiarity or coziness; it's formed to bring out the best of both parties for the benefit of the relationship and the organization.

Bad leaders rely on force to achieve false covenants. What bad leaders believe to be a covenant, followers view as oppression, because bad leaders use force to achieve it.

Bad leaders contextualize covenant in terms of a force to take or to take back rather than a persuasive influence to win over (or win back) the hearts and minds of followers.

I suggest you strive to be the good leader with whom others want to be in covenant, but your other positive attributes of leadership must be evident for covenant to occur.

You can remain in covenant and still disagree on tactics. Disagreements do not automatically default or annul covenant because it is built on agreements and goals.

Bad leaders sometimes seek to destroy their prior covenants among fellow workers. These covenants may have taken decades to build and contain a sense of mutual history within them. It is through a leader's self-centeredness or lack of emotional intelligence that covenants are devalued, and the benefits of covenants disappear.

Bad leaders seek ways to be disaffected by covenant. Being in covenant places mutual interests ahead of individual interests, creates too much intimacy, and makes bad leaders vulnerable to the feelings and aspirations of others.

Conclusion

hen you learn the lessons of adversity, you have learned good lessons about how to avoid the attitudes, actions, and negative results that bad leaders produce. People can call you many good things throughout life but being justifiably labeled as a bad leader is not one of them. Avoid it at all costs by learning how to learn good lessons to achieve good success.

Many people come to the end of their service with a particular employer—or at the end of their working lives completely—and realize they have underperformed and not advanced to the level of their talent or performance capacity. They might feel they just *worked* and did not develop to the intellectual capacity they could have.

Extracting good lessons from the bad leaders they encountered is a means of compensating for these emotions and increasing their sense of achievement.

There is no exact timetable for learning good lessons and achieving good success from bad leaders, but the sooner the better if you want less internal conflict and backward-glancing regret.

You waste time and energy continuing to rehearse and ruminate on the negativity you have encountered while being exposed to bad leaders without extracting good lessons. Achieving a deep level of personal resolution and benefit *in spite of NOORTS* is an intentional choice.

Good lessons are not easily won, because they are likely to require you to have gone through consternation or pain to learn. Great leaders don't become great by chance and pain alone, but by choice, circumstantial need, the will to be great, and having learned from both good *and* bad leaders.

Merely to condemn a bad leader is not the point. Rather, you want to adopt and live out the **Good Lessons Affirmation**. Truly, there is no *Failure, Experience, Anxiety,* or *Roadblock* created by a bad leader from which you cannot learn a good lesson or achieve good success.

Embracing this perspective and fully integrating the **Good Lessons Affirmation** requires you have the heart and motives of the fully aware, committed teacher. Truly great teachers live as though they have a cosmic responsibility to teach learners essential, enduring lessons rather than non-essential, transitory content. They teach what is to be avoided and what is to be modeled.

Because you are the only one to have lived in your skin and interfaced with the bad leaders as you have, you must become a teacher to yourself, so you can realize the full benefit of the good lessons.

Like great teachers, truly great leaders are great learners who have developed the ability to assess bad leaders in order to find *good lessons*. Their discernment produces benefits for everyone they lead. They know what and how to evaluate, what to teach and not teach, what to concentrate on and what deserves to be ignored.

> **It is not the certain reality that you will encounter bad leaders or the degree of badness they create by their failures that determines your well-being, energy, and initiative. Rather, it's the pledge you make to yourself that you will do better, produce more, and treat people better than bad leaders do.**

This, then, is truly a good lesson learned.

Let me briefly revisit two concepts and the G.R.A.C.E. GRID mentioned in Chapter 1 under the headings Trending to or from G.R.A.C.E. and Capitalizing on Your G.R.A.C.E to Overcome Your Lack of Experience.

It is the nature of your G.R.A.C.E. and the direction in which you are trending that comprise the important elements of your competitive advantage and what you offer to your employer, the market, and the world. To do that, you must separate yourself from the behaviors of bad leaders and associate yourself with the behaviors of good ones.

Often, as people's expertise and employability are evaluated, they are linked to those with whom they have studied and worked. They're also linked with schools attended and experiences they have had. The assumption is that these relationships with good people, good places, and good experiences have been of great benefit and that some of their goodness has rubbed off on you.

If you had the opportunity to be an understudy to great business leaders such as Warren Buffet or Steve Jobs, great coaches such as Bill Belichick and Tom Izzo, and great actors such as Meryl Streep and Tom Hanks, then your association with them provides identity and credibility.

The same can be said of bad influences and bad leaders. They too will rub off and influence the nature of your G.R.A.C.E. Thus, the direction of your trending will be affected by the positive or negative nature of your relationships. If you learn the *good lessons* available from bad leaders and have the proper influences rub off, then success and significance will follow.

Merging all that you have learned about bad leaders, what you need to avoid, what to emulate, and the direction of your G.R.A.C.E. GRID, then you have the characteristics necessary for the positive trending you desire. When this happens, you will have the best of what the best leaders have, which are these characteristics:

- Good leaders have a calming influence on the people they lead. They don't make people anxious.
- Good leaders are trustworthy.
- Good leaders are not wasteful of time, effort, financial resources, or opportunities.
- Good leaders have an abundance mentality rather than a scarcity mentality.
- Good leaders show their competency and humanity in how they do little things.
- Good leaders are not reckless and foolhardy under or without pressure.
- Good leaders display rationality and wisdom, and they evoke these qualities in others.

- Good leaders focus on mission first, then profitability and people (or people and profitability depending on the circumstance). Always, they focus on mission first.
- Good leaders take the right risks.
- Good leaders use data and love their people, not use people and love their data.

G.R.A.C.E. GRID

Deficiency	Proficiency
Wasteful	Frugal
Scarcity	Abundance
Insensitive: unaware of importance of little things	Sensitive: aware of importance of little things
Foolish	Wise
Unfocused	Focused
Inappropriate or no risk	Appropriate/right risk
Emotionally shallow	Emotionally deep

1. Running the Table

Running the table is a phrase that means putting every pool ball in a pocket without a miss or a scratch. It also means that a person or a team cannot be beaten in a game or series of games.

When you take to heart and train yourself with each of the fifty-two lessons presented in this book, you will indeed run the table and remove yourself from the chaos created by bad leaders. Running the table will allow you to learn the best from your boss's worst.

The fifty-two individual lessons should have identified the direction in which you trend and enabled you to fix your leadership deficiencies (inabilities, willingness, refusals) before they threaten your peace of mind, livelihood, and career. Self-correction is the key to doing so. If you do this, you can be assured to achieve the following:

- Achieving Self-mastery to not behave and lead like the bad guys.
- Gaining proper self-evaluation and progress-evaluation skills.

- Acquiring an unmatched vocational skillset.
- Gaining peace of mind and peace of place.
- Knowledge to grow your confidence and contain your arrogance.
- An ability to observe and recall human behaviors that are appropriate and inappropriate.
- Acting like you have driven the dangerous road before.
- Knowledge to not place yourself in a bad situation, and skill to extract yourself if you do.
- Lessons on what it means to be self-reliant.
- Developing the full set of EI, CI, and SI skills.
- Growing your contributory value and its impact.
- Casting a bigger shadow by your ability and status as an influencer.
- Creating the path to higher placement in the organization faster.
- Becoming a great reader of human and organizational behavior.
- Becoming a voracious reader of the right content created by the right sources.
- Learning the skills required by the sprint and the marathon.
- Creating deep awareness of the human capital side of value-creation.
- Expanding awareness of the balance between being person-centric and data-centric.
- Increasing your ability to focus and concentrate as an option to continuous distraction.

2. Commit to Grit

If there is a single, tidy way to wrap up all what good leaders do that should be emulated and what bad leaders do that should be avoided, it is perhaps this short phrase: Commit to Grit.

Grit is defined as "firmness of character; indomitable spirit; pluck."[45] One who has grit shows unyielding courage, backbone, fortitude, steadfastness, guts, and a willingness to persist. Grit can also be viewed as that which provides traction, such as sanding an icy or snow-covered intersection.

Grit is often the key characteristic of successful entrepreneurs and highly successful professional managers. It means working with courage on a minute-by-minute, hour-by-hour, day-by-day, month-by-month, and year-by-year basis with no gaps or pauses for distractions and diversions.

Good leaders have, at their core, emotional maturity, intellectual competency, and the ability and willingness to focus their grit to achieve a specific task or goal. Grit helps gain traction and focus on the object or status that is sought. Energy is the power to get one there; grit is the glue that keeps the focus and energy together, regardless of the challenge.

Grit matters in the following ways:

- Grit overcomes the 4 Fs (folly, frenzy, futility, and flight).
- Grit eliminates self-defeating behaviors (Nemesis).
- Grit replaces arrogance (Hubris).
- Grit aligns aspirations and energy.
- Grit supplants reluctance.
- Grit produces resilience.

Come to the Edge

He said "Come to the edge" They said "We can't, we're afraid and we might fall"
He said "Come to the edge" They said "We're afraid, we might fall"
He said "Come to the edge" They said "We might fall"
They came to the edge. He pushed them and they flew.[46]

I'm open to conversations about this book and available for speaking and consulting engagements. I've helped many individuals and organizations improve their effectiveness by charting a new and better course and by improving their performance through the concepts found in this book.

Please access www.GoodLessonsGroup.com or my Facebook and Linked-In pages for my contact data, to schedule a conversation, and to see when I will be in your area speaking and teaching.

ALL BLESSINGS!

About the Author

E. Arthur "Woody" Self, Ph.D., has nearly forty years of experience successfully blending a leadership career in higher education with business theory and organizational practice.

The combination of the theoretical and the pragmatic has led to transformative solutions to difficult problems for his business clients and the academic institutions he has served.

Dr. Self's academic preparation was in Higher Education Administration, Organizational Communication and Speech. (Ph.D., M.A. Michigan State University, B.A. Olivet Nazarene University) He has held positions in community colleges as well as doctoral-degree-granting institutions and has been the president of two institutions of higher learning: Malone University of Canton, Ohio, and Seattle Pacific University. He also served as the founding Dean of the School of Business at Northwest University.

Dr. Self has served as a strategic opportunity and planning analyst for scores of early- and mid-stage companies. Currently a business strategist and confidant to senior managers, board members, and investors, he enables the increased performance of both high-achieving and under-achieving organizations.

Known as Woody, Dr. Self is a voracious reader and writer who authored *Good Lessons from Bad Leaders: Discovering Courage Beyond the Chaos*. He spends his leisure hours bicycling, weightlifting, and riding his touring motorcycle.

Woody and his wife Carol reside in Oro Valley, Arizona, and are parents of Adam in Chicago, Illinois, and Eric in Atlanta, Georgia.

Endnotes

1   https://www.linkedin.com/pulse/employees-dont-leave-companies-managers-brigette-hyacinth

2   http://theconversation.com/what-is-full-employment-an-economist-explains-the-latest-jobs-data-95

3   https://www.usatoday.com/story/news/2019/05/25/boeing-737-max-8-autopilot-automation-pilots-skills-flying-hours-safety/1219147001/

4   What Is Big Data? Gartner IT Glossary–Big Data, https://www.gartner.com/it-glossary/big-data/

5   What Is Big Data? | Oracle https://www.oracle.com/big-data/guide/what-is-big-data.html

6   Locus of Control. There is a concept in the psychological literature known as locus of control that is unfamiliar to most people, even though, once defined, is commonly understood. Locus of control is an individual's belief system regarding the causes of his or her experiences and the factors to which that person attributes success or failure. https://www.psychologytoday.com/us/blog/moments-matter/201708/locus-control

7   *The New Yorker*, July 11, 1983, http://www.newyorker.com/archive/1983/07/11/1983_07_11_036_TNY_CARDS_000341303

8   L.B.Cowman, ed. James Reiman, *Streams in the Desert* (Grand Rapids: Zondervan, 1997.PDF 30book.) 367-368

9   Ella Wheeler Wilcox, https://www.goodreads.com/quotes/83455-one-ship-drives-east-and-another-drives-west-with-the

10 Laurence J. Peter and Raymond Hall, *The Peter Principle: Why Things Always Go Wrong* (New York: Harper Collins, 1969, reprint 2011)

11 Adapted from Charles E. Cowman, "It Must Be Bought." July 26, 2013, http://www.serminindex.net/modules/artilces/index.Php?view=article&aid=9486

12 Gospel according to St. Matthew 10:16 NIV

13 Fredrick Herzberg, Two-Factor Theory, https://www.mindtools.com › Team Management › Motivating Your Team

14 Joaquin Miller, Columbus, https://www.bartleby.com/248/798.html

15 "After Years of Delays, Boeing 787 Dreamliner Gets FAA Certification." Seattle PI, August 26, 2011

16 https://www.coursehero.com/file/38021561/2018-cmo-09-11pdf/

17 https://www.bloomberg.com/news/articles/2019-04-02/boeing-s-grounded-737-max-the-story-so-far-quicktake

18 https://www.ft.com/content/e8e17f4-91d5-11e9-aea1-2b1d33ac3271

19 Alfred Lansing, *Endurance*, (New York, Basic Books, 2014)

20 *Hacksaw Ridge,* (Universal Studios, 2016)

21 Robert J. Herbold, *Seduced By Success*, (New York, McGraw-Hill, 2007)

22 The National Oceanic and Atmospheric Administration (NOAA)

23 https://www.songfacts.com/lyrics/bruce-springsteen/hungry-heart

24 University of Washington, Libraries. White Pass: "Dead Horse Trail." Exhibit: Klondike Gold Rush-The Perilous Journey North. July 26, 2003. http://www.lib.washinton.edu/special collection/collections/exhibits/klondike/case6

25 https://en.wikipedia.org/wiki/Costa_Concordia

26 https://en.wikipedia.org/wiki/Taken_(film)

27 Margaret Thatcher. "Speech at Monash University (1981 Sir Robert Menzies Lecture)." October 6, 1981, http://margaretthatcher.org/document/104712

28 Henri Fayol, General and Industrial Management. (Paris, H. Dunod et. E.Pinat, 1917, OCLC 40224931)

29 https://en.wikipedia.org/wiki/The_Devil_Wears_Prada_(film)

30 Influencers, Urban Dictionary www.urbandictionary.com

31 Graham Johnson, May 20, 2013. http://kirotv.com/news.news/mercer-mess-lane-opening-not-so-messy/nXxrX/

32 *Saving Private Ryan*, Movie Quotation from Abraham Lincoln, https://www.imdb.com/title/tt0120815/

33 https://www.imdb.com/title/tt0109830/

34 Ken Blanchard and Spencer Johnson, *The One Minute Manager*, (New York, Harper Collins Publishers, Ltd., 1994)

35 Lambert's Cafe Sikeston, MO., https://throwedrolls.com ...https://throwedrolls.com

36 https://www.history.com/topics/world-war-i/battle-of-gallipoli-1

37 D. Justhy, *The Billion Dollar Byte*, (New York, Morgan James Publishers, 2018) 224

38 https://www.gartner.com/it-glossary/data-monetization

39 https://www.accenture.com/us-en/insights/security/cost-cybercrime-study

40 https://www.google.com/search?client=firefox-b-1-d&q=Climb+to+Safety+lyrics

41 Dennis F. Kinlaw, *This Day with the Master*, (Grand Rapids, Zondervan, 2002)

42 https://www.dictionary.com/browse/apotheosis?s=t

43 Daniel Goleman, *Emotional Intelligence*, (New York, Bantam Books, 1997)

44 Justin Bariso, 13 Signs of Emotional Intelligence, https://www.inc.com/justin-bariso/13-things-emotionally intelligent-people-do.html

45 https://www.dictionary.com/browse/grit?s=t

46 Adapted from a poem by Guillaume Apollinaire: https://www.goodreads.com/quotes/17760-come-to-the-edge-he-said-we-can-t-we-re-afraid

CPSIA information can be obtained
at www.ICGtesting.com
Printed in the USA
JSHW031406210820
7397JS00001B/16